Just The facts101
Textbook Key Facts

Textbook Outlines, Highlights, and Practice Quizzes

Economics: Private and Public Choice

by James D. Gwartney, 14th Edition

All "Just the Facts101" Material Written or Prepared by Cram101 Publishing

Title Page

Visit Cram101.com for full Practice Exams

WHY STOP HERE... THERE'S MORE ONLINE

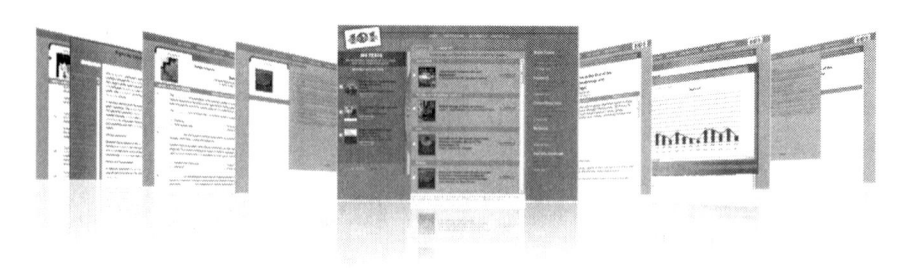

With technology and experience, we've developed tools that make studying easier and efficient. Like this Cram101 textbook notebook, Cram101.com offers you the highlights from every chapter of your actual textbook. However, unlike this notebook, Cram101.com gives you practice tests for each of the chapters. You also get access to in-depth reference material for writing essays and papers.

By purchasing this book, you get 50% off the normal subscription free!. Just enter the promotional code **'DK73DW20514'** on the Cram101.com registration screen.

CRAM101.COM FEATURES:

Outlines & Highlights
Just like the ones in this notebook, but with links to additional information.

Integrated Note Taking
Add your class notes to the Cram101 notes, print them and maximize your study time.

Problem Solving
Step-by-step walk throughs for math, stats and other disciplines.

Practice Exams
Five different test taking formats for every chapter.

Easy Access
Study any of your books, on any computer, anywhere.

Unlimited Textbooks
All the features above for virtually all your textbooks, just add them to your account at no additional cost.

Be sure to use the promo code above when registering on Cram101.com to get 50% off your membership fees.

Visit Cram101.com for full Practice Exams

STUDYING MADE EASY

This Cram101 notebook is designed to make studying easier and increase your comprehension of the textbook material. Instead of starting with a blank notebook and trying to write down everything discussed in class lectures, you can use this Cram101 textbook notebook and annotate your notes along with the lecture.

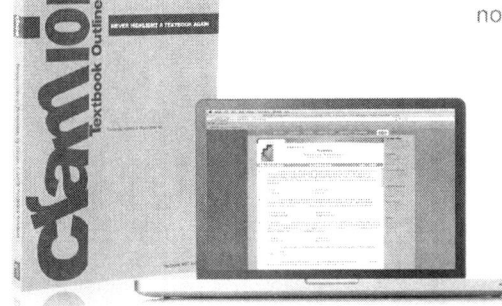

Our goal is to give you the best tools for success.

For a supreme understanding of the course, pair your notebook with our online tools. Should you decide you prefer Cram101.com as your study tool,

we'd like to offer you a trade...

Our Trade In program is a simple way for us to keep our promise and provide you the best studying tools, regardless of where you purchased your Cram101 textbook notebook. As long as your notebook is in *Like New Condition**, you can send it back to us and we will immediately give you a Cram101.com account free for 120 days!

Let The *Trade In* Begin!

THREE SIMPLE STEPS TO TRADE:

1. Go to www.cram101.com/tradein and fill out the packing slip information.
2. Submit and print the packing slip and mail it in with your Cram101 textbook notebook.
3. Activate your account after you receive your email confirmation.

* Books must be returned in *Like New Condition*, meaning there is no damage to the book including, but not limited to: ripped or torn pages, markings or writing on pages, or folded / creased pages. Upon receiving the book, Cram101 will inspect it and reserves the right to terminate your free Cram101.com account and return your textbook notebook at the owners expense.

Visit Cram101.com for full Practice Exams

Cram101
LEARNING SYSTEM

"Just the Facts101" is a Cram101 publication and tool designed to give you all the facts from your textbooks. Visit Cram101.com for the full practice test for each of your chapters for virtually any of your textbooks.

Cram101 has built custom study tools specific to your textbook. We provide all of the factual testable information and unlike traditional study guides, we will never send you back to your textbook for more information.

YOU WILL NEVER HAVE TO HIGHLIGHT A BOOK AGAIN!

Cram101 StudyGuides
All of the information in this StudyGuide is written specifically for your textbook. We include the key terms, places, people, and concepts... the information you can expect on your next exam!

Want to take a practice test?
Throughout each chapter of this StudyGuide you will find links to cram101.com where you can select specific chapters to take a complete test on, or you can subscribe and get practice tests for up to 12 of your textbooks, along with other exclusive cram101.com tools like problem solving labs and reference libraries.

Cram101.com
Only cram101.com gives you the outlines, highlights, and PRACTICE TESTS specific to your textbook. Cram101.com is an online application where you'll discover study tools designed to make the most of your limited study time.

By purchasing this book, you get 50% off the normal subscription free!. Just enter the promotional code **'DK73DW20514'** on the Cram101.com registration screen.

www.Cram101.com

Copyright © 2012 by Cram101, Inc. All rights reserved.
"Just the FACTS101"®, "Cram101"® and "Never Highlight a Book Again!"® are registered trademarks of Cram101, Inc.
ISBN(s): 9781478416333. PUBE-1.201299

Learning System

facts101

Economics: Private and Public Choice
James D. Gwartney, 14th

CONTENTS

1. The Economic Approach 5
2. Some Tools of the Economist 14
3. Supply, Demand, and the Market Process 23
4. Supply and Demand: Applications and Extensions 34
5. Difficult Cases for the Market, and the Role of Government 45
6. The Economics of Collective Decision-Making 54
7. Taking the Nation`s Economic Pulse 67
8. Economic Fluctuations, Unemployment, and Inflation 76
9. An Introduction to Basic Macroeconomic Markets 87
10. Dynamic Change, Economic Fluctuations, and the AD-AS Model 98
11. Fiscal Policy: The Keynesian View and Historical Perspective 106
12. Fiscal Policy, Incentives, and Secondary Effects 114
13. Money and the Banking System 123
14. Modern Macroeconomics and Monetary Policy 135
15. Stabilization Policy, Output, and Employment 144
16. Creating an Environment for Growth and Prosperity 153
17. Institutions, Policies, and Cross-Country Differences in Income and Growth 163
18. Gaining from International Trade 171
19. International Finance and the Foreign Exchange Market 182
20. Consumer Choice and Elasticity 194
21. Costs and the Supply of Goods 202
22. Price Takers and the Competitive Process 211
23. Price-Searcher Markets with Low Entry Barriers 217
24. Price-Searcher Markets with High Entry Barriers 225
25. The Supply of and Demand for Productive Resources 236
26. Earnings, Productivity, and the Job Market 244
27. Investment, the Capital Market, and the Wealth of Nations 251
28. Income, Inequaltiy and Poverty 261

Visit Cram101.com for full Practice Exams

Chapter 1. The Economic Approach

CHAPTER OUTLINE: KEY TERMS, PEOPLE, PLACES, CONCEPTS

- Human capital
- Labor relations
- Phillips curve
- Natural resource
- Renewable resource
- Scarcity
- Trade-off
- Poverty
- Rationing
- Structural unemployment
- Social security
- Opportunity cost
- Utility
- Incentive
- International trade
- Unintended consequences
- Normative economics
- Positive economics
- Environmental protection

Chapter 1. The Economic Approach
CHAPTER OUTLINE: KEY TERMS, PEOPLE, PLACES, CONCEPTS

| | Total cost |

CHAPTER HIGHLIGHTS & NOTES: KEY TERMS, PEOPLE, PLACES, CONCEPTS

Human capital	Human capital is the stock of competencies, knowledge, social and personality attributes, including creativity, embodied in the ability to perform labor so as to produce economic value. It is an aggregate economic view of the human being acting within economies, which is an attempt to capture the social, biological, cultural and psychological complexity as they interact in explicit and/or economic transactions. It was assumed in early economic theories, reflecting the context in which the secondary sector of the economy was producing much more than the tertiary sector was able to produce at the time in most countries - to be a fungible resource, homogeneous, and easily interchangeable, and it was referred to simply as workforce or labor, one of three factors of production (the others being land, and assumed-interchangeable assets of money and physical equipment).
Labor relations	Labor relations is the study and practice of managing unionized employment situations. In academia, labor relations is frequently a subarea within industrial relations, though scholars from many disciplines--including economics, sociology, history, law, and political science--also study labor unions and labor movements. In practice, labor relations is frequently a subarea within human resource management.
Phillips curve	In economics, the Phillips curve is a historical inverse relationship between the rate of unemployment and the rate of inflation in an economy. Stated simply, the lower the unemployment in an economy, the higher the rate of inflation. While it has been observed that there is a stable short run tradeoff between unemployment and inflation, this has not been observed in the long run.
Natural resource	Natural resources occur naturally within environments that exist relatively undisturbed by mankind, in a natural form. A natural resource is often characterized by amounts of biodiversity and geodiversity existent in various ecosystems. Natural resources are derived from the environment.

Visit Cram101.com for full Practice Exams

Chapter 1. The Economic Approach

CHAPTER HIGHLIGHTS & NOTES: KEY TERMS, PEOPLE, PLACES, CONCEPTS

Renewable resource	A renewable resource is a natural resource with the ability to reproduce through biological or natural processes and replenished with the passage of time. Renewable resources are part of our natural environment and form our eco-system. In 1962, within a report to the committee on natural resources which was forwarded to the President of the United States, Paul Weiss defined Renewable Resources as: 'The total range of living organisms providing man with food, fibers, drugs, etc...'.
Scarcity	Scarcity is the fundamental economic problem of having humans who have wants and needs in a world of limited resources. It states that society has insufficient productive resources to fulfill all human wants and needs. Alternatively, scarcity implies that not all of society's goals can be pursued at the same time; trade-offs are made of one good against others.
Trade-off	A trade-off is a situation that involves losing one quality or aspect of something in return for gaining another quality or aspect. It implies a decision to be made with full comprehension of both the upside and downside of a particular choice. And you are giving something away to get something back.
Poverty	Poverty is the state of one who lacks a certain amount of material possessions or money. Absolute poverty or destitution refers to the one who lacks basic human needs, which commonly includes clean and fresh water, nutrition, health care, education, clothing and shelter. About 1.7 billion people are estimated to live in absolute poverty today.
Rationing	Rationing is the controlled distribution of scarce resources, goods, or services. Rationing controls the size of the ration, one's allotted portion of the resources being distributed on a particular day or at a particular time. In economics, rationing is an artificial restriction of demand.
Structural unemployment	Structural unemployment is a form of unemployment resulting from a mismatch between demand in the labour market and the skills and locations of the workers seeking employment. Even though the number of vacancies may be equal to, or greater than, the number of the unemployed, the unemployed workers may lack the skills needed for the jobs, or they may not live in the part of the country or world where the jobs are available. Structural unemployment is a result of the dynamics of the labor market, such as agricultural workers being displaced by mechanized agriculture, unskilled laborers displaced by both mechanization and automation, or industries with declining employment.

Visit Cram101.com for full Practice Exams

Chapter 1. The Economic Approach

CHAPTER HIGHLIGHTS & NOTES: KEY TERMS, PEOPLE, PLACES, CONCEPTS

Social security	Social security is a concept enshrined in Article 22 of the Universal Declaration of Human Rights which states that Everyone, as a member of society, has the right to social security and is entitled to realization, through national effort and international co-operation and in accordance with the organization and resources of each State, of the economic, social and cultural rights indispensable for his dignity and the free development of his personality. In simple term, this means that the signatories agree that society in which a person lives should help them to develop and to make the most of all the advantages (culture, work, social welfare) which are offered to them in the country. Social security may also refer to the action programs of government intended to promote the welfare of the population through assistance measures guaranteeing access to sufficient resources for food and shelter and to promote health and wellbeing for the population at large and potentially vulnerable segments such as children, the elderly, the sick and the unemployed.
Opportunity cost	Opportunity cost is the cost of any activity measured in terms of the value of the next best alternative forgone (that is not chosen). It is the sacrifice related to the second best choice available to someone, or group, who has picked among several mutually exclusive choices. The opportunity cost is also the 'cost' (as a lost benefit) of the forgone products after making a choice.
Utility	In economics, utility is a representation of preferences over some set of goods and services. Preferences have a utility representation so long as they are transitive, complete, and continuous. Utility is usually applied by economists in such constructs as the indifference curve, which plot the combination of commodities that an individual or a society would accept to maintain a given level of satisfaction.
Incentive	Since human beings are purposeful creatures, the study of incentive structures is central to the study of all economic activity (both in terms of individual decision-making and in terms of co-operation and competition within a larger institutional structure). Economic analysis, then, of the differences between societies (and between different organizations within a society) largely amounts to characterizing the differences in incentive structures faced by individuals involved in these collective efforts. Ultimately, incentives aim to provide value for money and contribute to organizational success.
International trade	International trade is the exchange of capital, goods, and services across international borders or territories. In most countries, such trade represents a significant share of gross domestic product (GDP). While international trade has been present throughout much of history , its economic, social, and political importance has been on the rise in recent centuries.

Visit Cram101.com for full Practice Exams

Chapter 1. The Economic Approach

CHAPTER HIGHLIGHTS & NOTES: KEY TERMS, PEOPLE, PLACES, CONCEPTS

Unintended consequences	In the social sciences, unintended consequences are outcomes that are not the ones intended by a purposeful action. The concept has long existed but was named and popularised in the 20th century by American sociologist Robert K. Merton. Unintended consequences can be roughly grouped into three types:•A positive, unexpected benefit (usually referred to as luck, serendipity or a windfall).•A negative, unexpected detriment occurring in addition to the desired effect of the policy .•A perverse effect contrary to what was originally intended (when an intended solution makes a problem worse), such as when a policy has a perverse incentive that causes actions opposite to what was intended.History The idea of unintended consequences dates back at least to Adam Smith, the Scottish Enlightenment, and consequentialism (judging by results).
Normative economics	Normative economics is that part of economics that expresses value judgments (normative judgments) about economic fairness or what the economy ought to be like or what goals of public policy ought to be. It is common to distinguish normative economics from positive economics ('what is'). But many normative (value) judgments are held conditionally, to be given up if facts or knowledge of facts changes, so that a change of values may be purely scientific.
Positive economics	Positive economics is the branch of economics that concerns the description and explanation of economic phenomena. It focuses on facts and cause-and-effect behavioral relationships and includes the development and testing of economics theories. Earlier terms were value-free economics and its German counterpart wertfrei economics.
Environmental protection	Environmental protection is a practice of protecting the environment, on individual, organizational or governmental levels, for the benefit of the natural environment and (or) humans. Due to the pressures of population and technology, the biophysical environment is being degraded, sometimes permanently. This has been recognized, and governments have begun placing restraints on activities that cause environmental degradation.
Total cost	In economics, and cost accounting, total cost describes the total economic cost of production and is made up of variable costs, which vary according to the quantity of a good produced and include inputs such as labor and raw materials, plus fixed costs, which are independent of the quantity of a good produced and include inputs (capital) that cannot be varied in the short term, such as buildings and machinery. Total cost in economics includes the total opportunity cost of each factor of production as part of its fixed or variable costs. The rate at which total cost changes as the amount produced changes is called marginal cost.

Visit Cram101.com for full Practice Exams

Chapter 1. The Economic Approach

CHAPTER QUIZ: KEY TERMS, PEOPLE, PLACES, CONCEPTS

1. _____ is the controlled distribution of scarce resources, goods, or services. _____ controls the size of the ration, one's allotted portion of the resources being distributed on a particular day or at a particular time.

   In economics, _____ is an artificial restriction of demand.

   a. 2007 Gasoline Rationing Plan in Iran
   b. CC41
   c. First-come, first-served
   d. Rationing

2. _____ is a concept enshrined in Article 22 of the Universal Declaration of Human Rights which states that Everyone, as a member of society, has the right to _____ and is entitled to realization, through national effort and international co-operation and in accordance with the organization and resources of each State, of the economic, social and cultural rights indispensable for his dignity and the free development of his personality. In simple term, this means that the signatories agree that society in which a person lives should help them to develop and to make the most of all the advantages (culture, work, social welfare) which are offered to them in the country.

   _____ may also refer to the action programs of government intended to promote the welfare of the population through assistance measures guaranteeing access to sufficient resources for food and shelter and to promote health and wellbeing for the population at large and potentially vulnerable segments such as children, the elderly, the sick and the unemployed.

   a. Social Security Agency
   b. Social welfare function
   c. Social security
   d. Suits index

3. A _____ is a natural resource with the ability to reproduce through biological or natural processes and replenished with the passage of time. _____s are part of our natural environment and form our eco-system.

   In 1962, within a report to the committee on natural resources which was forwarded to the President of the United States, Paul Weiss defined _____s as: 'The total range of living organisms providing man with food, fibers, drugs, etc...'.

   a. Sustainable yield
   b. Renewable resource
   c. Resource allocation
   d. Resource nationalism

4. . _____ is the stock of competencies, knowledge, social and personality attributes, including creativity, embodied in the ability to perform labor so as to produce economic value. It is an aggregate economic view of the human being acting within economies, which is an attempt to capture the social, biological, cultural and psychological complexity as they interact in explicit and/or economic transactions.

Chapter 1. The Economic Approach

CHAPTER QUIZ: KEY TERMS, PEOPLE, PLACES, CONCEPTS

It was assumed in early economic theories, reflecting the context in which the secondary sector of the economy was producing much more than the tertiary sector was able to produce at the time in most countries - to be a fungible resource, homogeneous, and easily interchangeable, and it was referred to simply as workforce or labor, one of three factors of production (the others being land, and assumed-interchangeable assets of money and physical equipment).

a. Knowledge capital
b. Human capital
c. Means of production
d. Natural capital

5. In the social sciences, _____ are outcomes that are not the ones intended by a purposeful action. The concept has long existed but was named and popularised in the 20th century by American sociologist Robert K. Merton.

    _____ can be roughly grouped into three types:•A positive, unexpected benefit (usually referred to as luck, serendipity or a windfall).•A negative, unexpected detriment occurring in addition to the desired effect of the policy .•A perverse effect contrary to what was originally intended (when an intended solution makes a problem worse), such as when a policy has a perverse incentive that causes actions opposite to what was intended.History

    The idea of _____ dates back at least to Adam Smith, the Scottish Enlightenment, and consequentialism (judging by results).

    a. 15th century
    b. Laffey Matrix
    c. Law costs draftsman
    d. Unintended consequences

ANSWER KEY
Chapter 1. The Economic Approach

1. d
2. c
3. b
4. b
5. d

You can take the complete Chapter Practice Test

for Chapter 1. The Economic Approach
on all key terms, persons, places, and concepts.

Online 99 Cents

http://www.epub40.13.20514.1.cram101.com/

Use www.Cram101.com for all your study needs

including Cram101's online interactive problem solving labs in

chemistry, statistics, mathematics, and more.

Chapter 2. Some Tools of the Economist

CHAPTER OUTLINE: KEY TERMS, PEOPLE, PLACES, CONCEPTS

- _____ Opportunity cost
- _____ Social security
- _____ Exchange
- _____ Great Depression
- _____ Derived demand
- _____ Environmental protection
- _____ Labor relations
- _____ Entrepreneur
- _____ Invention
- _____ Investment
- _____ Renewable resource
- _____ Gains from trade
- _____ Total cost
- _____ AD-AS model
- _____ Comparative advantage
- _____ Human capital
- _____ Mass production
- _____ Phillips curve
- _____ Capitalism

Visit Cram101.com for full Practice Exams

Chapter 2. Some Tools of the Economist

CHAPTER OUTLINE: KEY TERMS, PEOPLE, PLACES, CONCEPTS

Climate change

CHAPTER HIGHLIGHTS & NOTES: KEY TERMS, PEOPLE, PLACES, CONCEPTS

Opportunity cost	Opportunity cost is the cost of any activity measured in terms of the value of the next best alternative forgone (that is not chosen). It is the sacrifice related to the second best choice available to someone, or group, who has picked among several mutually exclusive choices. The opportunity cost is also the 'cost' (as a lost benefit) of the forgone products after making a choice.
Social security	Social security is a concept enshrined in Article 22 of the Universal Declaration of Human Rights which states that Everyone, as a member of society, has the right to social security and is entitled to realization, through national effort and international co-operation and in accordance with the organization and resources of each State, of the economic, social and cultural rights indispensable for his dignity and the free development of his personality. In simple term, this means that the signatories agree that society in which a person lives should help them to develop and to make the most of all the advantages (culture, work, social welfare) which are offered to them in the country. Social security may also refer to the action programs of government intended to promote the welfare of the population through assistance measures guaranteeing access to sufficient resources for food and shelter and to promote health and wellbeing for the population at large and potentially vulnerable segments such as children, the elderly, the sick and the unemployed.
Exchange	In the tactics and strategy in the board game of chess, an exchange (exchanging) or trade (trading) of chess pieces is series of closely related moves, typically sequential, in which the two players capture each other's pieces. Any types of pieces except the kings may possibly be exchanged, i.e. captured in an exchange, although a king can capture an opponent's piece. Either the player of the white or the black pieces may make the first capture of the other player's piece in an exchange, followed by the other player capturing a piece of the first player, often referred to as a recapture.
Great Depression	The Great Depression was a severe worldwide economic depression in the decade preceding World War II.

Chapter 2. Some Tools of the Economist

CHAPTER HIGHLIGHTS & NOTES: KEY TERMS, PEOPLE, PLACES, CONCEPTS

	The timing of the Great Depression varied across nations, but in most countries it started in 1930 after the passage of the Smoot-Hawley Tariff bill (June 17), and lasted until the late 1930s or early 1940s. It was the longest, most widespread, and deepest depression of the 20th century.

In the 21st century, the Great Depression is commonly used as an example of how far the world's economy can decline. |
Derived demand	Derived demand is a term in economics, where demand for one good or service occurs as a result of the demand for another intermediate/ final good or service. This may occur as the former is a part of production of the second. For example, demand for coal leads to derived demand for mining, as coal must be mined for coal to be consumed.
Environmental protection	Environmental protection is a practice of protecting the environment, on individual, organizational or governmental levels, for the benefit of the natural environment and (or) humans. Due to the pressures of population and technology, the biophysical environment is being degraded, sometimes permanently. This has been recognized, and governments have begun placing restraints on activities that cause environmental degradation.
Labor relations	Labor relations is the study and practice of managing unionized employment situations. In academia, labor relations is frequently a subarea within industrial relations, though scholars from many disciplines--including economics, sociology, history, law, and political science--also study labor unions and labor movements. In practice, labor relations is frequently a subarea within human resource management.
Entrepreneur	An entrepreneur is an enterprising individual who builds capital through risk and/or initiative. The term was originally a loanword from French and was first defined by the Irish-French economist Richard Cantillon. Entrepreneur in English is a term applied to a person who is willing to help launch a new venture or enterprise and accept full responsibility for the outcome.
Invention	An invention is a unique or novel device, method, composition or process. It may also be an improvement upon a machine or product, or alternate means of achieving a process. An invention that is not derived from an existing model or idea, or that achieves a completely unique function or result, may be a radical breakthrough.
Investment	Investment has different meanings in finance and economics. Finance investment is putting money into something with the expectation of gain, that upon thorough analysis, has a high degree of security for the principal amount, as well as security of return, within an expected period of time.

Visit Cram101.com for full Practice Exams

Chapter 2. Some Tools of the Economist

CHAPTER HIGHLIGHTS & NOTES: KEY TERMS, PEOPLE, PLACES, CONCEPTS

Renewable resource	A renewable resource is a natural resource with the ability to reproduce through biological or natural processes and replenished with the passage of time. Renewable resources are part of our natural environment and form our eco-system. In 1962, within a report to the committee on natural resources which was forwarded to the President of the United States, Paul Weiss defined Renewable Resources as: 'The total range of living organisms providing man with food, fibers, drugs, etc...'.
Gains from trade	Gains from trade in economics refers to net benefits to agents from allowing an increase in voluntary trading with each other. In technical terms, it is the increase of consumer surplus plus producer surplus from lower tariffs or otherwise liberalizing trade. Gains from trade are commonly described as resulting from:•specialization in production from division of labor, economies of scale, scope, and agglomeration and relative availability of factor resources in types of output by farms, businesses, location and economies•a resulting increase in total output possibilities•trade through markets from sale of one type of output for other, more highly valued goods. Market incentives, such as reflected in prices of outputs and inputs, are theorized to attract factors of production, including labor, into activities according to comparative advantage, that is, for which they each have a low opportunity cost.
Total cost	In economics, and cost accounting, total cost describes the total economic cost of production and is made up of variable costs, which vary according to the quantity of a good produced and include inputs such as labor and raw materials, plus fixed costs, which are independent of the quantity of a good produced and include inputs (capital) that cannot be varied in the short term, such as buildings and machinery. Total cost in economics includes the total opportunity cost of each factor of production as part of its fixed or variable costs. The rate at which total cost changes as the amount produced changes is called marginal cost.
AD-AS model	The AD-AS or Aggregate Demand-Aggregate Supply model is a macroeconomic model that explains price level and output through the relationship of aggregate demand and aggregate supply. It is based on the theory of John Maynard Keynes presented in his work The General Theory of Employment, Interest, and Money. It is one of the primary simplified representations in the modern field of macroeconomics, and is used by a broad array of economists, from libertarian, Monetarist supporters of laissez-faire, such as Milton Friedman to Post-Keynesian supporters of economic interventionism, such as Joan Robinson. The conventional 'aggregate supply and demand' model is, in actuality, a Keynesian visualization that has come to be a widely accepted image of the theory.

Visit Cram101.com for full Practice Exams

Chapter 2. Some Tools of the Economist

CHAPTER HIGHLIGHTS & NOTES: KEY TERMS, PEOPLE, PLACES, CONCEPTS

	The Classical supply and demand model, which is largely based on Say's Law, or that supply creates its own demand, depicts the aggregate supply curve as being vertical at all times (not just in the long-run)Modeling
	The AD/AS model is used to illustrate the Keynesian model of the business cycle. Movements of the two curves can be used to predict the effects that various exogenous events will have on two variables: real GDP and the price level. Furthermore, the model can be incorporated as a component in any of a variety of dynamic models (models of how variables like the price level and others evolve over time). The AD-AS model can be related to the Phillips curve model of wage or price inflation and unemployment.
Comparative advantage	In economics, the theory of comparative advantage refers to the ability of a person or a country to produce a particular good or service at a lower marginal and opportunity cost over another. Even if one country is more efficient in the production of all goods (absolute advantage in all goods) than the other, both countries will still gain by trading with each other, as long as they have different relative efficiencies.
	For example, if, using machinery, a worker in one country can produce both shoes and shirts at 6 per hour, and a worker in a country with less machinery can produce either 2 shoes or 4 shirts in an hour, each country can gain from trade because their internal trade-offs between shoes and shirts are different.
Human capital	Human capital is the stock of competencies, knowledge, social and personality attributes, including creativity, embodied in the ability to perform labor so as to produce economic value. It is an aggregate economic view of the human being acting within economies, which is an attempt to capture the social, biological, cultural and psychological complexity as they interact in explicit and/or economic transactions.
	It was assumed in early economic theories, reflecting the context in which the secondary sector of the economy was producing much more than the tertiary sector was able to produce at the time in most countries - to be a fungible resource, homogeneous, and easily interchangeable, and it was referred to simply as workforce or labor, one of three factors of production (the others being land, and assumed-interchangeable assets of money and physical equipment).
Mass production	Mass production is the production of large amounts of standardized products, including and especially on assembly lines.
Phillips curve	In economics, the Phillips curve is a historical inverse relationship between the rate of unemployment and the rate of inflation in an economy. Stated simply, the lower the unemployment in an economy, the higher the rate of inflation.

Visit Cram101.com for full Practice Exams

Chapter 2. Some Tools of the Economist

CHAPTER HIGHLIGHTS & NOTES: KEY TERMS, PEOPLE, PLACES, CONCEPTS

Capitalism	Capitalism is generally considered to be an economic system that is based on private ownership of the means of production and the creation of goods or services for profit by privately-owned business enterprises. Some have also used the term as a synonym for competitive markets, wage labor, capital accumulation, voluntary exchange, and personal finance. The designation is applied to a variety of historical cases, varying in time, geography, politics, and culture.
Climate change	Climate change is a significant and lasting change in the statistical distribution of weather patterns over periods ranging from decades to millions of years. It may be a change in average weather conditions, or in the distribution of weather around the average conditions (i.e., more or fewer extreme weather events). Climate change is caused by factors that include oceanic processes (such as oceanic circulation), variations in solar radiation received by Earth, plate tectonics and volcanic eruptions, and human-induced alterations of the natural world; these latter effects are currently causing global warming, and 'climate change' is often used to describe human-specific impacts.

CHAPTER QUIZ: KEY TERMS, PEOPLE, PLACES, CONCEPTS

1. In economics, the theory of _____ refers to the ability of a person or a country to produce a particular good or service at a lower marginal and opportunity cost over another. Even if one country is more efficient in the production of all goods (absolute advantage in all goods) than the other, both countries will still gain by trading with each other, as long as they have different relative efficiencies.

    For example, if, using machinery, a worker in one country can produce both shoes and shirts at 6 per hour, and a worker in a country with less machinery can produce either 2 shoes or 4 shirts in an hour, each country can gain from trade because their internal trade-offs between shoes and shirts are different.

    a. Competitiveness Policy Council
    b. Comparative advantage
    c. Confirming house
    d. Country of origin

2. _____ is a term in economics, where demand for one good or service occurs as a result of the demand for another intermediate/ final good or service. This may occur as the former is a part of production of the second. For example, demand for coal leads to _____ for mining, as coal must be mined for coal to be consumed.

    a. Hicksian demand function
    b. Joint demand
    c. Derived demand
    d. Law of demand

Visit Cram101.com for full Practice Exams

Chapter 2. Some Tools of the Economist

CHAPTER QUIZ: KEY TERMS, PEOPLE, PLACES, CONCEPTS

3. In economics, and cost accounting, _____ describes the total economic cost of production and is made up of variable costs, which vary according to the quantity of a good produced and include inputs such as labor and raw materials, plus fixed costs, which are independent of the quantity of a good produced and include inputs (capital) that cannot be varied in the short term, such as buildings and machinery. _____ in economics includes the total opportunity cost of each factor of production as part of its fixed or variable costs.

   The rate at which _____ changes as the amount produced changes is called marginal cost.

   a. Total cost of ownership
   b. Total value of ownership
   c. Total cost
   d. Value

4. _____ is the cost of any activity measured in terms of the value of the next best alternative forgone (that is not chosen). It is the sacrifice related to the second best choice available to someone, or group, who has picked among several mutually exclusive choices. The _____ is also the 'cost' (as a lost benefit) of the forgone products after making a choice.

   a. Overchoice
   b. Opportunity cost
   c. Agricultural Wages (Regulation) Act 1924
   d. Abnormal Importations (Customs Duties) Act 1931

5. _____ is a concept enshrined in Article 22 of the Universal Declaration of Human Rights which states that Everyone, as a member of society, has the right to _____ and is entitled to realization, through national effort and international co-operation and in accordance with the organization and resources of each State, of the economic, social and cultural rights indispensable for his dignity and the free development of his personality. In simple term, this means that the signatories agree that society in which a person lives should help them to develop and to make the most of all the advantages (culture, work, social welfare) which are offered to them in the country.

   _____ may also refer to the action programs of government intended to promote the welfare of the population through assistance measures guaranteeing access to sufficient resources for food and shelter and to promote health and wellbeing for the population at large and potentially vulnerable segments such as children, the elderly, the sick and the unemployed.

   a. Social Security Agency
   b. Social security
   c. Structural adjustment loan
   d. Suits index

Visit Cram101.com for full Practice Exams

ANSWER KEY
Chapter 2. Some Tools of the Economist

1. b
2. c
3. c
4. b
5. b

You can take the complete Chapter Practice Test

for Chapter 2. Some Tools of the Economist
on all key terms, persons, places, and concepts.

Online 99 Cents

http://www.epub40.13.20514.2.cram101.com/

Use www.Cram101.com for all your study needs

including Cram101's online interactive problem solving labs in

chemistry, statistics, mathematics, and more.

Chapter 3. Supply, Demand, and the Market Process

CHAPTER OUTLINE: KEY TERMS, PEOPLE, PLACES, CONCEPTS

- Aggregate supply
- AD-AS model
- Social security
- Consumer choice
- Law of demand
- Supply and demand
- Consumer
- Marginal utility
- Marginal value
- Total cost
- Aggregate demand
- Demand curve
- Renewable resource
- Game theory
- Opportunity cost
- Product market
- Entrepreneur
- Market economy
- Law of supply

Visit Cram101.com for full Practice Exams

Chapter 3. Supply, Demand, and the Market Process

CHAPTER OUTLINE: KEY TERMS, PEOPLE, PLACES, CONCEPTS

_____	Phillips curve
_____	Environmental protection
_____	New York Stock Exchange
_____	Stock exchange
_____	Economic efficiency
_____	Income tax
_____	Tax credit
_____	Invisible hand
_____	Market price

CHAPTER HIGHLIGHTS & NOTES: KEY TERMS, PEOPLE, PLACES, CONCEPTS

Aggregate supply	In economics, aggregate supply is the total supply of goods and services that firms in a national economy plan on selling during a specific time period. It is the total amount of goods and services that firms are willing to sell at a given price level in an economy. There are two main reasons why Q^s might rise as P rises, i.e., why the AS curve is upward sloping:•aggregate supply is usually inadequate to supply ample opportunity.
AD-AS model	The AD-AS or Aggregate Demand-Aggregate Supply model is a macroeconomic model that explains price level and output through the relationship of aggregate demand and aggregate supply. It is based on the theory of John Maynard Keynes presented in his work The General Theory of Employment, Interest, and Money. It is one of the primary simplified representations in the modern field of macroeconomics, and is used by a broad array of economists, from libertarian, Monetarist supporters of laissez-faire, such as Milton Friedman to Post-Keynesian supporters of economic interventionism, such as Joan Robinson.

Visit Cram101.com for full Practice Exams

Chapter 3. Supply, Demand, and the Market Process

	The conventional 'aggregate supply and demand' model is, in actuality, a Keynesian visualization that has come to be a widely accepted image of the theory. The Classical supply and demand model, which is largely based on Say's Law, or that supply creates its own demand, depicts the aggregate supply curve as being vertical at all times (not just in the long-run)Modeling
	The AD/AS model is used to illustrate the Keynesian model of the business cycle. Movements of the two curves can be used to predict the effects that various exogenous events will have on two variables: real GDP and the price level. Furthermore, the model can be incorporated as a component in any of a variety of dynamic models (models of how variables like the price level and others evolve over time). The AD-AS model can be related to the Phillips curve model of wage or price inflation and unemployment.
Social security	Social security is a concept enshrined in Article 22 of the Universal Declaration of Human Rights which states that Everyone, as a member of society, has the right to social security and is entitled to realization, through national effort and international co-operation and in accordance with the organization and resources of each State, of the economic, social and cultural rights indispensable for his dignity and the free development of his personality. In simple term, this means that the signatories agree that society in which a person lives should help them to develop and to make the most of all the advantages (culture, work, social welfare) which are offered to them in the country.
	Social security may also refer to the action programs of government intended to promote the welfare of the population through assistance measures guaranteeing access to sufficient resources for food and shelter and to promote health and wellbeing for the population at large and potentially vulnerable segments such as children, the elderly, the sick and the unemployed.
Consumer choice	Consumer choice is a theory of microeconomics that relates preferences for consumption goods and services to consumption expenditures and ultimately to consumer demand curves. The link between personal preferences, consumption, and the demand curve is one of the most closely studied relations in economics. Consumer choice theory is a way of analyzing how consumers may achieve equilibrium between preferences and expenditures by maximizing utility as subject to consumer budget constraints.
Law of demand	In economics, the law of demand is an economic law, which states that consumers buy more of a good when its price decreases and less when its price increases (ceteris paribus).
	The greater the amount to be sold, the smaller the price at which it is offered must be, in order for it to find purchasers.

Chapter 3. Supply, Demand, and the Market Process

CHAPTER HIGHLIGHTS & NOTES: KEY TERMS, PEOPLE, PLACES, CONCEPTS

Supply and demand	Supply and demand is an economic model of price determination in a market. It concludes that in a competitive market, the unit price for a particular good will vary until it settles at a point where the quantity demanded by consumers (at current price) will equal the quantity supplied by producers (at current price), resulting in an economic equilibrium of price and quantity. The four basic laws of supply and demand are:•If demand increases and supply remains unchanged, then it leads to higher equilibrium price and higher quantity.•If demand decreases and supply remains unchanged, then it leads to lower equilibrium price and lower quantity.•If supply increases and demand remains unchanged, then it leads to lower equilibrium price and higher quantity.•If supply decreases and demand remains unchanged, then it leads to higher equilibrium price and lower quantity.Graphical representation of supply and demand Although it is normal to regard the quantity demanded and the quantity supplied as functions of the price of the good, the standard graphical representation, usually attributed to Alfred Marshall, has price on the vertical axis and quantity on the horizontal axis, the opposite of the standard convention for the representation of a mathematical function.
Consumer	A consumer is a person or group of people that are the final users of products and or services generated within a social system. A consumer may be a person or group, such as a household. The concept of a consumer may vary significantly by context.
Marginal utility	In economics, the marginal utility of a good or service is the gain from an increase in the consumption of that good or service. Economists sometimes speak of a law of diminishing marginal utility, meaning that the first unit of consumption of a good or service yields more utility than the second and subsequent units. The concept of marginal utility played a crucial role in the marginal revolution of the late 19th century, and led to the replacement of the labor theory of value by neoclassical value theory in which the relative prices of goods and services are simultaneously determined by marginal rates of substitution in consumption and marginal rates of transformation in production, which are equal in economic equilibrium.
Marginal value	A marginal value is•a value that holds true given particular constraints,•the change in a value associated with a specific change in some independent variable, whether it be of that variable or of a dependent variable, or•[when underlying values are quantified] the ratio of the change of a dependent variable to that of the independent variable. (This third case is actual a special case of the second). In the case of differentiability, at the limit, a marginal change is a mathematical differential, or the corresponding mathematical derivative.

Chapter 3. Supply, Demand, and the Market Process

CHAPTER HIGHLIGHTS & NOTES: KEY TERMS, PEOPLE, PLACES, CONCEPTS

Total cost	In economics, and cost accounting, total cost describes the total economic cost of production and is made up of variable costs, which vary according to the quantity of a good produced and include inputs such as labor and raw materials, plus fixed costs, which are independent of the quantity of a good produced and include inputs (capital) that cannot be varied in the short term, such as buildings and machinery. Total cost in economics includes the total opportunity cost of each factor of production as part of its fixed or variable costs. The rate at which total cost changes as the amount produced changes is called marginal cost.
Aggregate demand	In macroeconomics, aggregate demand is the total demand for final goods and services in the economy (Y) at a given time and price level. It is the amount of goods and services in the economy that will be purchased at all possible price levels. This is the demand for the gross domestic product of a country when inventory levels are static.
Demand curve	In economics, the demand curve is the graph depicting the relationship between the price of a certain commodity and the amount of it that consumers are willing and able to purchase at that given price. It is a graphic representation of a demand schedule. The demand curve for all consumers together follows from the demand curve of every individual consumer: the individual demands at each price are added together.
Renewable resource	A renewable resource is a natural resource with the ability to reproduce through biological or natural processes and replenished with the passage of time. Renewable resources are part of our natural environment and form our eco-system. In 1962, within a report to the committee on natural resources which was forwarded to the President of the United States, Paul Weiss defined Renewable Resources as: 'The total range of living organisms providing man with food, fibers, drugs, etc...'.
Game theory	Game theory is the study of strategic decision making. More formally, it is 'the study of mathematical models of conflict and cooperation between intelligent rational decision-makers.' An alternative term suggested 'as a more descriptive name for the discipline' is interactive decision theory. Game theory is mainly used in economics, political science, and psychology, as well as logic and biology.
Opportunity cost	Opportunity cost is the cost of any activity measured in terms of the value of the next best alternative forgone (that is not chosen). It is the sacrifice related to the second best choice available to someone, or group, who has picked among several mutually exclusive choices. The opportunity cost is also the 'cost' (as a lost benefit) of the forgone products after making a choice.
Product market	Product market is a mechanism that allows people to easily buy and sell products.

Visit Cram101.com for full Practice Exams

Chapter 3. Supply, Demand, and the Market Process

CHAPTER HIGHLIGHTS & NOTES: KEY TERMS, PEOPLE, PLACES, CONCEPTS

	Services are often included in the scope of the term. Product market regulation is an economic term that describes restrictions in the market.
Entrepreneur	An entrepreneur is an enterprising individual who builds capital through risk and/or initiative. The term was originally a loanword from French and was first defined by the Irish-French economist Richard Cantillon. Entrepreneur in English is a term applied to a person who is willing to help launch a new venture or enterprise and accept full responsibility for the outcome.
Market economy	A Market Economy is an economy in which decisions regarding investment, production and distribution are based on supply and demand and the prices of goods and services are determined in a free price system. This is contrasted with a planned economy, where investment and production decisions are embodied in a plan of production. Market economies can range from hypothetical laissez-faire and free market variants to regulated markets and interventionist variants.
Law of supply	The Law of Supply states that (all other things unchanged) an increase in price results in an increase in quantity supplied. This means that producers are willing to offer more products for sale on the market at higher prices by increasing production as a way of increasing profits.
Phillips curve	In economics, the Phillips curve is a historical inverse relationship between the rate of unemployment and the rate of inflation in an economy. Stated simply, the lower the unemployment in an economy, the higher the rate of inflation. While it has been observed that there is a stable short run tradeoff between unemployment and inflation, this has not been observed in the long run.
Environmental protection	Environmental protection is a practice of protecting the environment, on individual, organizational or governmental levels, for the benefit of the natural environment and (or) humans. Due to the pressures of population and technology, the biophysical environment is being degraded, sometimes permanently. This has been recognized, and governments have begun placing restraints on activities that cause environmental degradation.
New York Stock Exchange	The New York Stock Exchange, commonly referred to as NYSE is a stock exchange located at 11 Wall Street, Lower Manhattan, New York City, New York, United States. It is by far the world's largest stock exchange by market capitalization of its listed companies at US$14.242 trillion as of Dec 2011. Average daily trading value was approximately US$153 billion in 2008. The NYSE is operated by NYSE Euronext (NYSE: NYX), which was formed by the NYSE's 2007 merger with the fully electronic stock exchange Euronext.
Stock exchange	A stock exchange is a form of exchange which provides services for stock brokers and traders to trade stocks, bonds, and other securities.

Chapter 3. Supply, Demand, and the Market Process

	Stock exchanges also provide facilities for issue and redemption of securities and other financial instruments, and capital events including the payment of income and dividends. Securities traded on a stock exchange include shares issued by companies, unit trusts, derivatives, pooled investment products and bonds.
Economic efficiency	In economics, the term economic efficiency refers to the use of resources so as to maximize the production of goods and services. An economic system is said to be more efficient than another (in relative terms) if it can provide more goods and services for society without using more resources. In absolute terms, a situation can be called economically efficient if:•No one can be made better off without making someone else worse off (commonly referred to as Pareto efficiency).•No additional output can be obtained without increasing the amount of inputs.•Production proceeds at the lowest possible per-unit cost. These definitions of efficiency are not exactly equivalent, but they are all encompassed by the idea that a system is efficient if nothing more can be achieved given the resources available.
Income tax	An income tax is a tax levied on the income of individuals or businesses (corporations or other legal entities). Various income tax systems exist, with varying degrees of tax incidence. Income taxation can be progressive, proportional, or regressive.
Tax credit	A tax credit is a sum deducted from the total amount a taxpayer owes to the state. A tax credit may be granted for various types of taxes, such as an income tax, property tax, or VAT. It may be granted in recognition of taxes already paid, as a subsidy, or to encourage investment or other behaviors. In some systems tax credits are 'refundable' to the extent they exceed the relevant tax.
Invisible hand	In economics, invisible hand is the term economists use to describe the self-regulating nature of the marketplace. This is a metaphor first coined by the economist Adam Smith. The exact phrase is used just three times in his writings, but has come to capture his important claim that by trying to maximize their own gains in a free market, individual ambition benefits society, even if the ambitious have no benevolent intentions.
Market price	In economics, market price is the economic price for which a good or service is offered in the marketplace. It is of interest mainly in the study of microeconomics. Market value and market price are equal only under conditions of market efficiency, equilibrium, and rational expectations.

Chapter 3. Supply, Demand, and the Market Process

CHAPTER QUIZ: KEY TERMS, PEOPLE, PLACES, CONCEPTS

1. A _____ is a person or group of people that are the final users of products and or services generated within a social system. A _____ may be a person or group, such as a household. The concept of a _____ may vary significantly by context.

    a. Consumer complaint
    b. Consumer unit
    c. Consumer
    d. Cost-of-living index

2. In economics, _____ is the total supply of goods and services that firms in a national economy plan on selling during a specific time period. It is the total amount of goods and services that firms are willing to sell at a given price level in an economy.

    There are two main reasons why Q^s might rise as P rises, i.e., why the AS curve is upward sloping:• _____ is usually inadequate to supply ample opportunity.

    a. Aggregation problem
    b. Effective demand
    c. Arbitrista
    d. Aggregate supply

3. _____ is the study of strategic decision making. More formally, it is 'the study of mathematical models of conflict and cooperation between intelligent rational decision-makers.' An alternative term suggested 'as a more descriptive name for the discipline' is interactive decision theory. _____ is mainly used in economics, political science, and psychology, as well as logic and biology.

    a. Grammar systems theory
    b. Lexical density
    c. Logic
    d. Game theory

4. . A _____ is•a value that holds true given particular constraints,•the change in a value associated with a specific change in some independent variable, whether it be of that variable or of a dependent variable, or•[when underlying values are quantified] the ratio of the change of a dependent variable to that of the independent variable.

    (This third case is actual a special case of the second).

    In the case of differentiability, at the limit, a marginal change is a mathematical differential, or the corresponding mathematical derivative.

    These uses of the term 'marginal' are especially common in economics, and result from conceptualizing constraints as borders or as margins.

    a. Market cannibalism
    b. Marginal value

Chapter 3. Supply, Demand, and the Market Process

CHAPTER QUIZ: KEY TERMS, PEOPLE, PLACES, CONCEPTS

    c. Maximum sustainable yield
    d. Mechanism

5. In economics, the _____ of a good or service is the gain from an increase in the consumption of that good or service. Economists sometimes speak of a law of diminishing _____, meaning that the first unit of consumption of a good or service yields more utility than the second and subsequent units.

    The concept of _____ played a crucial role in the marginal revolution of the late 19th century, and led to the replacement of the labor theory of value by neoclassical value theory in which the relative prices of goods and services are simultaneously determined by marginal rates of substitution in consumption and marginal rates of transformation in production, which are equal in economic equilibrium.

    a. Means test
    b. Mincome
    c. Missing market
    d. Marginal utility

Visit Cram101.com for full Practice Exams

ANSWER KEY
Chapter 3. Supply, Demand, and the Market Process

1. c
2. d
3. d
4. b
5. d

You can take the complete Chapter Practice Test

for Chapter 3. Supply, Demand, and the Market Process
on all key terms, persons, places, and concepts.

Online 99 Cents

http://www.epub40.13.20514.3.cram101.com/

Use www.Cram101.com for all your study needs

including Cram101's online interactive problem solving labs in

chemistry, statistics, mathematics, and more.

Chapter 4. Supply and Demand: Applications and Extensions

CHAPTER OUTLINE: KEY TERMS, PEOPLE, PLACES, CONCEPTS

_____ AD-AS model

_____ Social security

_____ Product market

_____ Renewable resource

_____ Kyoto Protocol

_____ Price ceiling

_____ Price controls

_____ Human capital

_____ Black market

_____ Rent control

_____ Great Depression

_____ Price floor

_____ Fair Labor Standards Act

_____ Minimum wage

_____ Entry-level job

_____ Unemployment

_____ Tax incidence

_____ Tax rate

_____ Deadweight loss

Visit Cram101.com for full Practice Exams

Chapter 4. Supply and Demand: Applications and Extensions

CHAPTER OUTLINE: KEY TERMS, PEOPLE, PLACES, CONCEPTS

|_____ | Tax revenue
|_____ | Excess burden of taxation
|_____ | Game theory
|_____ | Progressive tax
|_____ | Proportional tax
|_____ | Regressive tax
|_____ | Laffer curve
|_____ | Health insurance
|_____ | Structural unemployment

CHAPTER HIGHLIGHTS & NOTES: KEY TERMS, PEOPLE, PLACES, CONCEPTS

AD-AS model	The AD-AS or Aggregate Demand-Aggregate Supply model is a macroeconomic model that explains price level and output through the relationship of aggregate demand and aggregate supply. It is based on the theory of John Maynard Keynes presented in his work The General Theory of Employment, Interest, and Money. It is one of the primary simplified representations in the modern field of macroeconomics, and is used by a broad array of economists, from libertarian, Monetarist supporters of laissez-faire, such as Milton Friedman to Post-Keynesian supporters of economic interventionism, such as Joan Robinson. The conventional 'aggregate supply and demand' model is, in actuality, a Keynesian visualization that has come to be a widely accepted image of the theory. The Classical supply and demand model, which is largely based on Say's Law, or that supply creates its own demand, depicts the aggregate supply curve as being vertical at all times (not just in the long-run)Modeling

Visit Cram101.com for full Practice Exams

Chapter 4. Supply and Demand: Applications and Extensions

CHAPTER HIGHLIGHTS & NOTES: KEY TERMS, PEOPLE, PLACES, CONCEPTS

	The AD/AS model is used to illustrate the Keynesian model of the business cycle. Movements of the two curves can be used to predict the effects that various exogenous events will have on two variables: real GDP and the price level. Furthermore, the model can be incorporated as a component in any of a variety of dynamic models (models of how variables like the price level and others evolve over time). The AD-AS model can be related to the Phillips curve model of wage or price inflation and unemployment.
Social security	Social security is a concept enshrined in Article 22 of the Universal Declaration of Human Rights which states that Everyone, as a member of society, has the right to social security and is entitled to realization, through national effort and international co-operation and in accordance with the organization and resources of each State, of the economic, social and cultural rights indispensable for his dignity and the free development of his personality. In simple term, this means that the signatories agree that society in which a person lives should help them to develop and to make the most of all the advantages (culture, work, social welfare) which are offered to them in the country. Social security may also refer to the action programs of government intended to promote the welfare of the population through assistance measures guaranteeing access to sufficient resources for food and shelter and to promote health and wellbeing for the population at large and potentially vulnerable segments such as children, the elderly, the sick and the unemployed.
Product market	Product market is a mechanism that allows people to easily buy and sell products. Services are often included in the scope of the term. Product market regulation is an economic term that describes restrictions in the market.
Renewable resource	A renewable resource is a natural resource with the ability to reproduce through biological or natural processes and replenished with the passage of time. Renewable resources are part of our natural environment and form our eco-system. In 1962, within a report to the committee on natural resources which was forwarded to the President of the United States, Paul Weiss defined Renewable Resources as: 'The total range of living organisms providing man with food, fibers, drugs, etc...'.
Kyoto Protocol	The Kyoto Protocol is a protocol to the United Nations Framework Convention on Climate Change (UNFCCC or FCCC), aimed at fighting global warming. The UNFCCC is an international environmental treaty with the goal of achieving the 'stabilisation of greenhouse gas concentrations in the atmosphere at a level that would prevent dangerous anthropogenic interference with the climate system.'

Chapter 4. Supply and Demand: Applications and Extensions

CHAPTER HIGHLIGHTS & NOTES: KEY TERMS, PEOPLE, PLACES, CONCEPTS

	The Protocol was initially adopted on 11 December 1997 in Kyoto, Japan, and entered into force on 16 February 2005. As of September 2011, 191 states have signed and ratified the protocol. The only remaining signatory not to have ratified the protocol is the United States.
Price ceiling	A price ceiling is a government-imposed limit on the price charged for a product. Governments intend price ceilings to protect consumers from conditions that could make necessary commodities unattainable. However, a price ceiling can cause problems if imposed for a long period without controlled rationing.
Price controls	Price controls are governmental restrictions on the prices that can be charged for goods and services in a market. The intent behind implementing such controls can stem from the desire to maintain affordability of staple foods and goods, to prevent price gouging during shortages, and to slow inflation, or, alternatively, to insure a minimum income for providers of certain goods. There are two primary forms of price control, a price ceiling, the maximum price that can be charged, and a price floor, the minimum price that can be charged.
Human capital	Human capital is the stock of competencies, knowledge, social and personality attributes, including creativity, embodied in the ability to perform labor so as to produce economic value. It is an aggregate economic view of the human being acting within economies, which is an attempt to capture the social, biological, cultural and psychological complexity as they interact in explicit and/or economic transactions.
	It was assumed in early economic theories, reflecting the context in which the secondary sector of the economy was producing much more than the tertiary sector was able to produce at the time in most countries - to be a fungible resource, homogeneous, and easily interchangeable, and it was referred to simply as workforce or labor, one of three factors of production (the others being land, and assumed-interchangeable assets of money and physical equipment).
Black market	A black market is a market in goods or services which operates outside the formal one(s) supported by established state powerg. 'the black market in bush meat' or the state jurisdiction 'the black market in China'.
	It is distinct from the grey market, in which commodities are distributed through channels which, while legal, are unofficial, unauthorized, or unintended by the original manufacturer, and the white market, the legal market for goods and services.
Rent control	Rent control refers to laws or ordinances that set price controls on the renting of residential housing. It functions as a price ceiling. Rent control exists in approximately 40 countries around the world.

Visit Cram101.com for full Practice Exams

Chapter 4. Supply and Demand: Applications and Extensions

CHAPTER HIGHLIGHTS & NOTES: KEY TERMS, PEOPLE, PLACES, CONCEPTS

Great Depression	The Great Depression was a severe worldwide economic depression in the decade preceding World War II. The timing of the Great Depression varied across nations, but in most countries it started in 1930 after the passage of the Smoot-Hawley Tariff bill (June 17), and lasted until the late 1930s or early 1940s. It was the longest, most widespread, and deepest depression of the 20th century. In the 21st century, the Great Depression is commonly used as an example of how far the world's economy can decline.
Price floor	A price floor is a government- or group-imposed limit on how low a price can be charged for a product. For a price floor to be effective, it must be greater than the equilibrium price. A price floor can be set below the free-market equilibrium price.
Fair Labor Standards Act	The Fair Labor Standards Act 1938 is a federal statute of the United States. The FLSA established a national minimum wage, guaranteed 'time-and-a-half' for overtime in certain jobs, and prohibited most employment of minors in 'oppressive child labor,' a term that is defined in the statute. It applies to employees engaged in interstate commerce or employed by an enterprise engaged in commerce or in the production of goods for commerce, unless the employer can claim an exemption from coverage.
Minimum wage	A minimum wage is the lowest hourly, daily or monthly remuneration that employers may legally pay to workers. Equivalently, it is the lowest wage at which workers may sell their labor. Although minimum wage laws are in effect in many jurisdictions, differences of opinion exist about the benefits and drawbacks of a minimum wage.
Entry-level job	An entry-level job is a job that is normally designed or designated for recent graduates of a given discipline, and does not require prior experience in the field or profession. These may require some on-site training. Many entry-level jobs are part-time, and do not include employee benefits.
Unemployment	Unemployment, as defined by the International Labour Organization, occurs when people are without jobs and they have actively sought work within the past four weeks. The unemployment rate is a measure of the prevalence of unemployment and it is calculated as a percentage by dividing the number of unemployed individuals by all individuals currently in the labor force. In a 2011 news story, BusinessWeek reported, 'More than 200 million people globally are out of work, a record high, as almost two-thirds of advanced economies and half of developing countries are experiencing a slowdown in employment growth'.
Tax incidence	In economics, tax incidence is the analysis of the effect of a particular tax on the distribution of economic welfare. Tax incidence is said to 'fall' upon the group that, at the end of the day, bears the burden of the tax.

Chapter 4. Supply and Demand: Applications and Extensions

CHAPTER HIGHLIGHTS & NOTES: KEY TERMS, PEOPLE, PLACES, CONCEPTS

Tax rate	In a tax system and in economics, the tax rate describes the burden ratio (usually expressed as a percentage) at which a business or person is taxed. There are several methods used to present a tax rate: statutory, average, marginal, and effective. These rates can also be presented using different definitions applied to a tax base: inclusive and exclusive.
Deadweight loss	In economics, a deadweight loss is a loss of economic efficiency that can occur when equilibrium for a good or service is not Pareto optimal. In other words, either people who would have more marginal benefit than marginal cost are not buying the product, or people who have more marginal cost than marginal benefit are buying the product. Causes of deadweight loss can include monopoly pricing (in the case of artificial scarcity), externalities, taxes or subsidies, and binding price ceilings or floors.
Tax revenue	Tax revenue is the income that is gained by governments through taxation. Just as there are different types of tax, the form in which tax revenue is collected also differs; furthermore, the agency that collects the tax may not be part of central government, but may be an alternative third-party licenced to collect tax which they themselves will use. For example:•In the UK, the DVLA collects vehicle excise duty, which is then passed onto the treasury. Tax revenues on purchases can come from two forms: 'tax' itself is a percentage of the price added to the purchase (such as sales tax in US states, or VAT in the UK), while 'duty' is a fixed amount added to the purchase price (such as is commonly found on cigarettes).
Excess burden of taxation	In economics, the excess burden of taxation, is one of the economic losses that society suffers as the result of a tax. Economic theory posits that distortions changes the amount and type of economic behavior from that which would occur in a free market without the tax. Excess burdens can be measured using the average cost of funds or the marginal cost of funds (MCF).
Game theory	Game theory is the study of strategic decision making. More formally, it is 'the study of mathematical models of conflict and cooperation between intelligent rational decision-makers.' An alternative term suggested 'as a more descriptive name for the discipline' is interactive decision theory. Game theory is mainly used in economics, political science, and psychology, as well as logic and biology.
Progressive tax	A progressive tax is a tax by which the tax rate increases as the taxable base amount increases. 'Progressive' describes a distribution effect on income or expenditure, referring to the way the rate progresses from low to high, where the average tax rate is less than the marginal tax rate. It can be applied to individual taxes or to a tax system as a whole; a year, multi-year, or lifetime.
Proportional tax	A proportional tax is a tax imposed so that the tax rate is fixed.

Chapter 4. Supply and Demand: Applications and Extensions

CHAPTER HIGHLIGHTS & NOTES: KEY TERMS, PEOPLE, PLACES, CONCEPTS

	The amount of the tax is in proportion to the amount subject to taxation. 'Proportional' describes a distribution effect on income or expenditure, referring to the way the rate remains consistent (does not progress from 'low to high' or 'high to low' as income or consumption changes), where the marginal tax rate is equal to the average tax rate.
Regressive tax	A regressive tax is a tax imposed in such a manner that the tax rate decreases as the amount subject to taxation increases. 'Regressive' describes a distribution effect on income or expenditure, referring to the way the rate progresses from high to low, where the average tax rate exceeds the marginal tax rate. In terms of individual income and wealth, a regressive tax imposes a greater burden (relative to resources) on the poor than on the rich -- there is an inverse relationship between the tax rate and the taxpayer's ability to pay as measured by assets, consumption, or income.
Laffer curve	In economics, the Laffer curve is a hypothetical representation of the relationship between government revenue raised by taxation and all possible rates of taxation. It is used to illustrate the concept of taxable income elasticity - that taxable income will change in response to changes in the rate of taxation. The Laffer curve postulates that no tax revenue will be raised at the extreme tax rates of 0% and 100%.
Health insurance	Health insurance is insurance against the risk of incurring medical expenses among individuals. By estimating the overall risk of health care expenses among a targeted group, an insurer can develop a routine finance structure, such as a monthly premium or payroll tax, to ensure that money is available to pay for the health care benefits specified in the insurance agreement. The benefit is administered by a central organization such as a government agency, private business, or not-for-profit entity.
Structural unemployment	Structural unemployment is a form of unemployment resulting from a mismatch between demand in the labour market and the skills and locations of the workers seeking employment. Even though the number of vacancies may be equal to, or greater than, the number of the unemployed, the unemployed workers may lack the skills needed for the jobs, or they may not live in the part of the country or world where the jobs are available.
	Structural unemployment is a result of the dynamics of the labor market, such as agricultural workers being displaced by mechanized agriculture, unskilled laborers displaced by both mechanization and automation, or industries with declining employment.

Chapter 4. Supply and Demand: Applications and Extensions

CHAPTER QUIZ: KEY TERMS, PEOPLE, PLACES, CONCEPTS

1. _____ is the stock of competencies, knowledge, social and personality attributes, including creativity, embodied in the ability to perform labor so as to produce economic value. It is an aggregate economic view of the human being acting within economies, which is an attempt to capture the social, biological, cultural and psychological complexity as they interact in explicit and/or economic transactions.

    It was assumed in early economic theories, reflecting the context in which the secondary sector of the economy was producing much more than the tertiary sector was able to produce at the time in most countries - to be a fungible resource, homogeneous, and easily interchangeable, and it was referred to simply as workforce or labor, one of three factors of production (the others being land, and assumed-interchangeable assets of money and physical equipment).

    a. Human capital
    b. Liquid capital
    c. Means of production
    d. Natural capital

2. _____ is a concept enshrined in Article 22 of the Universal Declaration of Human Rights which states that Everyone, as a member of society, has the right to _____ and is entitled to realization, through national effort and international co-operation and in accordance with the organization and resources of each State, of the economic, social and cultural rights indispensable for his dignity and the free development of his personality. In simple term, this means that the signatories agree that society in which a person lives should help them to develop and to make the most of all the advantages (culture, work, social welfare) which are offered to them in the country.

    _____ may also refer to the action programs of government intended to promote the welfare of the population through assistance measures guaranteeing access to sufficient resources for food and shelter and to promote health and wellbeing for the population at large and potentially vulnerable segments such as children, the elderly, the sick and the unemployed.

    a. Social Security Agency
    b. Social welfare function
    c. Structural adjustment loan
    d. Social security

3. . The AD-AS or Aggregate Demand-Aggregate Supply model is a macroeconomic model that explains price level and output through the relationship of aggregate demand and aggregate supply. It is based on the theory of John Maynard Keynes presented in his work The General Theory of Employment, Interest, and Money. It is one of the primary simplified representations in the modern field of macroeconomics, and is used by a broad array of economists, from libertarian, Monetarist supporters of laissez-faire, such as Milton Friedman to Post-Keynesian supporters of economic interventionism, such as Joan Robinson.

    The conventional 'aggregate supply and demand' model is, in actuality, a Keynesian visualization that has come to be a widely accepted image of the theory. The Classical supply and demand model, which is largely based on Say's Law, or that supply creates its own demand, depicts the aggregate supply curve as being vertical at all times (not just in the long-run)Modeling

    The AD/AS model is used to illustrate the Keynesian model of the business cycle.

Visit Cram101.com for full Practice Exams

Chapter 4. Supply and Demand: Applications and Extensions

CHAPTER QUIZ: KEY TERMS, PEOPLE, PLACES, CONCEPTS

Movements of the two curves can be used to predict the effects that various exogenous events will have on two variables: real GDP and the price level. Furthermore, the model can be incorporated as a component in any of a variety of dynamic models (models of how variables like the price level and others evolve over time). The _____ can be related to the Phillips curve model of wage or price inflation and unemployment.

a. AD-IA model
b. AK model
c. E2m.org
d. AD-AS model

4. The _____ is a protocol to the United Nations Framework Convention on Climate Change (UNFCCC or FCCC), aimed at fighting global warming. The UNFCCC is an international environmental treaty with the goal of achieving the 'stabilisation of greenhouse gas concentrations in the atmosphere at a level that would prevent dangerous anthropogenic interference with the climate system.'

The Protocol was initially adopted on 11 December 1997 in Kyoto, Japan, and entered into force on 16 February 2005. As of September 2011, 191 states have signed and ratified the protocol. The only remaining signatory not to have ratified the protocol is the United States.

a. The London Accord
b. Marginal abatement cost
c. Plant A Tree Today Foundation
d. Kyoto Protocol

5. In a tax system and in economics, the _____ describes the burden ratio (usually expressed as a percentage) at which a business or person is taxed. There are several methods used to present a _____: statutory, average, marginal, and effective. These rates can also be presented using different definitions applied to a tax base: inclusive and exclusive.

a. Tax refund
b. Tax revenue
c. Tax rate
d. Tax taking

ANSWER KEY
Chapter 4. Supply and Demand: Applications and Extensions

1. a
2. d
3. d
4. d
5. c

You can take the complete Chapter Practice Test

for Chapter 4. Supply and Demand: Applications and Extensions
on all key terms, persons, places, and concepts.

Online 99 Cents

http://www.epub40.13.20514.4.cram101.com/

Use www.Cram101.com for all your study needs

including Cram101's online interactive problem solving labs in

chemistry, statistics, mathematics, and more.

Chapter 5. Difficult Cases for the Market, and the Role of Government

CHAPTER OUTLINE: KEY TERMS, PEOPLE, PLACES, CONCEPTS

_____ Economic efficiency

_____ Cost curve

_____ Marginal cost

_____ Government

_____ AD-AS model

_____ Market price

_____ Monetary policy

_____ Monetary system

_____ Sherman Antitrust Act

_____ Phillips curve

_____ International trade

_____ Spillover effect

_____ Public good

_____ Renewable resource

_____ Consumer choice

_____ Free rider problem

_____ Climate change

_____ Quality control

_____ Government debt

Visit Cram101.com for full Practice Exams

Chapter 5. Difficult Cases for the Market, and the Role of Government

CHAPTER OUTLINE: KEY TERMS, PEOPLE, PLACES, CONCEPTS

Market failure

CHAPTER HIGHLIGHTS & NOTES: KEY TERMS, PEOPLE, PLACES, CONCEPTS

Economic efficiency	In economics, the term economic efficiency refers to the use of resources so as to maximize the production of goods and services. An economic system is said to be more efficient than another (in relative terms) if it can provide more goods and services for society without using more resources. In absolute terms, a situation can be called economically efficient if:•No one can be made better off without making someone else worse off (commonly referred to as Pareto efficiency).•No additional output can be obtained without increasing the amount of inputs.•Production proceeds at the lowest possible per-unit cost. These definitions of efficiency are not exactly equivalent, but they are all encompassed by the idea that a system is efficient if nothing more can be achieved given the resources available.
Cost curve	In economics, a cost curve is a graph of the costs of production as a function of total quantity produced. In a free market economy, productively efficient firms use these curves to find the optimal point of production (minimising cost), and profit maximizing firms can use them to decide output quantities to achieve those aims. There are various types of cost curves, all related to each other, including total and average cost curves, and marginal ('for each additional unit') cost curves, which are the equal to the differential of the total cost curves.
Marginal cost	In economics and finance, marginal cost is the change in total cost that arises when the quantity produced changes by one unit. That is, it is the cost of producing one more unit of a good. If the good being produced is infinitely divisible, so the size of a marginal cost will change with volume, as a non-linear and non-proportional cost function includes the following:•variable terms dependent to volume,•constant terms independent to volume and occurring with the respective lot size,•jump fix cost increase or decrease dependent to steps of volume increase. In practice the above definition of marginal cost as the change in total cost as a result of an increase in output of one unit is inconsistent with the calculation of marginal cost as $MC = dTC/dQ$ for virtually all non-linear functions.

Chapter 5. Difficult Cases for the Market, and the Role of Government

CHAPTER HIGHLIGHTS & NOTES: KEY TERMS, PEOPLE, PLACES, CONCEPTS

Government	Government, refers to the legislators, administrators, and arbitrators in the administrative bureaucracy who control a state at a given time, and to the system of government by which they are organized (Referred : More to govern than control). Government is the means by which state policy is enforced, as well as the mechanism for determining the policy of the state. A form of government, or form of state governance, refers to the set of political institutions by which a government of a state is organized.
AD-AS model	The AD-AS or Aggregate Demand-Aggregate Supply model is a macroeconomic model that explains price level and output through the relationship of aggregate demand and aggregate supply. It is based on the theory of John Maynard Keynes presented in his work The General Theory of Employment, Interest, and Money. It is one of the primary simplified representations in the modern field of macroeconomics, and is used by a broad array of economists, from libertarian, Monetarist supporters of laissez-faire, such as Milton Friedman to Post-Keynesian supporters of economic interventionism, such as Joan Robinson. The conventional 'aggregate supply and demand' model is, in actuality, a Keynesian visualization that has come to be a widely accepted image of the theory. The Classical supply and demand model, which is largely based on Say's Law, or that supply creates its own demand, depicts the aggregate supply curve as being vertical at all times (not just in the long-run)Modeling The AD/AS model is used to illustrate the Keynesian model of the business cycle. Movements of the two curves can be used to predict the effects that various exogenous events will have on two variables: real GDP and the price level. Furthermore, the model can be incorporated as a component in any of a variety of dynamic models (models of how variables like the price level and others evolve over time). The AD-AS model can be related to the Phillips curve model of wage or price inflation and unemployment.
Market price	In economics, market price is the economic price for which a good or service is offered in the marketplace. It is of interest mainly in the study of microeconomics. Market value and market price are equal only under conditions of market efficiency, equilibrium, and rational expectations.
Monetary policy	Monetary policy is the process by which the monetary authority of a country controls the supply of money, often targeting a rate of interest for the purpose of promoting economic growth and stability. The official goals usually include relatively stable prices and low unemployment. Monetary theory provides insight into how to craft optimal monetary policy.
Monetary system	A monetary system is anything that is accepted as a standard of value and measure of wealth in a particular region.

Chapter 5. Difficult Cases for the Market, and the Role of Government

CHAPTER HIGHLIGHTS & NOTES: KEY TERMS, PEOPLE, PLACES, CONCEPTS

	However, the current trend is to use international trade and investment to alter the policy and legislation of individual governments. The best recent example of this policy is the European Union's creation of the euro as a common currency for many of its individual states.
Sherman Antitrust Act	The Sherman Antitrust Act is a landmark federal statute on competition law passed by Congress in 1890. It prohibits certain business activities that reduce competition in the marketplace, and requires the United States federal government to investigate and pursue trusts, companies, and organizations suspected of being in violation. It was the first Federal statute to limit cartels and monopolies, and today still forms the basis for most antitrust litigation by the United States federal government. However, for the most part, politicians were unwilling to refer to the law until Theodore Roosevelt's presidency (1901-1909).
Phillips curve	In economics, the Phillips curve is a historical inverse relationship between the rate of unemployment and the rate of inflation in an economy. Stated simply, the lower the unemployment in an economy, the higher the rate of inflation. While it has been observed that there is a stable short run tradeoff between unemployment and inflation, this has not been observed in the long run.
International trade	International trade is the exchange of capital, goods, and services across international borders or territories. In most countries, such trade represents a significant share of gross domestic product (GDP). While international trade has been present throughout much of history, its economic, social, and political importance has been on the rise in recent centuries.
Spillover effect	Spillover effects are externalities of economic activity or processes that affect those who are not directly involved. Odours from a rendering plant are negative spillover effects upon its neighbours; the beauty of a homeowner's flower garden is a positive spillover effect upon neighbours. In the same way, the economic benefits of increased trade are the spillover effects anticipated in the formation of multilateral alliances of many of the regional nation states: e.g. SARC (South Asian Regional Cooperation), ASEAN (Association of South East Asian Nations) In reference to psychology, the spillover effect is when one's emotions affect the way they perceive other events.
Public good	In economics, a public good is a good that is both non-excludable and non-rivalrous in that individuals can not be effectively excluded from use and where use by one individual does not reduce availability to others. Examples of public goods include fresh air, clean water, knowledge, lighthouses, open source software, radio and television broadcasts, roads, street lighting.

Chapter 5. Difficult Cases for the Market, and the Role of Government

CHAPTER HIGHLIGHTS & NOTES: KEY TERMS, PEOPLE, PLACES, CONCEPTS

Renewable resource	A renewable resource is a natural resource with the ability to reproduce through biological or natural processes and replenished with the passage of time. Renewable resources are part of our natural environment and form our eco-system. In 1962, within a report to the committee on natural resources which was forwarded to the President of the United States, Paul Weiss defined Renewable Resources as: 'The total range of living organisms providing man with food, fibers, drugs, etc...'.
Consumer choice	Consumer choice is a theory of microeconomics that relates preferences for consumption goods and services to consumption expenditures and ultimately to consumer demand curves. The link between personal preferences, consumption, and the demand curve is one of the most closely studied relations in economics. Consumer choice theory is a way of analyzing how consumers may achieve equilibrium between preferences and expenditures by maximizing utility as subject to consumer budget constraints.
Free rider problem	In economics, collective bargaining, psychology, and political science, a free rider is someone who enjoys the benefits of an activity without paying for it. The free rider may withhold effort or resources, or may impose the costs of his or her activities on others. The free rider problem is the question of how to limit free riding.
Climate change	Climate change is a significant and lasting change in the statistical distribution of weather patterns over periods ranging from decades to millions of years. It may be a change in average weather conditions, or in the distribution of weather around the average conditions (i.e., more or fewer extreme weather events). Climate change is caused by factors that include oceanic processes (such as oceanic circulation), variations in solar radiation received by Earth, plate tectonics and volcanic eruptions, and human-induced alterations of the natural world; these latter effects are currently causing global warming, and 'climate change' is often used to describe human-specific impacts.
Quality control	Quality control, is a process by which entities review the quality of all factors involved in production. This approach places an emphasis on three aspects:•Elements such as controls, job management, defined and well managed processes, performance and integrity criteria, and identification of records•Competence, such as knowledge, skills, experience, and qualifications•Soft elements, such as personnel integrity, confidence, organizational culture, motivation, team spirit, and quality relationships. Controls include product inspection, where every product is examined visually, and often using a stereo microscope for fine detail before the product is sold into the external market. Inspectors will be provided with lists and descriptions of unacceptable product defects such as cracks or surface blemishes for example.

Visit Cram101.com for full Practice Exams

Chapter 5. Difficult Cases for the Market, and the Role of Government

CHAPTER HIGHLIGHTS & NOTES: KEY TERMS, PEOPLE, PLACES, CONCEPTS

Government debt	Government debt is the debt owed by a central government. (In the U.S. and other federal states, 'government debt' may also refer to the debt of a state or provincial government, municipal or local government). By contrast, the annual 'government deficit' refers to the difference between government receipts and spending in a single year, that is, the increase of debt over a particular year.
Market failure	Market failure is a concept within economic theory describing when the allocation of goods and services by a free market is not efficient. That is, there exists another conceivable outcome where a market participant may be made better-off without making someone else worse-off. (The outcome is not Pareto optimal).

CHAPTER QUIZ: KEY TERMS, PEOPLE, PLACES, CONCEPTS

1. In economics and finance, _____ is the change in total cost that arises when the quantity produced changes by one unit. That is, it is the cost of producing one more unit of a good. If the good being produced is infinitely divisible, so the size of a _____ will change with volume, as a non-linear and non-proportional cost function includes the following:•variable terms dependent to volume,•constant terms independent to volume and occurring with the respective lot size,•jump fix cost increase or decrease dependent to steps of volume increase.

   In practice the above definition of _____ as the change in total cost as a result of an increase in output of one unit is inconsistent with the calculation of _____ as MC=dTC/dQ for virtually all non-linear functions.

   a. Marginal product
   b. Marginal cost
   c. Marginal rate of technical substitution
   d. Means of production

2. _____ is the debt owed by a central government. (In the U.S. and other federal states, '_____' may also refer to the debt of a state or provincial government, municipal or local government). By contrast, the annual 'government deficit' refers to the difference between government receipts and spending in a single year, that is, the increase of debt over a particular year.

   a. BTAN
   b. Commissioners for the Reduction of the National Debt
   c. Government debt
   d. Debt-based monetary system

3. In economics, the _____ is a historical inverse relationship between the rate of unemployment and the rate of inflation in an economy. Stated simply, the lower the unemployment in an economy, the higher the rate of inflation. While it has been observed that there is a stable short run tradeoff between unemployment and inflation, this has not been observed in the long run.

Chapter 5. Difficult Cases for the Market, and the Role of Government

Visit Cram101.com for full Practice Exams

a. Recession-proof job
b. Reserve army of labour
c. Structural unemployment
d. Phillips curve

4. In economics, a _____ is a good that is both non-excludable and non-rivalrous in that individuals can not be effectively excluded from use and where use by one individual does not reduce availability to others. Examples of _____s include fresh air, clean water, knowledge, lighthouses, open source software, radio and television broadcasts, roads, street lighting. _____s that are available everywhere are sometimes referred to as global _____s.

a. Public sector
b. Quasi-market
c. Redistribution of wealth
d. Public good

5. In economics, the term _____ refers to the use of resources so as to maximize the production of goods and services. An economic system is said to be more efficient than another (in relative terms) if it can provide more goods and services for society without using more resources. In absolute terms, a situation can be called economically efficient if:•No one can be made better off without making someone else worse off (commonly referred to as Pareto efficiency).•No additional output can be obtained without increasing the amount of inputs.•Production proceeds at the lowest possible per-unit cost.

These definitions of efficiency are not exactly equivalent, but they are all encompassed by the idea that a system is efficient if nothing more can be achieved given the resources available.

a. Allocative efficiency
b. American Information Exchange
c. Economic efficiency
d. Inefficiency

ANSWER KEY
Chapter 5. Difficult Cases for the Market, and the Role of Government

1. b
2. c
3. d
4. d
5. c

You can take the complete Chapter Practice Test

for Chapter 5. Difficult Cases for the Market, and the Role of Government

on all key terms, persons, places, and concepts.

Online 99 Cents

http://www.epub40.13.20514.5.cram101.com/

Use www.Cram101.com for all your study needs

including Cram101's online interactive problem solving labs in

chemistry, statistics, mathematics, and more.

Visit Cram101.com for full Practice Exams

Chapter 6. The Economics of Collective Decision-Making

CHAPTER OUTLINE: KEY TERMS, PEOPLE, PLACES, CONCEPTS

- Social security
- Government
- Government revenue
- Transfer payment
- Opportunity cost
- Private sector
- Public policy
- Public sector
- Scarcity
- James M. Buchanan
- Phillips curve
- Fiscal policy
- Monetary policy
- Rational ignorance
- User charge
- Inefficiency
- Renewable resource
- Rent-seeking
- Bank reserves

Visit Cram101.com for full Practice Exams

Chapter 6. The Economics of Collective Decision-Making

CHAPTER OUTLINE: KEY TERMS, PEOPLE, PLACES, CONCEPTS

- Bankruptcy
- Crony capitalism
- Total cost
- Bear Stearns
- Fannie Mae
- Lehman Brothers
- Mortgage loan
- Government debt
- Market failure
- Monetary system
- Economic freedom
- Great Depression
- Economic growth
- Macroeconomics

Visit Cram101.com for full Practice Exams

Chapter 6. The Economics of Collective Decision-Making

CHAPTER HIGHLIGHTS & NOTES: KEY TERMS, PEOPLE, PLACES, CONCEPTS

Social security	Social security is a concept enshrined in Article 22 of the Universal Declaration of Human Rights which states that Everyone, as a member of society, has the right to social security and is entitled to realization, through national effort and international co-operation and in accordance with the organization and resources of each State, of the economic, social and cultural rights indispensable for his dignity and the free development of his personality. In simple term, this means that the signatories agree that society in which a person lives should help them to develop and to make the most of all the advantages (culture, work, social welfare) which are offered to them in the country. Social security may also refer to the action programs of government intended to promote the welfare of the population through assistance measures guaranteeing access to sufficient resources for food and shelter and to promote health and wellbeing for the population at large and potentially vulnerable segments such as children, the elderly, the sick and the unemployed.
Government	Government, refers to the legislators, administrators, and arbitrators in the administrative bureaucracy who control a state at a given time, and to the system of government by which they are organized (Referred : More to govern than control). Government is the means by which state policy is enforced, as well as the mechanism for determining the policy of the state. A form of government, or form of state governance, refers to the set of political institutions by which a government of a state is organized.
Government revenue	Government revenue is revenue received by a government. Its opposite is government spending. Yet, governments coin money.Government revenue is an important part of fiscal policy.
Transfer payment	In economics, a transfer payment is a redistribution of income in the market system. These payments are considered to be exhaustive because they do not directly absorb resources or create output. Examples of certain transfer payments include welfare (financial aid), social security, and government making subsidies for certain businesses (firms).
Opportunity cost	Opportunity cost is the cost of any activity measured in terms of the value of the next best alternative forgone (that is not chosen). It is the sacrifice related to the second best choice available to someone, or group, who has picked among several mutually exclusive choices. The opportunity cost is also the 'cost' (as a lost benefit) of the forgone products after making a choice.
Private sector	In economics, the private sector is that part of the economy, sometimes referred to as the citizen sector, which is run by private individuals or groups, usually as a means of enterprise for profit, and is not controlled by the state. By contrast, enterprises that are part of the state are part of the public sector; private, non-profit organizations are regarded as part of the voluntary sector.

Chapter 6. The Economics of Collective Decision-Making

CHAPTER HIGHLIGHTS & NOTES: KEY TERMS, PEOPLE, PLACES, CONCEPTS

Public policy	Public policy as government action is generally the principled guide to action taken by the administrative or executive branches of the state with regard to a class of issues in a manner consistent with law and institutional customs. In general, the foundation is the pertinent national and substantial constitutional law and implementing legislation such as the US Federal code. Further substrates include both judicial interpretations and regulations which are generally authorized by legislation.
Public sector	The public sector, is a part of the state that deals with either the production, ownership, sale, provision, delivery and allocation of goods and services by and for the government or its citizens, whether national, regional or localmunicipal. Examples of public sector activity range from delivering social security, administering urban planning and organizing national defense. The organization of the public sector can take several forms, including:•Direct administration funded through taxation; the delivering organization generally has no specific requirement to meet commercial success criteria, and production decisions are determined by government.•Publicly owned corporations (in some contexts, especially manufacturing, 'state-owned enterprises'); which differ from direct administration in that they have greater commercial freedoms and are expected to operate according to commercial criteria, and production decisions are not generally taken by government (although goals may be set for them by government).•Partial outsourcing (of the scale many businesses do, e.g. for IT services), is considered a public sector model. A borderline form is as follows**•Complete outsourcing or contracting out, with a privately owned corporation delivering the entire service on behalf of government.
Scarcity	Scarcity is the fundamental economic problem of having humans who have wants and needs in a world of limited resources. It states that society has insufficient productive resources to fulfill all human wants and needs. Alternatively, scarcity implies that not all of society's goals can be pursued at the same time; trade-offs are made of one good against others.
James M. Buchanan	James McGill Buchanan, Jr. is an American economist known for his work on public choice theory, for which he received the 1986 Nobel Memorial Prize in Economic Sciences. Buchanan's work initiated research on how politicians' self-interest and non-economic forces affect government economic policy. He is a Distinguished Senior Fellow of the Cato Institute. Biography

Chapter 6. The Economics of Collective Decision-Making

CHAPTER HIGHLIGHTS & NOTES: KEY TERMS, PEOPLE, PLACES, CONCEPTS

Buchanan graduated from Middle Tennessee State Teachers College, now known as Middle Tennessee State University, in 1940. Buchanan completed his M.S. from the University of Tennessee in 1941. He spent the war years on the staff of Admiral Nimitz in Honolulu, and it is during that time he met and married his wife Anne.

Buchanan received his Ph.D. from the University of Chicago in 1948, where he was much influenced by Frank H. Knight. It was also at Chicago that he read for the first time and found enlightening the work of Knut Wicksell. Photographs of Knight and Wicksell have hung from his office-walls ever since.

Buchanan is the founder of a new Virginia school of political economy. He taught at the University of Virginia, where he founded the Thomas Jefferson Center for the Protection of Free Expression; UCLA; Florida State University; the University of Tennessee; and the Virginia Polytechnic Institute ('Virginia Tech'), where he was affiliated with the Center for the Study of Public Choice (CSPC). In 1983, he followed CSPC to its new home at George Mason University. In 2001 Buchanan was honoured with an honorary doctoral degree at Universidad Francisco Marroquín due his contribution to economic theory.

Buchanan's work includes extensive writings on public finance, the public debt, voting, rigorous analysis of the theory of logrolling, macroeconomics, constitutional economics. and libertarian theory. Approach to economic analysis

Buchanan's important contribution to constitutionalism is his development of the sub-discipline of constitutional economics. Buchanan rejects 'any organic conception of the state as superior in wisdom, to the citizens of this state.' This philosophical position forms the basis of constitutional economics. Buchanan believes that every constitution is created for at least several generations of citizens. Therefore, it must be able to balance interests of the state, society, and each individual. List of publications •The Collected Works of James M. Buchanan by James M. Buchanan, at the Library of Economics and Liberty. Twenty-volume work, copyrighted but nine of the 20 volumes are free to read and access; fully searchable online. Includes:•A list of Buchanan's Publications from 1949 to 1986 can be found at The Scandinavian Journal Of Economics, 1987, Vol. 39. No. 1, pp. 17-37.•Public Principles of Public Debt: A Defense and Restatement, by James M. Buchanan, at the Library of Economics and Liberty•The Calculus of Consent: Logical Foundations of Constitutional Democracy, by James M. Buchanan and Gordon Tullock, at the Library of Economics and Liberty•Public Finance in Democratic Process: Fiscal Institutions and Individual Choice, by James M. Buchanan, at the Library of Economics and Liberty•The Demand and Supply of Public Goods, by James M. Buchanan, at the Library of Economics and Liberty•Cost and Choice: An Inquiry in Economic Theory, by James M. Buchanan, at the Library of Economics and Liberty•The Limits of Liberty: Between Anarchy and Leviathan, by James M.

Chapter 6. The Economics of Collective Decision-Making

CHAPTER HIGHLIGHTS & NOTES: KEY TERMS, PEOPLE, PLACES, CONCEPTS

	Buchanan, at the Library of Economics and Liberty•Democracy in Deficit: The Political Legacy of Lord Keynes, by James M. Buchanan and Richard E. Wagner, at the Library of Economics and Liberty•The Power to Tax: Analytical Foundations of a Fiscal Constitution, by Geoffrey Brennan and James M. Buchanan, at the Library of Economics and Liberty•The Reason of Rules: Constitutional Political Economy, by Geoffrey Brennan and James M. Buchanan, at the Library of Economics and Liberty•Complete 20-volume list of The Collected Works of James M. Buchanan by James M. Buchanan, at the publisher, Liberty Fund.•Why I, Too, Am Not a Conservative: The Normative Vision of Classical Liberalism (Cheltenham UK: Edward Elgar, 2005)•Economics from the Outside In: Better than Plowing and Beyond (College Station: Texas A&M Press, 2007).
Phillips curve	In economics, the Phillips curve is a historical inverse relationship between the rate of unemployment and the rate of inflation in an economy. Stated simply, the lower the unemployment in an economy, the higher the rate of inflation. While it has been observed that there is a stable short run tradeoff between unemployment and inflation, this has not been observed in the long run.
Fiscal policy	In economics and political science, fiscal policy is the use of government revenue collection (taxation) and expenditure (spending) to influence the economy. The two main instruments of fiscal policy are government taxation and expenditure. Changes in the level and composition of taxation and government spending can impact the following variables in the economy:•Aggregate demand and the level of economic activity;•The pattern of resource allocation;•The distribution of income.

Fiscal policy refers to the use of the government budget to influence economic activity. |
| Monetary policy | Monetary policy is the process by which the monetary authority of a country controls the supply of money, often targeting a rate of interest for the purpose of promoting economic growth and stability. The official goals usually include relatively stable prices and low unemployment. Monetary theory provides insight into how to craft optimal monetary policy. |
| Rational ignorance | Rational ignorance occurs when the cost of educating oneself on an issue exceeds the potential benefit that the knowledge would provide.

Ignorance about an issue is said to be 'rational' when the cost of educating oneself about the issue sufficiently to make an informed decision can outweigh any potential benefit one could reasonably expect to gain from that decision, and so it would be irrational to waste time doing so. This has consequences for the quality of decisions made by large numbers of people, such as general elections, where the probability of any one vote changing the outcome is very small. |
| User charge | A user charge is a charge for the use of a product or service. A user charge may apply per use of the good or service or for the use of the good or service. |

Chapter 6. The Economics of Collective Decision-Making

CHAPTER HIGHLIGHTS & NOTES: KEY TERMS, PEOPLE, PLACES, CONCEPTS

Inefficiency	The term inefficiency has several meanings depending on the context in which its used:•Allocative inefficiency - Allocative inefficiency theory says that the distribution of resources between alternatives does not fit with consumer taste (perceptions of costs and benefits). For example, a company may have the lowest costs in 'productive' terms, but the result may be inefficient in allocative terms because the 'true' or social cost exceeds the price that consumers are willing to pay for an extra unit of the product. This is true, for example, if the firm produces pollution .
Renewable resource	A renewable resource is a natural resource with the ability to reproduce through biological or natural processes and replenished with the passage of time. Renewable resources are part of our natural environment and form our eco-system. In 1962, within a report to the committee on natural resources which was forwarded to the President of the United States, Paul Weiss defined Renewable Resources as: 'The total range of living organisms providing man with food, fibers, drugs, etc...'.
Rent-seeking	In economics, rent-seeking is an attempt to obtain economic rent by manipulating the social or political environment in which economic activities occur, rather than by creating new wealth, for example, spending money on political lobbying in order to be given a share of wealth that has already been created. A famous example of rent-seeking is the limiting of access to lucrative occupations, as by medieval guilds or modern state certifications and licensures. People accused of rent seeking typically argue that they are indeed creating new wealth by improving quality controls, guaranteeing that charlatans do not prey on a gullible public, and preventing bubbles.
Bank reserves	Bank reserves are banks' holdings of deposits in accounts with their central bank (for instance the European Central Bank or the Federal Reserve, in the latter case including federal funds), plus currency that is physically held in the bank's vault (vault cash). The central banks of some nations set minimum reserve requirements. Even when no requirements are set, banks commonly wish to hold some reserves, called desired reserves, against unexpected events such as unusually large net withdrawals by customers or even bank runs.
Bankruptcy	Bankruptcy is a legal status of an insolvent person or an organisation, that is, one who cannot repay the debts they owe to creditors. In most jurisdictions bankruptcy is imposed by a court order, often initiated by the debtor. Bankruptcy is not the only legal status that an insolvent person or organisation may have, and the term bankruptcy is therefore not the same as insolvency.
Crony capitalism	Crony capitalism is a term describing an economy in which success in business depends on close relationships between business people and government officials.

Chapter 6. The Economics of Collective Decision-Making

CHAPTER HIGHLIGHTS & NOTES: KEY TERMS, PEOPLE, PLACES, CONCEPTS

	It may be exhibited by favoritism in the distribution of legal permits, government grants, special tax breaks, and so forth. Crony capitalism is believed to arise when political cronyism spills over into the business world; self-serving friendships and family ties between businessmen and the government influence the economy and society to the extent that it corrupts public-serving economic and political ideals.
Total cost	In economics, and cost accounting, total cost describes the total economic cost of production and is made up of variable costs, which vary according to the quantity of a good produced and include inputs such as labor and raw materials, plus fixed costs, which are independent of the quantity of a good produced and include inputs (capital) that cannot be varied in the short term, such as buildings and machinery. Total cost in economics includes the total opportunity cost of each factor of production as part of its fixed or variable costs. The rate at which total cost changes as the amount produced changes is called marginal cost.
Bear Stearns	The Bear Stearns Companies, Inc. (former NYSE ticker symbol BSC) based in New York City, was a global investment bank and securities trading and brokerage, until its sale to JPMorgan Chase in 2008 during the global financial crisis and recession. Its main business areas, based on 2006 net revenue distributions, were capital markets (equities, fixed income, investment banking; just under 80%), wealth management (under 10%), and global clearing services (12%).
Fannie Mae	The Federal National Mortgage Association (FNMA; OTCQB: FNMA), commonly known as Fannie Mae, was founded in 1938 during the Great Depression as part of the New Deal. It is a government-sponsored enterprise (GSE), though it has been a publicly traded company since 1968. The corporation's purpose is to expand the secondary mortgage market by securitizing mortgages in the form of mortgage-backed securities (MBS), allowing lenders to reinvest their assets into more lending and in effect increasing the number of lenders in the mortgage market by reducing the reliance on thrifts. The Federal National Mortgage Association (FNMA), colloquially known as Fannie Mae, was established in 1938 by amendments to the National Housing Act after the Great Depression as part of Franklin Delano Roosevelt's New Deal.
Lehman Brothers	Lehman Brothers Holdings Inc. (former NYSE ticker symbol LEH) ( ) was a global financial services firm. Before declaring bankruptcy in 2008, Lehman was the fourth largest investment bank in the USA (behind Goldman Sachs, Morgan Stanley, and Merrill Lynch), doing business in investment banking, equity and fixed-income sales and trading (especially U.S.

Visit Cram101.com for full Practice Exams

Chapter 6. The Economics of Collective Decision-Making

CHAPTER HIGHLIGHTS & NOTES: KEY TERMS, PEOPLE, PLACES, CONCEPTS

Mortgage loan	A mortgage loan is a loan secured by real property through the use of a mortgage note which evidences the existence of the loan and the encumbrance of that realty through the granting of a mortgage which secures the loan. However, the word mortgage alone, in everyday usage, is most often used to mean mortgage loan. The word mortgage is a Law French term meaning 'death contract,' meaning that the pledge ends (dies) when either the obligation is fulfilled or the property is taken through foreclosure.
Government debt	Government debt is the debt owed by a central government. (In the U.S. and other federal states, 'government debt' may also refer to the debt of a state or provincial government, municipal or local government). By contrast, the annual 'government deficit' refers to the difference between government receipts and spending in a single year, that is, the increase of debt over a particular year.
Market failure	Market failure is a concept within economic theory describing when the allocation of goods and services by a free market is not efficient. That is, there exists another conceivable outcome where a market participant may be made better-off without making someone else worse-off. (The outcome is not Pareto optimal).
Monetary system	A monetary system is anything that is accepted as a standard of value and measure of wealth in a particular region. However, the current trend is to use international trade and investment to alter the policy and legislation of individual governments. The best recent example of this policy is the European Union's creation of the euro as a common currency for many of its individual states.
Economic freedom	Economic freedom is a term used in economic and policy debates. As with freedom generally, there are various definitions, but no universally accepted concept of economic freedom. One major approach to economic freedom comes from classical liberal and libertarian traditions emphasizing free markets and private property, while another extends the welfare economics study of individual choice, with greater economic freedom coming from a 'larger' (in some technical sense) set of possible choices.
Great Depression	The Great Depression was a severe worldwide economic depression in the decade preceding World War II. The timing of the Great Depression varied across nations, but in most countries it started in 1930 after the passage of the Smoot-Hawley Tariff bill (June 17), and lasted until the late 1930s or early 1940s. It was the longest, most widespread, and deepest depression of the 20th century.

Chapter 6. The Economics of Collective Decision-Making

CHAPTER HIGHLIGHTS & NOTES: KEY TERMS, PEOPLE, PLACES, CONCEPTS

Economic growth	Economic growth is the increase in the amount of the goods and services produced by an economy over time. It is conventionally measured as the percent rate of increase in real gross domestic product, or real GDP. Growth is usually calculated in real terms, i.e. inflation-adjusted terms, in order to net out the effect of inflation on the price of the goods and services produced. In economics, 'economic growth' or 'economic growth theory' typically refers to growth of potential output, i.e., production at 'full employment,' which is caused by growth in aggregate demand or observed output.
Macroeconomics	Macroeconomics is a branch of economics dealing with the performance, structure, behavior, and decision-making of the whole economy. This includes national, regional, and global economies. With microeconomics, macroeconomics is one of the two most general fields in economics.

CHAPTER QUIZ: KEY TERMS, PEOPLE, PLACES, CONCEPTS

1. _____ occurs when the cost of educating oneself on an issue exceeds the potential benefit that the knowledge would provide.

   Ignorance about an issue is said to be 'rational' when the cost of educating oneself about the issue sufficiently to make an informed decision can outweigh any potential benefit one could reasonably expect to gain from that decision, and so it would be irrational to waste time doing so. This has consequences for the quality of decisions made by large numbers of people, such as general elections, where the probability of any one vote changing the outcome is very small.

   a. Rational irrationality
   b. Rationalizability
   c. Rational ignorance
   d. Replicator equation

2. . _____ is a concept enshrined in Article 22 of the Universal Declaration of Human Rights which states that Everyone, as a member of society, has the right to _____ and is entitled to realization, through national effort and international co-operation and in accordance with the organization and resources of each State, of the economic, social and cultural rights indispensable for his dignity and the free development of his personality. In simple term, this means that the signatories agree that society in which a person lives should help them to develop and to make the most of all the advantages (culture, work, social welfare) which are offered to them in the country.

   _____ may also refer to the action programs of government intended to promote the welfare of the population through assistance measures guaranteeing access to sufficient resources for food and shelter and to promote health and wellbeing for the population at large and potentially vulnerable segments such as children, the elderly, the sick and the unemployed.

   a. Social security
   b. Social welfare function

CHAPTER QUIZ: KEY TERMS, PEOPLE, PLACES, CONCEPTS

    c. Structural adjustment loan
    d. Suits index

3. _____ is revenue received by a government. Its opposite is government spending. Yet, governments coin money._____ is an important part of fiscal policy.

    a. Government spending
    b. Great Moderation
    c. Growth recession
    d. Government revenue

4. _____ as government action is generally the principled guide to action taken by the administrative or executive branches of the state with regard to a class of issues in a manner consistent with law and institutional customs. In general, the foundation is the pertinent national and substantial constitutional law and implementing legislation such as the US Federal code. Further substrates include both judicial interpretations and regulations which are generally authorized by legislation.

    a. Public speaking
    b. Public policy
    c. Serfdom in Tibet controversy
    d. Social choice theory

5. _____ is the increase in the amount of the goods and services produced by an economy over time. It is conventionally measured as the percent rate of increase in real gross domestic product, or real GDP. Growth is usually calculated in real terms, i.e. inflation-adjusted terms, in order to net out the effect of inflation on the price of the goods and services produced. In economics, '_____' or '_____ theory' typically refers to growth of potential output, i.e., production at 'full employment,' which is caused by growth in aggregate demand or observed output.

    a. Edgeworth box
    b. Equity
    c. Economic growth
    d. Excess burden of taxation

Visit Cram101.com for full Practice Exams

Visit Cram101.com for full Practice Exams

ANSWER KEY
Chapter 6. The Economics of Collective Decision-Making

1. c
2. a
3. d
4. b
5. c

You can take the complete Chapter Practice Test

for **Chapter 6. The Economics of Collective Decision-Making**
on all key terms, persons, places, and concepts.

Online 99 Cents

http://www.epub40.13.20514.6.cram101.com/

Use www.Cram101.com for all your study needs

including Cram101's online interactive problem solving labs in

chemistry, statistics, mathematics, and more.

Chapter 7. Taking the Nation's Economic Pulse

CHAPTER OUTLINE: KEY TERMS, PEOPLE, PLACES, CONCEPTS

- Final goods
- Phillips curve
- Renewable resource
- Labor relations
- Depreciation
- Government
- Inventory investment
- Business cycle
- Great Depression
- Gross domestic product
- Social security
- Capital Consumption Allowance
- Net income
- Bureau of Labor Statistics
- Consumer Price Index
- GDP deflator
- Price index
- Inflation rate
- Game theory

Visit Cram101.com for full Practice Exams

Chapter 7. Taking the Nation's Economic Pulse
CHAPTER OUTLINE: KEY TERMS, PEOPLE, PLACES, CONCEPTS

	Purchasing power
	Demand destruction
	Derived demand

CHAPTER HIGHLIGHTS & NOTES: KEY TERMS, PEOPLE, PLACES, CONCEPTS

Final goods	In economics final goods are goods that are ultimately consumed rather than used in the production of another good. For example, a car sold to a consumer is a final good; the components such as tires sold to the car manufacturer are not; they are intermediate goods used to make the final good. When used in measures of national income and output the term final goods only includes new goods.
Phillips curve	In economics, the Phillips curve is a historical inverse relationship between the rate of unemployment and the rate of inflation in an economy. Stated simply, the lower the unemployment in an economy, the higher the rate of inflation. While it has been observed that there is a stable short run tradeoff between unemployment and inflation, this has not been observed in the long run.
Renewable resource	A renewable resource is a natural resource with the ability to reproduce through biological or natural processes and replenished with the passage of time. Renewable resources are part of our natural environment and form our eco-system. In 1962, within a report to the committee on natural resources which was forwarded to the President of the United States, Paul Weiss defined Renewable Resources as: 'The total range of living organisms providing man with food, fibers, drugs, etc...'.
Labor relations	Labor relations is the study and practice of managing unionized employment situations. In academia, labor relations is frequently a subarea within industrial relations, though scholars from many disciplines--including economics, sociology, history, law, and political science--also study labor unions and labor movements.

Chapter 7. Taking the Nation's Economic Pulse

CHAPTER HIGHLIGHTS & NOTES: KEY TERMS, PEOPLE, PLACES, CONCEPTS

Depreciation	In economics, depreciation is the gradual decrease in the economic value of the capital stock of a firm, nation or other entity, either through physical depreciation, obsolescence or changes in the demand for the services of the capital in question. If capital stock is C_0 at the beginning of a period, investment is I and depreciation D, the capital stock at the end of the period, C_1, is $C_0 + I - D$.

In economics, the value of a capital asset may be modeled as the present value of the flow of services the asset will generate in future, appropriately adjusted for uncertainty. |
| Government | Government, refers to the legislators, administrators, and arbitrators in the administrative bureaucracy who control a state at a given time, and to the system of government by which they are organized (Referred : More to govern than control). Government is the means by which state policy is enforced, as well as the mechanism for determining the policy of the state. A form of government, or form of state governance, refers to the set of political institutions by which a government of a state is organized. |
| Inventory investment | Inventory investment is a component of gross domestic product (GDP). What is produced in a certain country is naturally also sold eventually, but some of the goods produced in a given year may be sold in a later year rather than in the year they were produced. Conversely, some of the goods sold in a given year might have been produced in an earlier year. |
| Business cycle | The term business cycle refers to economy-wide fluctuations in production or economic activity over several months or years. These fluctuations occur around a long-term growth trend, and typically involve shifts over time between periods of relatively rapid economic growth (an expansion or boom), and periods of relative stagnation or decline (a contraction or recession).

Business cycles are usually measured by considering the growth rate of real gross domestic product. |
| Great Depression | The Great Depression was a severe worldwide economic depression in the decade preceding World War II. The timing of the Great Depression varied across nations, but in most countries it started in 1930 after the passage of the Smoot-Hawley Tariff bill (June 17), and lasted until the late 1930s or early 1940s. It was the longest, most widespread, and deepest depression of the 20th century.

In the 21st century, the Great Depression is commonly used as an example of how far the world's economy can decline. |
| Gross domestic product | Gross domestic product refers to the market value of all officially recognized final goods and services produced within a country in a given period. |

Visit Cram101.com for full Practice Exams

Chapter 7. Taking the Nation's Economic Pulse

CHAPTER HIGHLIGHTS & NOTES: KEY TERMS, PEOPLE, PLACES, CONCEPTS

	GDP per capita is often considered an indicator of a country's standard of living; GDP per capita is not a measure of personal income. Under economic theory, GDP per capita exactly equals the gross domestic income (GDI) per capita.
Social security	Social security is a concept enshrined in Article 22 of the Universal Declaration of Human Rights which states that Everyone, as a member of society, has the right to social security and is entitled to realization, through national effort and international co-operation and in accordance with the organization and resources of each State, of the economic, social and cultural rights indispensable for his dignity and the free development of his personality. In simple term, this means that the signatories agree that society in which a person lives should help them to develop and to make the most of all the advantages (culture, work, social welfare) which are offered to them in the country.
	Social security may also refer to the action programs of government intended to promote the welfare of the population through assistance measures guaranteeing access to sufficient resources for food and shelter and to promote health and wellbeing for the population at large and potentially vulnerable segments such as children, the elderly, the sick and the unemployed.
Capital Consumption Allowance	The Capital Consumption Allowance is the portion of the Gross Domestic Product (GDP) which is due to depreciation. The Capital Consumption Allowance measures the amount of expenditure that a country needs to undertake in order to maintain, as opposed to grow, its productivity. The CCA can be thought of as representing the wear-and-tear on the country's physical capital, together with the investment needed to maintain the level of human capital (e.g. to educate the workers needed to replace retirees).
Net income	Net income in accounting is an entity's income minus expenses for an accounting period. It is computed as the residual of all revenues and gains over all expenses and losses for the period, and has also been defined as the net increase in stockholder's equity that results from a company's operations. In the context of the presentation of financial statements, the IFRS Foundation defines net income as synonymous with profit and loss.
Bureau of Labor Statistics	The Bureau of Labor Statistics is a unit of the United States Department of Labor. It is the principal fact-finding agency for the U.S. government in the broad field of labor economics and statistics. The BLS is a governmental statistical agency that collects, processes, analyzes, and disseminates essential statistical data to the American public, the U.S. Congress, other Federal agencies, State and local governments, business, and labor representatives.
Consumer Price Index	The Consumer Price Index (CPI) is the official measure of inflation of consumer prices of the United Kingdom. It is also called the Harmonised Index of Consumer Prices (HICP).

Visit Cram101.com for full Practice Exams

Chapter 7. Taking the Nation's Economic Pulse

CHAPTER HIGHLIGHTS & NOTES: KEY TERMS, PEOPLE, PLACES, CONCEPTS

GDP deflator	In economics, the GDP deflator is a measure of the level of prices of all new, domestically produced, final goods and services in an economy. GDP stands for gross domestic product, the total value of all final goods and services produced within that economy during a specified period. Measurement in national accounts In most systems of national accounts the GDP deflator measures the ratio of nominal GDP to the real measure of GDP. The formula used to calculate the deflator is: $$\text{GDP deflator} = \frac{\text{Nominal GDP}}{\text{Real GDP}} \times 100$$ Dividing the nominal GDP by the GDP deflator and multiplying it by 100 would then give the figure for real GDP, hence deflating the nominal GDP into a real measure.
Price index	A price index is a normalized average (typically a weighted average) of prices for a given class of goods or services in a given region, during a given interval of time. It is a statistic designed to help to compare how these prices, taken as a whole, differ between time periods or geographical locations. Price indices have several potential uses.
Inflation rate	In economics, the inflation rate is a measure of inflation, or the rate of increase of a price index such as the consumer price index. It is the percentage rate of change in price level over time, usually one year. The rate of decrease in the purchasing power of money is approximately equal.
Game theory	Game theory is the study of strategic decision making. More formally, it is 'the study of mathematical models of conflict and cooperation between intelligent rational decision-makers.' An alternative term suggested 'as a more descriptive name for the discipline' is interactive decision theory. Game theory is mainly used in economics, political science, and psychology, as well as logic and biology.
Purchasing power	Purchasing power is the number of goods/services that can be purchased with a unit of currency. For example, if you had taken one dollar to a store in the 1950s, you would have been able to buy a greater number of items than you would today, indicating that you would have had a greater purchasing power in the 1950s. Currency can be either a commodity money, like gold or silver, or fiat currency, or free-floating market-valued currency like US dollars.
Demand destruction	Demand destruction is an economic term used to describe a permanent downward shift on the demand curve in the direction of lower demand of a commodity, such as energy products, induced by a prolonged period of high prices or constrained supply.

Visit Cram101.com for full Practice Exams

Chapter 7. Taking the Nation's Economic Pulse

CHAPTER HIGHLIGHTS & NOTES: KEY TERMS, PEOPLE, PLACES, CONCEPTS

	In the context of the oil industry, 'demand' generally refers to the quantity consumed, rather than any measure of a demand curve as used in mainstream economics.
	The term has come to some prominence lately as a result of the growing interest in the peak oil theory, where demand destruction is the reduction of demand for oil and oil-derived products.
Derived demand	Derived demand is a term in economics, where demand for one good or service occurs as a result of the demand for another intermediate/ final good or service. This may occur as the former is a part of production of the second. For example, demand for coal leads to derived demand for mining, as coal must be mined for coal to be consumed.

CHAPTER QUIZ: KEY TERMS, PEOPLE, PLACES, CONCEPTS

1. In economics _____ are goods that are ultimately consumed rather than used in the production of another good. For example, a car sold to a consumer is a final good; the components such as tires sold to the car manufacturer are not; they are intermediate goods used to make the final good.

    When used in measures of national income and output the term _____ only includes new goods.

    a. Goods and services
    b. Refined goods
    c. Final goods
    d. Philippe Kruchten

2. _____ is a term in economics, where demand for one good or service occurs as a result of the demand for another intermediate/ final good or service. This may occur as the former is a part of production of the second. For example, demand for coal leads to _____ for mining, as coal must be mined for coal to be consumed.

    a. Derived demand
    b. Joint demand
    c. Kinked demand
    d. Law of demand

3. . In economics, the _____ is a measure of inflation, or the rate of increase of a price index such as the consumer price index. It is the percentage rate of change in price level over time, usually one year. The rate of decrease in the purchasing power of money is approximately equal.

    a. Inflation swap
    b. Inflation rate
    c. Inflation-indexed bond

Visit Cram101.com for full Practice Exams

Chapter 7. Taking the Nation's Economic Pulse

CHAPTER QUIZ: KEY TERMS, PEOPLE, PLACES, CONCEPTS

4. In economics, the _____ is a historical inverse relationship between the rate of unemployment and the rate of inflation in an economy. Stated simply, the lower the unemployment in an economy, the higher the rate of inflation. While it has been observed that there is a stable short run tradeoff between unemployment and inflation, this has not been observed in the long run.

   a. Recession-proof job
   b. Reserve army of labour
   c. Phillips curve
   d. Technological unemployment

5. A _____ is a natural resource with the ability to reproduce through biological or natural processes and replenished with the passage of time. _____s are part of our natural environment and form our eco-system.

   In 1962, within a report to the committee on natural resources which was forwarded to the President of the United States, Paul Weiss defined _____s as: 'The total range of living organisms providing man with food, fibers, drugs, etc...'.

   a. Sustainable yield
   b. Renewable resource
   c. Structural unemployment
   d. Technological unemployment

Visit Cram101.com for full Practice Exams

ANSWER KEY
Chapter 7. Taking the Nation's Economic Pulse

1. c
2. a
3. b
4. c
5. b

You can take the complete Chapter Practice Test

for Chapter 7. Taking the Nation's Economic Pulse
on all key terms, persons, places, and concepts.

Online 99 Cents

http://www.epub40.13.20514.7.cram101.com/

Use www.Cram101.com for all your study needs

including Cram101's online interactive problem solving labs in

chemistry, statistics, mathematics, and more.

Chapter 8. Economic Fluctuations, Unemployment, and Inflation

CHAPTER OUTLINE: KEY TERMS, PEOPLE, PLACES, CONCEPTS

_____ Business cycle

_____ Great Depression

_____ Recession

_____ Kyoto Protocol

_____ Employment

_____ Labor force

_____ Unemployment

_____ Bureau of Labor Statistics

_____ Frictional unemployment

_____ International trade

_____ Open market

_____ Structural unemployment

_____ Renewable resource

_____ Social security

_____ Full employment

_____ Natural rate of unemployment

_____ Baby boomer

_____ Public policy

_____ AD-AS model

Visit Cram101.com for full Practice Exams

Chapter 8. Economic Fluctuations, Unemployment, and Inflation

CHAPTER OUTLINE: KEY TERMS, PEOPLE, PLACES, CONCEPTS

	Phillips curve
	Inflation
	Potential output
	Consumer Price Index
	GDP deflator
	Price index
	Hyperinflation
	Inflation rate
	Relative price

CHAPTER HIGHLIGHTS & NOTES: KEY TERMS, PEOPLE, PLACES, CONCEPTS

Business cycle	The term business cycle refers to economy-wide fluctuations in production or economic activity over several months or years. These fluctuations occur around a long-term growth trend, and typically involve shifts over time between periods of relatively rapid economic growth (an expansion or boom), and periods of relative stagnation or decline (a contraction or recession). Business cycles are usually measured by considering the growth rate of real gross domestic product.
Great Depression	The Great Depression was a severe worldwide economic depression in the decade preceding World War II. The timing of the Great Depression varied across nations, but in most countries it started in 1930 after the passage of the Smoot-Hawley Tariff bill (June 17), and lasted until the late 1930s or early 1940s. It was the longest, most widespread, and deepest depression of the 20th century.

Visit Cram101.com for full Practice Exams

Chapter 8. Economic Fluctuations, Unemployment, and Inflation

CHAPTER HIGHLIGHTS & NOTES: KEY TERMS, PEOPLE, PLACES, CONCEPTS

Recession	In economics, a recession is a business cycle contraction, a general slowdown in economic activity. Macroeconomic indicators such as GDP, employment, investment spending, capacity utilization, household income, business profits, and inflation fall, while bankruptcies and the unemployment rate rise. Recessions generally occur when there is a widespread drop in spending, often following an adverse supply shock or the bursting of an economic bubble.
Kyoto Protocol	The Kyoto Protocol is a protocol to the United Nations Framework Convention on Climate Change (UNFCCC or FCCC), aimed at fighting global warming. The UNFCCC is an international environmental treaty with the goal of achieving the 'stabilisation of greenhouse gas concentrations in the atmosphere at a level that would prevent dangerous anthropogenic interference with the climate system.' The Protocol was initially adopted on 11 December 1997 in Kyoto, Japan, and entered into force on 16 February 2005. As of September 2011, 191 states have signed and ratified the protocol. The only remaining signatory not to have ratified the protocol is the United States.
Employment	Employment is a contract between two parties, one being the employer and the other being the employee. An employee may be defined as: An employee contributes labor and expertise to an endeavor of an employer and is usually hired to perform specific duties which are packaged into a job. In most modern economies, the term 'employee' refers to a specific defined relationship between an individual and a corporation, which differs from those of customer or client.
Labor force	Normally, the labor force of a country consists of everyone of working age (typically above a certain age (around 14 to 16) and below retirement (around 65) who are participating workers, that is people actively employed or seeking employment. People not counted include students, retired people, stay-at-home parents, people in prisons or similar institutions, people employed in jobs or professions with unreported income, as well as discouraged workers who cannot find work. In the United States, the unemployment rate is estimated by a household survey called the Current Population Survey, conducted monthly by the Federal Bureau of Labor Statistics.
Unemployment	Unemployment, as defined by the International Labour Organization, occurs when people are without jobs and they have actively sought work within the past four weeks. The unemployment rate is a measure of the prevalence of unemployment and it is calculated as a percentage by dividing the number of unemployed individuals by all individuals currently in the labor force.

Chapter 8. Economic Fluctuations, Unemployment, and Inflation

CHAPTER HIGHLIGHTS & NOTES: KEY TERMS, PEOPLE, PLACES, CONCEPTS

Bureau of Labor Statistics	The Bureau of Labor Statistics is a unit of the United States Department of Labor. It is the principal fact-finding agency for the U.S. government in the broad field of labor economics and statistics. The BLS is a governmental statistical agency that collects, processes, analyzes, and disseminates essential statistical data to the American public, the U.S. Congress, other Federal agencies, State and local governments, business, and labor representatives.
Frictional unemployment	Frictional unemployment is the time period between jobs when a worker is searching for, or transitioning from one job to another. It is sometimes called search unemployment and can be voluntary based on the circumstances of the unemployed individual. Frictional unemployment exists because both jobs and workers are heterogeneous, and a mismatch can result between the characteristics of supply and demand.
International trade	International trade is the exchange of capital, goods, and services across international borders or territories. In most countries, such trade represents a significant share of gross domestic product (GDP). While international trade has been present throughout much of history, its economic, social, and political importance has been on the rise in recent centuries.
Open market	The term open market is used generally to refer to a situation close to free trade and in a more specific technical sense to interbank trade in securities. In a general sense used in economics and political economy, an open market refers to a market which is accessible to all economic actors. In an open market so defined, all economic actors have an equal opportunity of entry in that market.
Structural unemployment	Structural unemployment is a form of unemployment resulting from a mismatch between demand in the labour market and the skills and locations of the workers seeking employment. Even though the number of vacancies may be equal to, or greater than, the number of the unemployed, the unemployed workers may lack the skills needed for the jobs, or they may not live in the part of the country or world where the jobs are available. Structural unemployment is a result of the dynamics of the labor market, such as agricultural workers being displaced by mechanized agriculture, unskilled laborers displaced by both mechanization and automation, or industries with declining employment.
Renewable resource	A renewable resource is a natural resource with the ability to reproduce through biological or natural processes and replenished with the passage of time. Renewable resources are part of our natural environment and form our eco-system.

Visit Cram101.com for full Practice Exams

Chapter 8. Economic Fluctuations, Unemployment, and Inflation

CHAPTER HIGHLIGHTS & NOTES: KEY TERMS, PEOPLE, PLACES, CONCEPTS

Social security	Social security is a concept enshrined in Article 22 of the Universal Declaration of Human Rights which states that Everyone, as a member of society, has the right to social security and is entitled to realization, through national effort and international co-operation and in accordance with the organization and resources of each State, of the economic, social and cultural rights indispensable for his dignity and the free development of his personality. In simple term, this means that the signatories agree that society in which a person lives should help them to develop and to make the most of all the advantages (culture, work, social welfare) which are offered to them in the country. Social security may also refer to the action programs of government intended to promote the welfare of the population through assistance measures guaranteeing access to sufficient resources for food and shelter and to promote health and wellbeing for the population at large and potentially vulnerable segments such as children, the elderly, the sick and the unemployed.
Full employment	Full employment, in macroeconomics, is the level of employment rates when there is no cyclical unemployment. It is defined by the majority of mainstream economists as being an acceptable level of natural unemployment above 0%, the discrepancy from 0% being due to non-cyclical types of unemployment. Unemployment above 0% is advocated as necessary to control inflation, which has brought about the concept of the Non-Accelerating Inflation Rate of Unemployment (NAIRU); the majority of mainstream economists mean NAIRU when speaking of 'full' employment.
Natural rate of unemployment	The natural rate of unemployment (sometimes called the structural unemployment rate) is a concept of economic activity developed in particular by Milton Friedman and Edmund Phelps in the 1960s, both recipients of the Nobel prize in economics. In both cases, the development of the concept is cited as a main motivation behind the prize. It represents the hypothetical unemployment rate consistent with aggregate production being at the 'long-run' level.
Baby boomer	A baby boomer is a person who was born during the demographic Post-World War II baby boom and who grew up during the period between 1946 and 1964. The term 'baby boomer' is sometimes used in a cultural context. Therefore, it is impossible to achieve broad consensus of a precise definition, even within a given territory. Different groups, organizations, individuals, and scholars may have widely varying opinions on what constitutes a baby boomer, both technically and culturally.
Public policy	Public policy as government action is generally the principled guide to action taken by the administrative or executive branches of the state with regard to a class of issues in a manner consistent with law and institutional customs. In general, the foundation is the pertinent national and substantial constitutional law and implementing legislation such as the US Federal code.

Chapter 8. Economic Fluctuations, Unemployment, and Inflation

CHAPTER HIGHLIGHTS & NOTES: KEY TERMS, PEOPLE, PLACES, CONCEPTS

AD-AS model	The AD-AS or Aggregate Demand-Aggregate Supply model is a macroeconomic model that explains price level and output through the relationship of aggregate demand and aggregate supply. It is based on the theory of John Maynard Keynes presented in his work The General Theory of Employment, Interest, and Money. It is one of the primary simplified representations in the modern field of macroeconomics, and is used by a broad array of economists, from libertarian, Monetarist supporters of laissez-faire, such as Milton Friedman to Post-Keynesian supporters of economic interventionism, such as Joan Robinson. The conventional 'aggregate supply and demand' model is, in actuality, a Keynesian visualization that has come to be a widely accepted image of the theory. The Classical supply and demand model, which is largely based on Say's Law, or that supply creates its own demand, depicts the aggregate supply curve as being vertical at all times (not just in the long-run)Modeling The AD/AS model is used to illustrate the Keynesian model of the business cycle. Movements of the two curves can be used to predict the effects that various exogenous events will have on two variables: real GDP and the price level. Furthermore, the model can be incorporated as a component in any of a variety of dynamic models (models of how variables like the price level and others evolve over time). The AD-AS model can be related to the Phillips curve model of wage or price inflation and unemployment.
Phillips curve	In economics, the Phillips curve is a historical inverse relationship between the rate of unemployment and the rate of inflation in an economy. Stated simply, the lower the unemployment in an economy, the higher the rate of inflation. While it has been observed that there is a stable short run tradeoff between unemployment and inflation, this has not been observed in the long run.
Inflation	In economics, inflation is a rise in the general level of prices of goods and services in an economy over a period of time. When the general price level rises, each unit of currency buys fewer goods and services. Consequently, inflation also reflects an erosion in the purchasing power of money - a loss of real value in the internal medium of exchange and unit of account in the economy.
Potential output	In economics, potential output refers to the highest level of real Gross Domestic Product output that can be sustained over the long term. The existence of a limit is due to natural and institutional constraints. If actual GDP rises and stays above potential output, then (in the absence of wage and price controls) inflation tends to increase as demand exceeds supply.
Consumer Price Index	The Consumer Price Index (CPI) is the official measure of inflation of consumer prices of the United Kingdom. It is also called the Harmonised Index of Consumer Prices (HICP).

Visit Cram101.com for full Practice Exams

Chapter 8. Economic Fluctuations, Unemployment, and Inflation

CHAPTER HIGHLIGHTS & NOTES: KEY TERMS, PEOPLE, PLACES, CONCEPTS

GDP deflator	In economics, the GDP deflator is a measure of the level of prices of all new, domestically produced, final goods and services in an economy. GDP stands for gross domestic product, the total value of all final goods and services produced within that economy during a specified period. Measurement in national accounts In most systems of national accounts the GDP deflator measures the ratio of nominal GDP to the real measure of GDP. The formula used to calculate the deflator is: $$\text{GDP deflator} = \frac{\text{Nominal GDP}}{\text{Real GDP}} \times 100$$ Dividing the nominal GDP by the GDP deflator and multiplying it by 100 would then give the figure for real GDP, hence deflating the nominal GDP into a real measure.
Price index	A price index is a normalized average (typically a weighted average) of prices for a given class of goods or services in a given region, during a given interval of time. It is a statistic designed to help to compare how these prices, taken as a whole, differ between time periods or geographical locations. Price indices have several potential uses.
Hyperinflation	In economics, hyperinflation occurs when a country experiences very high and usually accelerating inflation. While the real values of the specific economic items generally stay the same in terms of relatively stable foreign currencies, in hyperinflationary conditions the general price level within a specific economy increases rapidly as the functional or internal currency, as opposed to a foreign currency, loses its real value very quickly, normally at an accelerating rate. Economists usually follow Cagan's description that hyperinflation occurs when the monthly inflation rate exceeds 50%.
Inflation rate	In economics, the inflation rate is a measure of inflation, or the rate of increase of a price index such as the consumer price index. It is the percentage rate of change in price level over time, usually one year. The rate of decrease in the purchasing power of money is approximately equal.
Relative price	A relative price is the price of a commodity such as a good or service in terms of another; i.e., the ratio of two prices. A relative price may be expressed in terms of a ratio between any two prices or the ratio between the price of one particular good and a weighted average of all other goods available in the market. A relative price is an opportunity cost.

Chapter 8. Economic Fluctuations, Unemployment, and Inflation

CHAPTER QUIZ: KEY TERMS, PEOPLE, PLACES, CONCEPTS

1. In economics, a _____ is a business cycle contraction, a general slowdown in economic activity. Macroeconomic indicators such as GDP, employment, investment spending, capacity utilization, household income, business profits, and inflation fall, while bankruptcies and the unemployment rate rise.

   _____s generally occur when there is a widespread drop in spending, often following an adverse supply shock or the bursting of an economic bubble.

   a. Recession index
   b. Recession
   c. Recession of 1953
   d. Recession of 1958

2. The term _____ refers to economy-wide fluctuations in production or economic activity over several months or years. These fluctuations occur around a long-term growth trend, and typically involve shifts over time between periods of relatively rapid economic growth (an expansion or boom), and periods of relative stagnation or decline (a contraction or recession).

   _____s are usually measured by considering the growth rate of real gross domestic product.

   a. Bank run
   b. Bull trap
   c. Business cycle
   d. Countercyclical

3. Normally, the _____ of a country consists of everyone of working age (typically above a certain age (around 14 to 16) and below retirement (around 65) who are participating workers, that is people actively employed or seeking employment. People not counted include students, retired people, stay-at-home parents, people in prisons or similar institutions, people employed in jobs or professions with unreported income, as well as discouraged workers who cannot find work. _____ in the United States

   In the United States, the unemployment rate is estimated by a household survey called the Current Population Survey, conducted monthly by the Federal Bureau of Labor Statistics.

   a. Labor market segmentation
   b. Labor mobility
   c. The labor problem
   d. Labor force

4. . The _____ was a severe worldwide economic depression in the decade preceding World War II. The timing of the _____ varied across nations, but in most countries it started in 1930 after the passage of the Smoot-Hawley Tariff bill (June 17), and lasted until the late 1930s or early 1940s. It was the longest, most widespread, and deepest depression of the 20th century.

   In the 21st century, the _____ is commonly used as an example of how far the world's economy can decline.

Visit Cram101.com for full Practice Exams

Chapter 8. Economic Fluctuations, Unemployment, and Inflation

CHAPTER QUIZ: KEY TERMS, PEOPLE, PLACES, CONCEPTS

   a. Bank Night
   b. Battle of Ballantyne Pier
   c. Great Depression
   d. Bloody Sunday

5. The _____ is a protocol to the United Nations Framework Convention on Climate Change (UNFCCC or FCCC), aimed at fighting global warming. The UNFCCC is an international environmental treaty with the goal of achieving the 'stabilisation of greenhouse gas concentrations in the atmosphere at a level that would prevent dangerous anthropogenic interference with the climate system.'

   The Protocol was initially adopted on 11 December 1997 in Kyoto, Japan, and entered into force on 16 February 2005. As of September 2011, 191 states have signed and ratified the protocol. The only remaining signatory not to have ratified the protocol is the United States.

   a. Kyoto Protocol
   b. Marginal abatement cost
   c. Plant A Tree Today Foundation
   d. Reducing Emissions from Deforestation and Forest Degradation

ANSWER KEY
Chapter 8. Economic Fluctuations, Unemployment, and Inflation

1. b
2. c
3. d
4. c
5. a

You can take the complete Chapter Practice Test

for Chapter 8. Economic Fluctuations, Unemployment, and Inflation

on all key terms, persons, places, and concepts.

Online 99 Cents

http://www.epub40.13.20514.8.cram101.com/

Use www.Cram101.com for all your study needs

including Cram101's online interactive problem solving labs in

chemistry, statistics, mathematics, and more.

Visit Cram101.com for full Practice Exams

Chapter 9. An Introduction to Basic Macroeconomic Markets

CHAPTER OUTLINE: KEY TERMS, PEOPLE, PLACES, CONCEPTS

- Macroeconomics
- Business cycle
- Economic freedom
- Federal Reserve System
- Great Depression
- Phillips curve
- Economic growth
- Fiscal policy
- Monetary policy
- Money supply
- Interest rate
- Macroeconomic model
- Renewable resource
- Loanable funds
- AD-AS model
- Social security
- Aggregate demand
- Demand curve
- Purchasing power

Visit Cram101.com for full Practice Exams

Chapter 9. An Introduction to Basic Macroeconomic Markets
CHAPTER OUTLINE: KEY TERMS, PEOPLE, PLACES, CONCEPTS

_____ Aggregate supply

_____ Environmental protection

_____ Full employment

_____ Potential output

_____ Price level

_____ Kyoto Protocol

_____ Inflation rate

_____ Real interest rate

_____ Appreciation

_____ Depreciation

Chapter 9. An Introduction to Basic Macroeconomic Markets

CHAPTER HIGHLIGHTS & NOTES: KEY TERMS, PEOPLE, PLACES, CONCEPTS

Macroeconomics	Macroeconomics is a branch of economics dealing with the performance, structure, behavior, and decision-making of the whole economy. This includes national, regional, and global economies. With microeconomics, macroeconomics is one of the two most general fields in economics.
Business cycle	The term business cycle refers to economy-wide fluctuations in production or economic activity over several months or years. These fluctuations occur around a long-term growth trend, and typically involve shifts over time between periods of relatively rapid economic growth (an expansion or boom), and periods of relative stagnation or decline (a contraction or recession). Business cycles are usually measured by considering the growth rate of real gross domestic product.
Economic freedom	Economic freedom is a term used in economic and policy debates. As with freedom generally, there are various definitions, but no universally accepted concept of economic freedom. One major approach to economic freedom comes from classical liberal and libertarian traditions emphasizing free markets and private property, while another extends the welfare economics study of individual choice, with greater economic freedom coming from a 'larger' (in some technical sense) set of possible choices.
Federal Reserve System	The Federal Reserve System is the central banking system of the United States. It was created on December 23, 1913 with the enactment of the Federal Reserve Act, largely in response to a series of financial panics, particularly a severe panic in 1907. Over time, the roles and responsibilities of the Federal Reserve System have expanded and its structure has evolved. Events such as the Great Depression were major factors leading to changes in the system.
Great Depression	The Great Depression was a severe worldwide economic depression in the decade preceding World War II. The timing of the Great Depression varied across nations, but in most countries it started in 1930 after the passage of the Smoot-Hawley Tariff bill (June 17), and lasted until the late 1930s or early 1940s. It was the longest, most widespread, and deepest depression of the 20th century. In the 21st century, the Great Depression is commonly used as an example of how far the world's economy can decline.
Phillips curve	In economics, the Phillips curve is a historical inverse relationship between the rate of unemployment and the rate of inflation in an economy. Stated simply, the lower the unemployment in an economy, the higher the rate of inflation. While it has been observed that there is a stable short run tradeoff between unemployment and inflation, this has not been observed in the long run.

Visit Cram101.com for full Practice Exams

Chapter 9. An Introduction to Basic Macroeconomic Markets

CHAPTER HIGHLIGHTS & NOTES: KEY TERMS, PEOPLE, PLACES, CONCEPTS

Economic growth	Economic growth is the increase in the amount of the goods and services produced by an economy over time. It is conventionally measured as the percent rate of increase in real gross domestic product, or real GDP. Growth is usually calculated in real terms, i.e. inflation-adjusted terms, in order to net out the effect of inflation on the price of the goods and services produced. In economics, 'economic growth' or 'economic growth theory' typically refers to growth of potential output, i.e., production at 'full employment,' which is caused by growth in aggregate demand or observed output.
Fiscal policy	In economics and political science, fiscal policy is the use of government revenue collection (taxation) and expenditure (spending) to influence the economy. The two main instruments of fiscal policy are government taxation and expenditure. Changes in the level and composition of taxation and government spending can impact the following variables in the economy:•Aggregate demand and the level of economic activity;•The pattern of resource allocation;•The distribution of income. Fiscal policy refers to the use of the government budget to influence economic activity.
Monetary policy	Monetary policy is the process by which the monetary authority of a country controls the supply of money, often targeting a rate of interest for the purpose of promoting economic growth and stability. The official goals usually include relatively stable prices and low unemployment. Monetary theory provides insight into how to craft optimal monetary policy.
Money supply	In economics, the money supply, is the total amount of money available in an economy at a specific time. There are several ways to define 'money,' but standard measures usually include currency in circulation and demand deposits (depositors' easily accessed assets on the books of financial institutions). Money supply data are recorded and published, usually by the government or the central bank of the country.
Interest rate	An interest rate is the rate at which interest is paid by a borrower for the use of money that they borrow from a lender. For example, a small company borrows capital from a bank to buy new assets for their business, and in return the lender receives interest at a predetermined interest rate for deferring the use of funds and instead lending it to the borrower. Interest rates are normally expressed as a percentage of the principal for a period of one year.
Macroeconomic model	A macroeconomic model is an analytical tool designed to describe the operation of the economy of a country or a region. These models are usually designed to examine the dynamics of aggregate quantities such as the total amount of goods and services produced, total income earned, the level of employment of productive resources, and the level of prices.

Chapter 9. An Introduction to Basic Macroeconomic Markets

CHAPTER HIGHLIGHTS & NOTES: KEY TERMS, PEOPLE, PLACES, CONCEPTS

Renewable resource	A renewable resource is a natural resource with the ability to reproduce through biological or natural processes and replenished with the passage of time. Renewable resources are part of our natural environment and form our eco-system. In 1962, within a report to the committee on natural resources which was forwarded to the President of the United States, Paul Weiss defined Renewable Resources as: 'The total range of living organisms providing man with food, fibers, drugs, etc...'.
Loanable funds	In economics, the loanable funds market is a hypothetical market that brings savers and borrowers together, also bringing together the money available in commercial banks and lending institutions available for firms and households to finance expenditures, either investments or consumption. Savers supply the loanable funds; for instance, buying bonds will transfer their money to the institution issuing the bond, which can be a firm or government. In return, borrowers demand loanable funds; when an institution sells a bond, it is demanding loanable funds.
AD-AS model	The AD-AS or Aggregate Demand-Aggregate Supply model is a macroeconomic model that explains price level and output through the relationship of aggregate demand and aggregate supply. It is based on the theory of John Maynard Keynes presented in his work The General Theory of Employment, Interest, and Money. It is one of the primary simplified representations in the modern field of macroeconomics, and is used by a broad array of economists, from libertarian, Monetarist supporters of laissez-faire, such as Milton Friedman to Post-Keynesian supporters of economic interventionism, such as Joan Robinson. The conventional 'aggregate supply and demand' model is, in actuality, a Keynesian visualization that has come to be a widely accepted image of the theory. The Classical supply and demand model, which is largely based on Say's Law, or that supply creates its own demand, depicts the aggregate supply curve as being vertical at all times (not just in the long-run)Modeling The AD/AS model is used to illustrate the Keynesian model of the business cycle. Movements of the two curves can be used to predict the effects that various exogenous events will have on two variables: real GDP and the price level. Furthermore, the model can be incorporated as a component in any of a variety of dynamic models (models of how variables like the price level and others evolve over time). The AD-AS model can be related to the Phillips curve model of wage or price inflation and unemployment.

Visit Cram101.com for full Practice Exams

Chapter 9. An Introduction to Basic Macroeconomic Markets

CHAPTER HIGHLIGHTS & NOTES: KEY TERMS, PEOPLE, PLACES, CONCEPTS

Social security	Social security is a concept enshrined in Article 22 of the Universal Declaration of Human Rights which states that Everyone, as a member of society, has the right to social security and is entitled to realization, through national effort and international co-operation and in accordance with the organization and resources of each State, of the economic, social and cultural rights indispensable for his dignity and the free development of his personality. In simple term, this means that the signatories agree that society in which a person lives should help them to develop and to make the most of all the advantages (culture, work, social welfare) which are offered to them in the country. Social security may also refer to the action programs of government intended to promote the welfare of the population through assistance measures guaranteeing access to sufficient resources for food and shelter and to promote health and wellbeing for the population at large and potentially vulnerable segments such as children, the elderly, the sick and the unemployed.
Aggregate demand	In macroeconomics, aggregate demand is the total demand for final goods and services in the economy (Y) at a given time and price level. It is the amount of goods and services in the economy that will be purchased at all possible price levels. This is the demand for the gross domestic product of a country when inventory levels are static.
Demand curve	In economics, the demand curve is the graph depicting the relationship between the price of a certain commodity and the amount of it that consumers are willing and able to purchase at that given price. It is a graphic representation of a demand schedule. The demand curve for all consumers together follows from the demand curve of every individual consumer: the individual demands at each price are added together.
Purchasing power	Purchasing power is the number of goods/services that can be purchased with a unit of currency. For example, if you had taken one dollar to a store in the 1950s, you would have been able to buy a greater number of items than you would today, indicating that you would have had a greater purchasing power in the 1950s. Currency can be either a commodity money, like gold or silver, or fiat currency, or free-floating market-valued currency like US dollars.
Aggregate supply	In economics, aggregate supply is the total supply of goods and services that firms in a national economy plan on selling during a specific time period. It is the total amount of goods and services that firms are willing to sell at a given price level in an economy. There are two main reasons why Q^S might rise as P rises, i.e., why the AS curve is upward sloping:•aggregate supply is usually inadequate to supply ample opportunity.
Environmental protection	Environmental protection is a practice of protecting the environment, on individual, organizational or governmental levels, for the benefit of the natural environment and (or) humans.

Chapter 9. An Introduction to Basic Macroeconomic Markets

CHAPTER HIGHLIGHTS & NOTES: KEY TERMS, PEOPLE, PLACES, CONCEPTS

	Due to the pressures of population and technology, the biophysical environment is being degraded, sometimes permanently. This has been recognized, and governments have begun placing restraints on activities that cause environmental degradation.
Full employment	Full employment, in macroeconomics, is the level of employment rates when there is no cyclical unemployment. It is defined by the majority of mainstream economists as being an acceptable level of natural unemployment above 0%, the discrepancy from 0% being due to non-cyclical types of unemployment. Unemployment above 0% is advocated as necessary to control inflation, which has brought about the concept of the Non-Accelerating Inflation Rate of Unemployment (NAIRU); the majority of mainstream economists mean NAIRU when speaking of 'full' employment.
Potential output	In economics, potential output refers to the highest level of real Gross Domestic Product output that can be sustained over the long term. The existence of a limit is due to natural and institutional constraints. If actual GDP rises and stays above potential output, then (in the absence of wage and price controls) inflation tends to increase as demand exceeds supply.
Price level	A price level is a hypothetical measure of overall prices for some set of goods and services, in a given region during a given interval, normalized relative to some base set. Typically, a price level is approximated with a price index. The classical dichotomy is the assumption that there is a relatively clean distinction between overall increases or decreases in prices and underlying, 'nominal' economic variables.
Kyoto Protocol	The Kyoto Protocol is a protocol to the United Nations Framework Convention on Climate Change (UNFCCC or FCCC), aimed at fighting global warming. The UNFCCC is an international environmental treaty with the goal of achieving the 'stabilisation of greenhouse gas concentrations in the atmosphere at a level that would prevent dangerous anthropogenic interference with the climate system.' The Protocol was initially adopted on 11 December 1997 in Kyoto, Japan, and entered into force on 16 February 2005. As of September 2011, 191 states have signed and ratified the protocol. The only remaining signatory not to have ratified the protocol is the United States.
Inflation rate	In economics, the inflation rate is a measure of inflation, or the rate of increase of a price index such as the consumer price index. It is the percentage rate of change in price level over time, usually one year. The rate of decrease in the purchasing power of money is approximately equal.
Real interest rate	The 'real interest rate' is the rate of interest an investor expects to receive after allowing for inflation. It can be described more formally by the Fisher equation, which states that the real interest rate is approximately the nominal interest rate minus the inflation rate.

Visit Cram101.com for full Practice Exams

Chapter 9. An Introduction to Basic Macroeconomic Markets

CHAPTER HIGHLIGHTS & NOTES: KEY TERMS, PEOPLE, PLACES, CONCEPTS

Appreciation	In accounting, appreciation of an asset is an increase in its value. In this sense it is the reverse of depreciation, which measures the fall in value of assets over their normal life-time. Generally, the term is reserved for property or, more specifically, land and buildings.
Depreciation	In economics, depreciation is the gradual decrease in the economic value of the capital stock of a firm, nation or other entity, either through physical depreciation, obsolescence or changes in the demand for the services of the capital in question. If capital stock is C_0 at the beginning of a period, investment is I and depreciation D, the capital stock at the end of the period, C_1, is $C_0 + I - D$. In economics, the value of a capital asset may be modeled as the present value of the flow of services the asset will generate in future, appropriately adjusted for uncertainty.

CHAPTER QUIZ: KEY TERMS, PEOPLE, PLACES, CONCEPTS

1. The _____ is a protocol to the United Nations Framework Convention on Climate Change (UNFCCC or FCCC), aimed at fighting global warming. The UNFCCC is an international environmental treaty with the goal of achieving the 'stabilisation of greenhouse gas concentrations in the atmosphere at a level that would prevent dangerous anthropogenic interference with the climate system.'

    The Protocol was initially adopted on 11 December 1997 in Kyoto, Japan, and entered into force on 16 February 2005. As of September 2011, 191 states have signed and ratified the protocol. The only remaining signatory not to have ratified the protocol is the United States.

    a. The London Accord
    b. Marginal abatement cost
    c. Kyoto Protocol
    d. Reducing Emissions from Deforestation and Forest Degradation

2. _____ is a branch of economics dealing with the performance, structure, behavior, and decision-making of the whole economy. This includes national, regional, and global economies. With microeconomics, _____ is one of the two most general fields in economics.

    a. Comparative statics
    b. Macroeconomics
    c. Foreign-exchange reserves
    d. Hydraulic macroeconomics

3. The _____ is the central banking system of the United States. It was created on December 23, 1913 with the enactment of the Federal Reserve Act, largely in response to a series of financial panics, particularly a severe panic in 1907. Over time, the roles and responsibilities of the _____ have expanded and its structure has evolved.

Chapter 9. An Introduction to Basic Macroeconomic Markets

Visit Cram101.com for full Practice Exams

Events such as the Great Depression were major factors leading to changes in the system.

- a. Federal Reserve Act
- b. Bank holding company
- c. Federal Reserve System
- d. Beige Book

4. In economics, the _____ is a measure of inflation, or the rate of increase of a price index such as the consumer price index. It is the percentage rate of change in price level over time, usually one year. The rate of decrease in the purchasing power of money is approximately equal.

- a. Inflation swap
- b. Inflation rate
- c. Inflation-indexed bond
- d. Inflationary gap

5. The term _____ refers to economy-wide fluctuations in production or economic activity over several months or years. These fluctuations occur around a long-term growth trend, and typically involve shifts over time between periods of relatively rapid economic growth (an expansion or boom), and periods of relative stagnation or decline (a contraction or recession).

_____s are usually measured by considering the growth rate of real gross domestic product.

- a. Business cycle
- b. Bull trap
- c. Conjuncture
- d. Countercyclical

ANSWER KEY
Chapter 9. An Introduction to Basic Macroeconomic Markets

1. c
2. b
3. c
4. b
5. a

You can take the complete Chapter Practice Test

for Chapter 9. An Introduction to Basic Macroeconomic Markets

on all key terms, persons, places, and concepts.

Online 99 Cents

http://www.epub40.13.20514.9.cram101.com/

Use www.Cram101.com for all your study needs

including Cram101's online interactive problem solving labs in

chemistry, statistics, mathematics, and more.

Chapter 10. Dynamic Change, Economic Fluctuations, and the AD-AS Mode

CHAPTER OUTLINE: KEY TERMS, PEOPLE, PLACES, CONCEPTS

_____ AD-AS model

_____ Social security

_____ Interest rate

_____ Real interest rate

_____ Inflation rate

_____ Aggregate supply

_____ Great Depression

_____ Renewable resource

_____ Supply shock

_____ Inflation

_____ Recession

_____ Foreclosure

_____ Game theory

Visit Cram101.com for full Practice Exams

Chapter 10. Dynamic Change, Economic Fluctuations, and the AD-AS Model

CHAPTER HIGHLIGHTS & NOTES: KEY TERMS, PEOPLE, PLACES, CONCEPTS

AD-AS model	The AD-AS or Aggregate Demand-Aggregate Supply model is a macroeconomic model that explains price level and output through the relationship of aggregate demand and aggregate supply. It is based on the theory of John Maynard Keynes presented in his work The General Theory of Employment, Interest, and Money. It is one of the primary simplified representations in the modern field of macroeconomics, and is used by a broad array of economists, from libertarian, Monetarist supporters of laissez-faire, such as Milton Friedman to Post-Keynesian supporters of economic interventionism, such as Joan Robinson.
	The conventional 'aggregate supply and demand' model is, in actuality, a Keynesian visualization that has come to be a widely accepted image of the theory. The Classical supply and demand model, which is largely based on Say's Law, or that supply creates its own demand, depicts the aggregate supply curve as being vertical at all times (not just in the long-run)Modeling
	The AD/AS model is used to illustrate the Keynesian model of the business cycle. Movements of the two curves can be used to predict the effects that various exogenous events will have on two variables: real GDP and the price level. Furthermore, the model can be incorporated as a component in any of a variety of dynamic models (models of how variables like the price level and others evolve over time). The AD-AS model can be related to the Phillips curve model of wage or price inflation and unemployment.
Social security	Social security is a concept enshrined in Article 22 of the Universal Declaration of Human Rights which states that Everyone, as a member of society, has the right to social security and is entitled to realization, through national effort and international co-operation and in accordance with the organization and resources of each State, of the economic, social and cultural rights indispensable for his dignity and the free development of his personality. In simple term, this means that the signatories agree that society in which a person lives should help them to develop and to make the most of all the advantages (culture, work, social welfare) which are offered to them in the country.
	Social security may also refer to the action programs of government intended to promote the welfare of the population through assistance measures guaranteeing access to sufficient resources for food and shelter and to promote health and wellbeing for the population at large and potentially vulnerable segments such as children, the elderly, the sick and the unemployed.
Interest rate	An interest rate is the rate at which interest is paid by a borrower for the use of money that they borrow from a lender. For example, a small company borrows capital from a bank to buy new assets for their business, and in return the lender receives interest at a predetermined interest rate for deferring the use of funds and instead lending it to the borrower. Interest rates are normally expressed as a percentage of the principal for a period of one year.

Chapter 10. Dynamic Change, Economic Fluctuations, and the AD-AS Model

CHAPTER HIGHLIGHTS & NOTES: KEY TERMS, PEOPLE, PLACES, CONCEPTS

Real interest rate	The 'real interest rate' is the rate of interest an investor expects to receive after allowing for inflation. It can be described more formally by the Fisher equation, which states that the real interest rate is approximately the nominal interest rate minus the inflation rate. If, for example, an investor were able to lock in a 5% interest rate for the coming year and anticipated a 2% rise in prices, he would expect to earn a real interest rate of 3%.
Inflation rate	In economics, the inflation rate is a measure of inflation, or the rate of increase of a price index such as the consumer price index. It is the percentage rate of change in price level over time, usually one year. The rate of decrease in the purchasing power of money is approximately equal.
Aggregate supply	In economics, aggregate supply is the total supply of goods and services that firms in a national economy plan on selling during a specific time period. It is the total amount of goods and services that firms are willing to sell at a given price level in an economy. There are two main reasons why Q^s might rise as P rises, i.e., why the AS curve is upward sloping:•aggregate supply is usually inadequate to supply ample opportunity.
Great Depression	The Great Depression was a severe worldwide economic depression in the decade preceding World War II. The timing of the Great Depression varied across nations, but in most countries it started in 1930 after the passage of the Smoot-Hawley Tariff bill (June 17), and lasted until the late 1930s or early 1940s. It was the longest, most widespread, and deepest depression of the 20th century. In the 21st century, the Great Depression is commonly used as an example of how far the world's economy can decline.
Renewable resource	A renewable resource is a natural resource with the ability to reproduce through biological or natural processes and replenished with the passage of time. Renewable resources are part of our natural environment and form our eco-system. In 1962, within a report to the committee on natural resources which was forwarded to the President of the United States, Paul Weiss defined Renewable Resources as: 'The total range of living organisms providing man with food, fibers, drugs, etc...'.
Supply shock	A supply shock is an event that suddenly changes the price of a commodity or service. It may be caused by a sudden increase or decrease in the supply of a particular good. This sudden change affects the equilibrium price.
Inflation	In economics, inflation is a rise in the general level of prices of goods and services in an economy over a period of time. When the general price level rises, each unit of currency buys fewer goods and services.

Visit Cram101.com for full Practice Exams

Chapter 10. Dynamic Change, Economic Fluctuations, and the AD-AS Model

CHAPTER HIGHLIGHTS & NOTES: KEY TERMS, PEOPLE, PLACES, CONCEPTS

Recession	In economics, a recession is a business cycle contraction, a general slowdown in economic activity. Macroeconomic indicators such as GDP, employment, investment spending, capacity utilization, household income, business profits, and inflation fall, while bankruptcies and the unemployment rate rise. Recessions generally occur when there is a widespread drop in spending, often following an adverse supply shock or the bursting of an economic bubble.
Foreclosure	Foreclosure is a specific legal process in which a lender attempts to recover the balance of a loan from a borrower who has stopped making payments to the lender by forcing the sale of the asset used as the collateral for the loan. Formally, a mortgage lender (mortgagee), or other lien holder, obtains a termination of a mortgage borrower (mortgagor)'s equitable right of redemption, either by court order or by operation of law (after following a specific statutory procedure). Usually a lender obtains a security interest from a borrower who mortgages or pledges an asset like a house to secure the loan.
Game theory	Game theory is the study of strategic decision making. More formally, it is 'the study of mathematical models of conflict and cooperation between intelligent rational decision-makers.' An alternative term suggested 'as a more descriptive name for the discipline' is interactive decision theory. Game theory is mainly used in economics, political science, and psychology, as well as logic and biology.

Visit Cram101.com for full Practice Exams

Chapter 10. Dynamic Change, Economic Fluctuations, and the AD-AS Model

CHAPTER QUIZ: KEY TERMS, PEOPLE, PLACES, CONCEPTS

1. The AD-AS or Aggregate Demand-Aggregate Supply model is a macroeconomic model that explains price level and output through the relationship of aggregate demand and aggregate supply. It is based on the theory of John Maynard Keynes presented in his work The General Theory of Employment, Interest, and Money. It is one of the primary simplified representations in the modern field of macroeconomics, and is used by a broad array of economists, from libertarian, Monetarist supporters of laissez-faire, such as Milton Friedman to Post-Keynesian supporters of economic interventionism, such as Joan Robinson.

    The conventional 'aggregate supply and demand' model is, in actuality, a Keynesian visualization that has come to be a widely accepted image of the theory. The Classical supply and demand model, which is largely based on Say's Law, or that supply creates its own demand, depicts the aggregate supply curve as being vertical at all times (not just in the long-run)Modeling

    The AD/AS model is used to illustrate the Keynesian model of the business cycle. Movements of the two curves can be used to predict the effects that various exogenous events will have on two variables: real GDP and the price level. Furthermore, the model can be incorporated as a component in any of a variety of dynamic models (models of how variables like the price level and others evolve over time). The _____ can be related to the Phillips curve model of wage or price inflation and unemployment.

    a. AD-IA model
    b. AK model
    c. AD-AS model
    d. Edgeworth box

2. A _____ is an event that suddenly changes the price of a commodity or service. It may be caused by a sudden increase or decrease in the supply of a particular good. This sudden change affects the equilibrium price.

    a. Sustainable national income
    b. Technology shock
    c. Supply shock
    d. Value added

3. . _____ is a concept enshrined in Article 22 of the Universal Declaration of Human Rights which states that Everyone, as a member of society, has the right to _____ and is entitled to realization, through national effort and international co-operation and in accordance with the organization and resources of each State, of the economic, social and cultural rights indispensable for his dignity and the free development of his personality. In simple term, this means that the signatories agree that society in which a person lives should help them to develop and to make the most of all the advantages (culture, work, social welfare) which are offered to them in the country.

    _____ may also refer to the action programs of government intended to promote the welfare of the population through assistance measures guaranteeing access to sufficient resources for food and shelter and to promote health and wellbeing for the population at large and potentially vulnerable segments such as children, the elderly, the sick and the unemployed.

    a. Social Security Agency
    b. Social welfare function

Chapter 10. Dynamic Change, Economic Fluctuations, and the AD-AS Model

CHAPTER QUIZ: KEY TERMS, PEOPLE, PLACES, CONCEPTS

   c. Social security
   d. Suits index

4. An _____ is the rate at which interest is paid by a borrower for the use of money that they borrow from a lender. For example, a small company borrows capital from a bank to buy new assets for their business, and in return the lender receives interest at a predetermined _____ for deferring the use of funds and instead lending it to the borrower. _____s are normally expressed as a percentage of the principal for a period of one year.

   a. Inverse demand function
   b. Interest rate
   c. Undervalued stock
   d. Suits index

5. The '_____' is the rate of interest an investor expects to receive after allowing for inflation. It can be described more formally by the Fisher equation, which states that the _____ is approximately the nominal interest rate minus the inflation rate. If, for example, an investor were able to lock in a 5% interest rate for the coming year and anticipated a 2% rise in prices, he would expect to earn a _____ of 3%.

   a. Redenomination
   b. Reflation
   c. Second-round effect
   d. Real interest rate

Visit Cram101.com for full Practice Exams

ANSWER KEY
Chapter 10. Dynamic Change, Economic Fluctuations, and the AD-AS Model

1. c
2. c
3. c
4. b
5. d

You can take the complete Chapter Practice Test

for Chapter 10. Dynamic Change, Economic Fluctuations, and the AD-AS Model

on all key terms, persons, places, and concepts.

Online 99 Cents

http://www.epub40.13.20514.10.cram101.com/

Use www.Cram101.com for all your study needs

including Cram101's online interactive problem solving labs in

chemistry, statistics, mathematics, and more.

Chapter 11. Fiscal Policy: The Keynesian View and Historical Perspective

CHAPTER OUTLINE: KEY TERMS, PEOPLE, PLACES, CONCEPTS

- Keynesian economics
- Phillips curve
- Fiscal policy
- Great Depression
- Marginal propensity to consume
- Social security
- Balanced budget
- Debt crisis
- Renewable resource
- Automatic stabilizer
- Income tax
- AD-AS model
- Paradox of thrift
- Household

Visit Cram101.com for full Practice Exams

Chapter 11. Fiscal Policy: The Keynesian View and Historical Perspective

CHAPTER HIGHLIGHTS & NOTES: KEY TERMS, PEOPLE, PLACES, CONCEPTS

Keynesian economics	Keynesian economics are the group of macroeconomic schools of thought based on the ideas of 20th-century economist John Maynard Keynes. Advocates of Keynesian economics argue that private sector decisions sometimes lead to inefficient macroeconomic outcomes which require active policy responses by the public sector, particularly monetary policy actions by the central bank and fiscal policy actions by the government to stabilize output over the business cycle. The theories forming the basis of Keynesian economics were first presented in The General Theory of Employment, Interest and Money, published in 1936. The interpretations of Keynes are contentious and several schools of thought claim his legacy.
Phillips curve	In economics, the Phillips curve is a historical inverse relationship between the rate of unemployment and the rate of inflation in an economy. Stated simply, the lower the unemployment in an economy, the higher the rate of inflation. While it has been observed that there is a stable short run tradeoff between unemployment and inflation, this has not been observed in the long run.
Fiscal policy	In economics and political science, fiscal policy is the use of government revenue collection (taxation) and expenditure (spending) to influence the economy. The two main instruments of fiscal policy are government taxation and expenditure. Changes in the level and composition of taxation and government spending can impact the following variables in the economy:•Aggregate demand and the level of economic activity;•The pattern of resource allocation;•The distribution of income. Fiscal policy refers to the use of the government budget to influence economic activity.
Great Depression	The Great Depression was a severe worldwide economic depression in the decade preceding World War II. The timing of the Great Depression varied across nations, but in most countries it started in 1930 after the passage of the Smoot-Hawley Tariff bill (June 17), and lasted until the late 1930s or early 1940s. It was the longest, most widespread, and deepest depression of the 20th century. In the 21st century, the Great Depression is commonly used as an example of how far the world's economy can decline.
Marginal propensity to consume	In economics, the marginal propensity to consume is an empirical metric that quantifies induced consumption, the concept that the increase in personal consumer spending (consumption) occurs with an increase in disposable income (income after taxes and transfers). The proportion of the disposable income which individuals desire to spend on consumption is known as propensity to consume.

Visit Cram101.com for full Practice Exams

Chapter 11. Fiscal Policy: The Keynesian View and Historical Perspective

CHAPTER HIGHLIGHTS & NOTES: KEY TERMS, PEOPLE, PLACES, CONCEPTS

Social security	Social security is a concept enshrined in Article 22 of the Universal Declaration of Human Rights which states that Everyone, as a member of society, has the right to social security and is entitled to realization, through national effort and international co-operation and in accordance with the organization and resources of each State, of the economic, social and cultural rights indispensable for his dignity and the free development of his personality. In simple term, this means that the signatories agree that society in which a person lives should help them to develop and to make the most of all the advantages (culture, work, social welfare) which are offered to them in the country. Social security may also refer to the action programs of government intended to promote the welfare of the population through assistance measures guaranteeing access to sufficient resources for food and shelter and to promote health and wellbeing for the population at large and potentially vulnerable segments such as children, the elderly, the sick and the unemployed.
Balanced budget	A balanced budget is when there is neither a budget deficit or a budget surplus - when revenues equal expenditure ('the accounts balance') - particularly by a government. More generally, it refers to when there is no deficit, but possibly a surplus. A cyclically balanced budget is a budget that is not necessarily balanced year-to-year, but is balanced over the economic cycle, running a surplus in boom years and running a deficit in lean years, with these offsetting over time.
Debt crisis	Debt crisis is the general term for a proliferation of massive public debt relative to tax revenues, especially in reference to Latin American countries during the 1980s, and the United States and the European Union since the mid-2000s. Europe •European sovereign debt crisis•Greek government debt crisis•Irish financial crisis•Portuguese economic crisisLatin America •Argentine debt restructuring•Latin American debt crisisNorth America •United States debt-ceiling crisis.
Renewable resource	A renewable resource is a natural resource with the ability to reproduce through biological or natural processes and replenished with the passage of time. Renewable resources are part of our natural environment and form our eco-system. In 1962, within a report to the committee on natural resources which was forwarded to the President of the United States, Paul Weiss defined Renewable Resources as: 'The total range of living organisms providing man with food, fibers, drugs, etc...'.
Automatic stabilizer	In macroeconomics, automatic stabilizers describes/refers on how modern government budget policies, particularly income taxes and welfare spending, act to dampen fluctuations in real GDP. The size of the government budget deficit tends to increase when a country enters a recession, which tends to keep national income higher by maintaining aggregate demand. There may also be a multiplier effect.

Chapter 11. Fiscal Policy: The Keynesian View and Historical Perspective

CHAPTER HIGHLIGHTS & NOTES: KEY TERMS, PEOPLE, PLACES, CONCEPTS

Income tax	An income tax is a tax levied on the income of individuals or businesses (corporations or other legal entities). Various income tax systems exist, with varying degrees of tax incidence. Income taxation can be progressive, proportional, or regressive.
AD-AS model	The AD-AS or Aggregate Demand-Aggregate Supply model is a macroeconomic model that explains price level and output through the relationship of aggregate demand and aggregate supply. It is based on the theory of John Maynard Keynes presented in his work The General Theory of Employment, Interest, and Money. It is one of the primary simplified representations in the modern field of macroeconomics, and is used by a broad array of economists, from libertarian, Monetarist supporters of laissez-faire, such as Milton Friedman to Post-Keynesian supporters of economic interventionism, such as Joan Robinson. The conventional 'aggregate supply and demand' model is, in actuality, a Keynesian visualization that has come to be a widely accepted image of the theory. The Classical supply and demand model, which is largely based on Say's Law, or that supply creates its own demand, depicts the aggregate supply curve as being vertical at all times (not just in the long-run)Modeling The AD/AS model is used to illustrate the Keynesian model of the business cycle. Movements of the two curves can be used to predict the effects that various exogenous events will have on two variables: real GDP and the price level. Furthermore, the model can be incorporated as a component in any of a variety of dynamic models (models of how variables like the price level and others evolve over time). The AD-AS model can be related to the Phillips curve model of wage or price inflation and unemployment.
Paradox of thrift	The paradox of thrift is a paradox of economics, popularized by John Maynard Keynes, though it had been stated as early as 1714 in The Fable of the Bees, and similar sentiments date to antiquity. The paradox states that if everyone tries to save more money during times of recession, then aggregate demand will fall and will in turn lower total savings in the population because of the decrease in consumption and economic growth. The paradox is, narrowly speaking, that total savings may fall even when individual savings attempt to rise, and, broadly speaking, that increase in savings may be harmful to an economy.
Household	The household is 'the basic residential unit in which economic production, consumption, inheritance, child rearing, and shelter are organized and carried out'; [the household] 'may or may not be synonymous with family'. The household is the basic unit of analysis in many social, microeconomic and government models. The term refers to all individuals who live in the same dwelling.

Visit Cram101.com for full Practice Exams

Chapter 11. Fiscal Policy: The Keynesian View and Historical Perspective

CHAPTER QUIZ: KEY TERMS, PEOPLE, PLACES, CONCEPTS

1. A _____ is when there is neither a budget deficit or a budget surplus - when revenues equal expenditure ('the accounts balance') - particularly by a government. More generally, it refers to when there is no deficit, but possibly a surplus. A cyclically _____ is a budget that is not necessarily balanced year-to-year, but is balanced over the economic cycle, running a surplus in boom years and running a deficit in lean years, with these offsetting over time.

    a. Bancor
    b. Birmingham School
    c. Balanced budget
    d. Deficit spending

2. An _____ is a tax levied on the income of individuals or businesses (corporations or other legal entities). Various _____ systems exist, with varying degrees of tax incidence. Income taxation can be progressive, proportional, or regressive.

    a. Income tax audit
    b. Indirect tax
    c. Inflation tax
    d. Income tax

3. _____ is the general term for a proliferation of massive public debt relative to tax revenues, especially in reference to Latin American countries during the 1980s, and the United States and the European Union since the mid-2000s. Europe •European sovereign _____ •Greek government _____ •Irish financial crisis•Portuguese economic crisisLatin America •Argentine debt restructuring•Latin American _____ North America •United States debt-ceiling crisis.

    a. Government financial statements
    b. Greek government-debt crisis
    c. Taxpayer groups
    d. Debt crisis

4. . _____ is a concept enshrined in Article 22 of the Universal Declaration of Human Rights which states that Everyone, as a member of society, has the right to _____ and is entitled to realization, through national effort and international co-operation and in accordance with the organization and resources of each State, of the economic, social and cultural rights indispensable for his dignity and the free development of his personality. In simple term, this means that the signatories agree that society in which a person lives should help them to develop and to make the most of all the advantages (culture, work, social welfare) which are offered to them in the country.

    _____ may also refer to the action programs of government intended to promote the welfare of the population through assistance measures guaranteeing access to sufficient resources for food and shelter and to promote health and wellbeing for the population at large and potentially vulnerable segments such as children, the elderly, the sick and the unemployed.

    a. Social Security Agency
    b. Social security
    c. Structural adjustment loan

Visit Cram101.com for full Practice Exams

Chapter 11. Fiscal Policy: The Keynesian View and Historical Perspective

5. In economics and political science, _____ is the use of government revenue collection (taxation) and expenditure (spending) to influence the economy. The two main instruments of _____ are government taxation and expenditure. Changes in the level and composition of taxation and government spending can impact the following variables in the economy:•Aggregate demand and the level of economic activity;•The pattern of resource allocation;•The distribution of income.

_____ refers to the use of the government budget to influence economic activity.

a. Fiscal sustainability
b. Flypaper effect
c. Funding Opportunity Announcement
d. Fiscal policy

ANSWER KEY
Chapter 11. Fiscal Policy: The Keynesian View and Historical Perspective

1. c
2. d
3. d
4. b
5. d

You can take the complete Chapter Practice Test

for Chapter 11. Fiscal Policy: The Keynesian View and Historical Perspective
on all key terms, persons, places, and concepts.

Online 99 Cents

http://www.epub40.13.20514.11.cram101.com/

Use www.Cram101.com for all your study needs

including Cram101's online interactive problem solving labs in

chemistry, statistics, mathematics, and more.

Chapter 12. Fiscal Policy, Incentives, and Secondary Effects

CHAPTER OUTLINE: KEY TERMS, PEOPLE, PLACES, CONCEPTS

- Keynesian economics
- Alternatives
- Fiscal policy
- Interest rate
- Renewable resource
- Appreciation
- Financial market
- Ricardian equivalence
- Barriers to entry
- Government spending
- Automatic stabilizer
- International trade
- Supply-side economics
- Tax rate
- Great Depression
- Health insurance
- Income bracket
- Laffer curve
- AD-AS model

Visit Cram101.com for full Practice Exams

Chapter 12. Fiscal Policy, Incentives, and Secondary Effects

CHAPTER OUTLINE: KEY TERMS, PEOPLE, PLACES, CONCEPTS

	Deadweight loss
	Government revenue
	Tax cut
	Troubled Asset Relief Program

CHAPTER HIGHLIGHTS & NOTES: KEY TERMS, PEOPLE, PLACES, CONCEPTS

Keynesian economics	Keynesian economics are the group of macroeconomic schools of thought based on the ideas of 20th-century economist John Maynard Keynes. Advocates of Keynesian economics argue that private sector decisions sometimes lead to inefficient macroeconomic outcomes which require active policy responses by the public sector, particularly monetary policy actions by the central bank and fiscal policy actions by the government to stabilize output over the business cycle. The theories forming the basis of Keynesian economics were first presented in The General Theory of Employment, Interest and Money, published in 1936. The interpretations of Keynes are contentious and several schools of thought claim his legacy.
Alternatives	Founded in 1994, Alternatives, Action and Communication Network for International Development, is a non-governmental, international solidarity organization based in Montreal, Quebec, Canada. Alternatives works to promote justice and equality amongst individuals and communities worldwide. Active in over 35 countries, Alternatives supports local, community-based initiatives working towards the greater economic, social, and political rights of people and communities affected by poverty, discrimination, exploitation, and violence.
Fiscal policy	In economics and political science, fiscal policy is the use of government revenue collection (taxation) and expenditure (spending) to influence the economy. The two main instruments of fiscal policy are government taxation and expenditure.

Visit Cram101.com for full Practice Exams

Chapter 12. Fiscal Policy, Incentives, and Secondary Effects

CHAPTER HIGHLIGHTS & NOTES: KEY TERMS, PEOPLE, PLACES, CONCEPTS

	Changes in the level and composition of taxation and government spending can impact the following variables in the economy:•Aggregate demand and the level of economic activity;•The pattern of resource allocation;•The distribution of income.
	Fiscal policy refers to the use of the government budget to influence economic activity.
Interest rate	An interest rate is the rate at which interest is paid by a borrower for the use of money that they borrow from a lender. For example, a small company borrows capital from a bank to buy new assets for their business, and in return the lender receives interest at a predetermined interest rate for deferring the use of funds and instead lending it to the borrower. Interest rates are normally expressed as a percentage of the principal for a period of one year.
Renewable resource	A renewable resource is a natural resource with the ability to reproduce through biological or natural processes and replenished with the passage of time. Renewable resources are part of our natural environment and form our eco-system.
	In 1962, within a report to the committee on natural resources which was forwarded to the President of the United States, Paul Weiss defined Renewable Resources as: 'The total range of living organisms providing man with food, fibers, drugs, etc...'.
Appreciation	In accounting, appreciation of an asset is an increase in its value. In this sense it is the reverse of depreciation, which measures the fall in value of assets over their normal life-time. Generally, the term is reserved for property or, more specifically, land and buildings.
Financial market	A financial market is a market in which people and entities can trade financial securities, commodities, and other fungible items of value at low transaction costs and at prices that reflect supply and demand. Securities include stocks and bonds, and commodities include precious metals or agricultural goods.
	There are both general markets (where many commodities are traded) and specialized markets (where only one commodity is traded).
Ricardian equivalence	The Ricardian equivalence proposition (also known as the Barro-Ricardo equivalence theorem) is an economic theory holding that consumers internalize the government's budget constraint: as a result, the timing of any tax change does not affect their change in spending. Consequently, Ricardian equivalence suggests that it does not matter whether a government finances its spending with debt or a tax increase, because the effect on the total level of demand in the economy is the same.
	In its simplest terms: governments can raise money either through taxes or by issuing bonds.

Visit Cram101.com for full Practice Exams

Chapter 12. Fiscal Policy, Incentives, and Secondary Effects

CHAPTER HIGHLIGHTS & NOTES: KEY TERMS, PEOPLE, PLACES, CONCEPTS

Barriers to entry	In theories of competition in economics, barriers to entry, are obstacles that make it difficult to enter a given market. The term can refer to hindrances a firm faces in trying to enter a market or industry - such as government regulation, or a large, established firm taking advantage of economies of scale - or those an individual faces in trying to gain entrance to a profession - such as education or licensing requirements. Because barriers to entry protect incumbent firms and restrict competition in a market, they can contribute to distortionary prices.
Government spending	Government spending includes all government consumption, investment but excludes transfer payments made by a state. Government acquisition of goods and services for current use to directly satisfy individual or collective needs of the members of the community is classed as government final consumption expenditure. Government acquisition of goods and services intended to create future benefits, such as infrastructure investment or research spending, is classed as government investment (gross fixed capital formation), which usually is the largest part of the government gross capital formation.
Automatic stabilizer	In macroeconomics, automatic stabilizers describes/refers on how modern government budget policies, particularly income taxes and welfare spending, act to dampen fluctuations in real GDP. The size of the government budget deficit tends to increase when a country enters a recession, which tends to keep national income higher by maintaining aggregate demand. There may also be a multiplier effect. This effect happens automatically depending on GDP and household income, without any explicit policy action by the government, and acts to reduce the severity of recessions.
International trade	International trade is the exchange of capital, goods, and services across international borders or territories. In most countries, such trade represents a significant share of gross domestic product (GDP). While international trade has been present throughout much of history , its economic, social, and political importance has been on the rise in recent centuries.
Supply-side economics	Supply-side economics is a school of macroeconomic thought that argues that economic growth can be most effectively created by lowering barriers for people to produce (supply) goods and services, such as lowering income tax and capital gains tax rates, and by allowing greater flexibility by reducing regulation. According to supply-side economics, consumers will then benefit from a greater supply of goods and services at lower prices. Typical policy recommendations of supply-side economists are lower marginal tax rates and less regulation.

Chapter 12. Fiscal Policy, Incentives, and Secondary Effects

CHAPTER HIGHLIGHTS & NOTES: KEY TERMS, PEOPLE, PLACES, CONCEPTS

Tax rate	In a tax system and in economics, the tax rate describes the burden ratio (usually expressed as a percentage) at which a business or person is taxed. There are several methods used to present a tax rate: statutory, average, marginal, and effective. These rates can also be presented using different definitions applied to a tax base: inclusive and exclusive.
Great Depression	The Great Depression was a severe worldwide economic depression in the decade preceding World War II. The timing of the Great Depression varied across nations, but in most countries it started in 1930 after the passage of the Smoot-Hawley Tariff bill (June 17), and lasted until the late 1930s or early 1940s. It was the longest, most widespread, and deepest depression of the 20th century. In the 21st century, the Great Depression is commonly used as an example of how far the world's economy can decline.
Health insurance	Health insurance is insurance against the risk of incurring medical expenses among individuals. By estimating the overall risk of health care expenses among a targeted group, an insurer can develop a routine finance structure, such as a monthly premium or payroll tax, to ensure that money is available to pay for the health care benefits specified in the insurance agreement. The benefit is administered by a central organization such as a government agency, private business, or not-for-profit entity.
Income bracket	Income bracket is the bandwidth from a basic wage towards all possible salary components and is used to give employees a career perspective and to give the employer the possibility to reward achievements.
Laffer curve	In economics, the Laffer curve is a hypothetical representation of the relationship between government revenue raised by taxation and all possible rates of taxation. It is used to illustrate the concept of taxable income elasticity - that taxable income will change in response to changes in the rate of taxation. The Laffer curve postulates that no tax revenue will be raised at the extreme tax rates of 0% and 100%.
AD-AS model	The AD-AS or Aggregate Demand-Aggregate Supply model is a macroeconomic model that explains price level and output through the relationship of aggregate demand and aggregate supply. It is based on the theory of John Maynard Keynes presented in his work The General Theory of Employment, Interest, and Money. It is one of the primary simplified representations in the modern field of macroeconomics, and is used by a broad array of economists, from libertarian, Monetarist supporters of laissez-faire, such as Milton Friedman to Post-Keynesian supporters of economic interventionism, such as Joan Robinson. The conventional 'aggregate supply and demand' model is, in actuality, a Keynesian visualization that has come to be a widely accepted image of the theory.

Chapter 12. Fiscal Policy, Incentives, and Secondary Effects

CHAPTER HIGHLIGHTS & NOTES: KEY TERMS, PEOPLE, PLACES, CONCEPTS

	The Classical supply and demand model, which is largely based on Say's Law, or that supply creates its own demand, depicts the aggregate supply curve as being vertical at all times (not just in the long-run)Modeling
	The AD/AS model is used to illustrate the Keynesian model of the business cycle. Movements of the two curves can be used to predict the effects that various exogenous events will have on two variables: real GDP and the price level. Furthermore, the model can be incorporated as a component in any of a variety of dynamic models (models of how variables like the price level and others evolve over time). The AD-AS model can be related to the Phillips curve model of wage or price inflation and unemployment.
Deadweight loss	In economics, a deadweight loss is a loss of economic efficiency that can occur when equilibrium for a good or service is not Pareto optimal. In other words, either people who would have more marginal benefit than marginal cost are not buying the product, or people who have more marginal cost than marginal benefit are buying the product.
	Causes of deadweight loss can include monopoly pricing (in the case of artificial scarcity), externalities, taxes or subsidies, and binding price ceilings or floors.
Government revenue	Government revenue is revenue received by a government. Its opposite is government spending. Yet, governments coin money.Government revenue is an important part of fiscal policy.
Tax cut	A tax cut is a reduction in taxes. The immediate effects of a tax cut are a decrease in the real income of the government and an increase in the real income of those whose tax rate has been lowered. Due to the perceived benefit in growing real incomes among tax payers politicians have sought to claim their proposed tax credits as tax cuts.
Troubled Asset Relief Program	The Troubled Asset Relief Program is a program of the United States government to purchase assets and equity from financial institutions to strengthen its financial sector that was signed into law by U.S. President George W. Bush on October 3, 2008. It was a component of the government's measures in 2008 to address the subprime mortgage crisis.
	The TARP program originally authorized expenditures of $700 billion and was expected to cost the U.S. taxpayers as much as $300 billion. The Dodd-Frank Wall Street Reform and Consumer Protection Act reduced the amount authorized to $475 billion.

Visit Cram101.com for full Practice Exams

Chapter 12. Fiscal Policy, Incentives, and Secondary Effects

CHAPTER QUIZ: KEY TERMS, PEOPLE, PLACES, CONCEPTS

1. _____ are the group of macroeconomic schools of thought based on the ideas of 20th-century economist John Maynard Keynes.

    Advocates of _____ argue that private sector decisions sometimes lead to inefficient macroeconomic outcomes which require active policy responses by the public sector, particularly monetary policy actions by the central bank and fiscal policy actions by the government to stabilize output over the business cycle. The theories forming the basis of _____ were first presented in The General Theory of Employment, Interest and Money, published in 1936. The interpretations of Keynes are contentious and several schools of thought claim his legacy.

    a. Hydraulic macroeconomics
    b. John Maynard Keynes
    c. Keynesian economics
    d. Neo-Keynesian economics

2. _____ is revenue received by a government. Its opposite is government spending. Yet, governments coin money. _____ is an important part of fiscal policy.

    a. Government spending
    b. Government revenue
    c. Growth recession
    d. Guns versus butter model

3. _____ includes all government consumption, investment but excludes transfer payments made by a state. Government acquisition of goods and services for current use to directly satisfy individual or collective needs of the members of the community is classed as government final consumption expenditure.

    Government acquisition of goods and services intended to create future benefits, such as infrastructure investment or research spending, is classed as government investment (gross fixed capital formation), which usually is the largest part of the government gross capital formation.

    a. Great Moderation
    b. Growth recession
    c. Government spending
    d. Hard money

4. . The _____ is a program of the United States government to purchase assets and equity from financial institutions to strengthen its financial sector that was signed into law by U.S. President George W. Bush on October 3, 2008. It was a component of the government's measures in 2008 to address the subprime mortgage crisis.

    The TARP program originally authorized expenditures of $700 billion and was expected to cost the U.S. taxpayers as much as $300 billion. The Dodd-Frank Wall Street Reform and Consumer Protection Act reduced the amount authorized to $475 billion.

    a. Troubled Asset Relief Program
    b. Capital Purchase Program

Chapter 12. Fiscal Policy, Incentives, and Secondary Effects

CHAPTER QUIZ: KEY TERMS, PEOPLE, PLACES, CONCEPTS

    c. Financial Crisis Responsibility Fee
    d. Public Law 110-343

5. A _____ is a reduction in taxes. The immediate effects of a _____ are a decrease in the real income of the government and an increase in the real income of those whose tax rate has been lowered. Due to the perceived benefit in growing real incomes among tax payers politicians have sought to claim their proposed tax credits as _____ s.

    a. Tax cut
    b. Tax deferral
    c. Tax expense
    d. Tax exporting

Visit Cram101.com for full Practice Exams

ANSWER KEY
Chapter 12. Fiscal Policy, Incentives, and Secondary Effects

1. c
2. b
3. c
4. a
5. a

You can take the complete Chapter Practice Test

for Chapter 12. Fiscal Policy, Incentives, and Secondary Effects

on all key terms, persons, places, and concepts.

Online 99 Cents

http://www.epub40.13.20514.12.cram101.com/

Use www.Cram101.com for all your study needs

including Cram101's online interactive problem solving labs in

chemistry, statistics, mathematics, and more.

Chapter 13. Money and the Banking System

CHAPTER OUTLINE: KEY TERMS, PEOPLE, PLACES, CONCEPTS

_____ Great Depression

_____ Fiat money

_____ Money supply

_____ Social security

_____ Currency crisis

_____ Demand deposit

_____ Purchasing power

_____ Depository institution

_____ Money market

_____ Mutual fund

_____ Federal Reserve System

_____ Credit union

_____ Financial institution

_____ Savings and loan association

_____ Bank reserves

_____ Fractional reserve banking

_____ Gold

_____ Renewable resource

_____ Deposit insurance

Visit Cram101.com for full Practice Exams

Chapter 13. Money and the Banking System

CHAPTER OUTLINE: KEY TERMS, PEOPLE, PLACES, CONCEPTS

_____ Bank run

_____ Excess reserves

_____ Phillips curve

_____ Federal Open Market Committee

_____ Home equity loan

_____ Open market

_____ Independence

_____ Reserve requirement

_____ Open market operation

_____ Discount rate

_____ Federal funds

_____ Monetary base

CHAPTER HIGHLIGHTS & NOTES: KEY TERMS, PEOPLE, PLACES, CONCEPTS

| Great Depression | The Great Depression was a severe worldwide economic depression in the decade preceding World War II. The timing of the Great Depression varied across nations, but in most countries it started in 1930 after the passage of the Smoot-Hawley Tariff bill (June 17), and lasted until the late 1930s or early 1940s. It was the longest, most widespread, and deepest depression of the 20th century. |

Chapter 13. Money and the Banking System

CHAPTER HIGHLIGHTS & NOTES: KEY TERMS, PEOPLE, PLACES, CONCEPTS

Fiat money	Fiat money is money that derives its value from government regulation or law: the initial value of fiat money is established by government decree. The term fiat currency is also used when the fiat money is used as the main currency of the country. The term derives from the Latin fiat, meaning 'let it be done' or 'it shall be'.
Money supply	In economics, the money supply, is the total amount of money available in an economy at a specific time. There are several ways to define 'money,' but standard measures usually include currency in circulation and demand deposits (depositors' easily accessed assets on the books of financial institutions).
	Money supply data are recorded and published, usually by the government or the central bank of the country.
Social security	Social security is a concept enshrined in Article 22 of the Universal Declaration of Human Rights which states that Everyone, as a member of society, has the right to social security and is entitled to realization, through national effort and international co-operation and in accordance with the organization and resources of each State, of the economic, social and cultural rights indispensable for his dignity and the free development of his personality. In simple term, this means that the signatories agree that society in which a person lives should help them to develop and to make the most of all the advantages (culture, work, social welfare) which are offered to them in the country.
	Social security may also refer to the action programs of government intended to promote the welfare of the population through assistance measures guaranteeing access to sufficient resources for food and shelter and to promote health and wellbeing for the population at large and potentially vulnerable segments such as children, the elderly, the sick and the unemployed.
Currency crisis	A currency crisis, which is also called a balance-of-payments crisis, is a sudden devaluation of a currency caused by chronic balance-of-payments deficits which usually ends in a speculative attack in the foreign exchange market. It occurs when the value of a currency changes quickly, undermining its ability to serve as a medium of exchange or a store of value. Currency crises usually affect fixed exchange rate regimes, rather than floating regimes.
Demand deposit	Demand deposits, bank money or scriptural money are funds held in demand deposit accounts in commercial banks. These account balances are usually considered money and form the greater part of the narrowly defined money supply of a country.
	In the United States, demand deposits arose following the 1865 tax of 10% on the issuance of state bank notes.

Chapter 13. Money and the Banking System

CHAPTER HIGHLIGHTS & NOTES: KEY TERMS, PEOPLE, PLACES, CONCEPTS

Purchasing power	Purchasing power is the number of goods/services that can be purchased with a unit of currency. For example, if you had taken one dollar to a store in the 1950s, you would have been able to buy a greater number of items than you would today, indicating that you would have had a greater purchasing power in the 1950s. Currency can be either a commodity money, like gold or silver, or fiat currency, or free-floating market-valued currency like US dollars.
Depository institution	A depository institution is a financial institution in the United States (such as a savings bank, commercial bank, savings and loan association, or credit union) that is legally allowed to accept monetary deposits from consumers. Federal depository institutions are regulated by the Federal Deposit Insurance Corporation (FDIC).
	An example of a non-depository institution might be a mortgage bank.
Money market	As money became a commodity, the money market is nowadays a component of the financial markets for assets involved in short-term borrowing, lending, buying and selling with original maturities of one year or less. Trading in the money markets is done over the counter, is wholesale. Various instruments like Treasury bills, commercial paper, bankers' acceptances, deposits, certificates of deposit, bills of exchange, repurchase agreements, federal funds, and short-lived mortgage- and asset-backed securities do exist.
Mutual fund	A mutual fund is a type of professionally-managed collective investment scheme that pools money from many investors to purchase securities. While there is no legal definition of mutual fund, the term is most commonly applied only to those collective investment schemes that are regulated, available to the general public and open-ended in nature. Hedge funds are not considered a type of mutual fund.
Federal Reserve System	The Federal Reserve System is the central banking system of the United States. It was created on December 23, 1913 with the enactment of the Federal Reserve Act, largely in response to a series of financial panics, particularly a severe panic in 1907. Over time, the roles and responsibilities of the Federal Reserve System have expanded and its structure has evolved. Events such as the Great Depression were major factors leading to changes in the system.
Credit union	A credit union is a member-owned financial cooperative, democratically controlled by its members, and operated for the purpose of promoting thrift, providing credit at competitive rates, and providing other financial services to its members.
	Many credit unions also provide services intended to support community development or sustainable international development on a local level, and could be considered community development financial institutions.

Visit Cram101.com for full Practice Exams

Chapter 13. Money and the Banking System

CHAPTER HIGHLIGHTS & NOTES: KEY TERMS, PEOPLE, PLACES, CONCEPTS

Financial institution	In financial economics, a financial institution is an institution that provides financial services for its clients or members. Probably the most important financial service provided by financial institutions is acting as financial intermediaries. Most financial institutions are regulated by the government.
Savings and loan association	A savings and loan association, also known as a thrift, is a financial institution that specializes in accepting savings deposits and making mortgage and other loans. The terms 'S&L' or 'thrift' are mainly used in the United States; similar institutions in the United Kingdom, Ireland and some Commonwealth countries include building societies and trustee savings banks. They are often mutually held (often called mutual savings banks), meaning that the depositors and borrowers are members with voting rights, and have the ability to direct the financial and managerial goals of the organization like the members of a credit union or the policyholders of a mutual insurance company.
Bank reserves	Bank reserves are banks' holdings of deposits in accounts with their central bank (for instance the European Central Bank or the Federal Reserve, in the latter case including federal funds), plus currency that is physically held in the bank's vault (vault cash). The central banks of some nations set minimum reserve requirements. Even when no requirements are set, banks commonly wish to hold some reserves, called desired reserves, against unexpected events such as unusually large net withdrawals by customers or even bank runs.
Fractional reserve banking	Fractional-reserve banking is a form of banking where banks maintain reserves (of cash and coin or deposits at the central bank) that are only a fraction of the customer's deposits. Funds deposited into a bank are mostly lent out, and a bank keeps only a fraction (called the reserve ratio) of the quantity of deposits as reserves. Some of the funds lent out are subsequently deposited with another bank, increasing deposits at that second bank and allowing further lending. As most bank deposits are treated as money in their own right, fractional reserve banking increases the money supply, and banks are said to create money.
Gold	Gold is a chemical element with the symbol Au and an atomic number of 79. Gold is a dense, soft, shiny, malleable and ductile metal. Pure gold has a bright yellow color and luster traditionally considered attractive, which it maintains without oxidizing in air or water. Chemically, gold is a transition metal and a group 11 element.
Renewable resource	A renewable resource is a natural resource with the ability to reproduce through biological or natural processes and replenished with the passage of time. Renewable resources are part of our natural environment and form our eco-system.

Visit Cram101.com for full Practice Exams

Chapter 13. Money and the Banking System

CHAPTER HIGHLIGHTS & NOTES: KEY TERMS, PEOPLE, PLACES, CONCEPTS

Deposit insurance	Explicit deposit insurance is a measure implemented in many countries to protect bank depositors, in full or in part, from losses caused by a bank's inability to pay its debts when due. Deposit insurance systems are one component of a financial system safety net that is meant to promote financial stability, but can in fact do the opposite. Banks are allowed (and usually encouraged) to lend or invest most of the money deposited with them instead of safe-keeping the full amounts.
Bank run	A bank run occurs when a large number of customers withdraw their deposits from a financial institution and either demand cash or transfer those funds into government bonds or a safer institution because they believe that financial institution is, or might become, insolvent. As a bank run progresses, it generates its own momentum, in a kind of self-fulfilling prophecy - as more people withdraw their deposits, the likelihood of default increases, thus triggering further withdrawals. This can destabilize the bank to the point where it runs out of cash and thus faces sudden bankruptcy.
Excess reserves	In banking, excess reserves are bank reserves in excess of the reserve requirement set by a central bank. They are reserves of cash more than the required amounts. Holding excess reserves has an opportunity cost if higher risk-adjusted interest can be earned by putting the funds elsewhere; the advantage of holding some funds in excess reserves is that doing so may provide enhanced liquidity and therefore flexibility in bank operations.
Phillips curve	In economics, the Phillips curve is a historical inverse relationship between the rate of unemployment and the rate of inflation in an economy. Stated simply, the lower the unemployment in an economy, the higher the rate of inflation. While it has been observed that there is a stable short run tradeoff between unemployment and inflation, this has not been observed in the long run.
Federal Open Market Committee	The Federal Open Market Committee a committee within the Federal Reserve System, is charged under United States law with overseeing the nation's open market operations (i.e., the Fed's buying and selling of United States Treasury securities). It is the Federal Reserve committee that makes key decisions about interest rates and the growth of the United States money supply. It is the principal organ of United States national monetary policy.
Home equity loan	A home equity loan is a type of loan in which the borrower uses the equity in their home as collateral. Home equity loans are often used to finance major expenses such as home repairs, medical bills or college education. A home equity loan creates a lien against the borrower's house, and reduces actual home equity.
Open market	The term open market is used generally to refer to a situation close to free trade and in a more specific technical sense to interbank trade in securities.

Visit Cram101.com for full Practice Exams

Chapter 13. Money and the Banking System

CHAPTER HIGHLIGHTS & NOTES: KEY TERMS, PEOPLE, PLACES, CONCEPTS

	In a general sense used in economics and political economy, an open market refers to a market which is accessible to all economic actors. In an open market so defined, all economic actors have an equal opportunity of entry in that market.
Independence	In probability theory, to say that two events are independent intuitively means that the occurrence of one event makes it neither more nor less probable that the other occurs. For example:•The event of getting a 6 the first time a die is rolled and the event of getting a 6 the second time are independent.•By contrast, the event of getting a 6 the first time a die is rolled and the event that the sum of the numbers seen on the first and second trials is 8 are not independent.•If two cards are drawn with replacement from a deck of cards, the event of drawing a red card on the first trial and that of drawing a red card on the second trial are independent.•By contrast, if two cards are drawn without replacement from a deck of cards, the event of drawing a red card on the first trial and that of drawing a red card on the second trial are again not independent.

Similarly, two random variables are independent if the conditional probability distribution of either given the observed value of the other is the same as if the other's value had not been observed. The concept of independence extends to dealing with collections of more than two events or random variables. |
| Reserve requirement | The reserve requirement is a central bank regulation that sets the minimum reserves each commercial bank must hold (rather than lend out) of customer deposits and notes. It is normally in the form of cash stored physically in a bank vault (vault cash) or deposits made with a central bank.

The required reserve ratio is sometimes used as a tool in monetary policy, influencing the country's borrowing and interest rates by changing the amount of funds available for banks to make loans with. |
| Open market operation | An open market operation is an activity by a central bank to buy or sell government bonds on the open market. A central bank uses them as the primary means of implementing monetary policy. The usual aim of open market operations is to control the short term interest rate and the supply of base money in an economy, and thus indirectly control the total money supply. |
| Discount rate | The discount rate can mean•an interest rate a central bank charges depository institutions that borrow reserves from it, for example for the use of the Federal Reserve's discount window.•the same as interest rate; the term 'discount' does not refer to the common meaning of the word, but to the meaning in computations of present value, e.g. |

Visit Cram101.com for full Practice Exams

Chapter 13. Money and the Banking System

CHAPTER HIGHLIGHTS & NOTES: KEY TERMS, PEOPLE, PLACES, CONCEPTS

	net present value or discounted cash flow•the annual effective discount rate, which is the annual interest divided by the capital including that interest; this rate is lower than the interest rate; it corresponds to using the value after a year as the nominal value, and seeing the initial value as the nominal value minus a discount; it is used for Treasury Bills and similar financial instrumentsAnnual effective discount rate The annual effective discount rate is the annual interest divided by the capital including that interest, which is the interest rate divided by 100% plus the interest rate. It is the annual discount factor to be applied to the future cash flow, to find the discount, subtracted from a future value to find the value one year earlier. For example, suppose there is a government bond that sells for $95 and pays $100 in a year's time.
Federal funds	In the United States, federal funds are overnight borrowings by banks to maintain their bank reserves at the Federal Reserve. Banks keep reserves at Federal Reserve Banks to meet their reserve requirements and to clear financial transactions. Transactions in the federal funds market enable depository institutions with reserve balances in excess of reserve requirements to lend reserves to institutions with reserve deficiencies.
Monetary base	In economics, the monetary base is a term relating to (but not being equivalent to) the money supply , the amount of money in the economy. The monetary base is highly liquid money that consists of coins, paper money, and commercial banks' reserves with the central bank. Measures of money are typically classified as levels of M, where the monetary base is smallest and lowest M-level: M0. Base money can be described as the most acceptable form of final payment.

Chapter 13. Money and the Banking System

CHAPTER QUIZ: KEY TERMS, PEOPLE, PLACES, CONCEPTS

1. Explicit _____ is a measure implemented in many countries to protect bank depositors, in full or in part, from losses caused by a bank's inability to pay its debts when due. _____ systems are one component of a financial system safety net that is meant to promote financial stability, but can in fact do the opposite.

    Banks are allowed (and usually encouraged) to lend or invest most of the money deposited with them instead of safe-keeping the full amounts .

    a. Directors and officers liability insurance
    b. Deposit insurance
    c. Fidelity bond
    d. Financial reinsurance

2. _____ is the number of goods/services that can be purchased with a unit of currency. For example, if you had taken one dollar to a store in the 1950s, you would have been able to buy a greater number of items than you would today, indicating that you would have had a greater _____ in the 1950s. Currency can be either a commodity money, like gold or silver, or fiat currency, or free-floating market-valued currency like US dollars.

    a. Quality of life
    b. Quality of working life
    c. Purchasing power
    d. Receiver operating characteristic

3. The _____ was a severe worldwide economic depression in the decade preceding World War II. The timing of the _____ varied across nations, but in most countries it started in 1930 after the passage of the Smoot-Hawley Tariff bill (June 17), and lasted until the late 1930s or early 1940s. It was the longest, most widespread, and deepest depression of the 20th century.

    In the 21st century, the _____ is commonly used as an example of how far the world's economy can decline.

    a. Bank Night
    b. Battle of Ballantyne Pier
    c. Great Depression
    d. Bloody Sunday

4. _____ is money that derives its value from government regulation or law: the initial value of _____ is established by government decree. The term fiat currency is also used when the _____ is used as the main currency of the country. The term derives from the Latin fiat, meaning 'let it be done' or 'it shall be'.

    a. Friedman rule
    b. Fiat money
    c. Fungibility
    d. Gemach

5. . In economics, the _____, is the total amount of money available in an economy at a specific time.

Visit Cram101.com for full Practice Exams

Chapter 13. Money and the Banking System

CHAPTER QUIZ: KEY TERMS, PEOPLE, PLACES, CONCEPTS

There are several ways to define 'money,' but standard measures usually include currency in circulation and demand deposits (depositors' easily accessed assets on the books of financial institutions).

_____ data are recorded and published, usually by the government or the central bank of the country.

a. Monopoly money
b. Money supply
c. Play money
d. Polushka

ANSWER KEY
Chapter 13. Money and the Banking System

1. b
2. c
3. c
4. b
5. b

You can take the complete Chapter Practice Test

for Chapter 13. Money and the Banking System
on all key terms, persons, places, and concepts.

Online 99 Cents

http://www.epub40.13.20514.13.cram101.com/

Use www.Cram101.com for all your study needs

including Cram101's online interactive problem solving labs in

chemistry, statistics, mathematics, and more.

Chapter 14. Modern Macroeconomics and Monetary Policy

CHAPTER OUTLINE: KEY TERMS, PEOPLE, PLACES, CONCEPTS

- Phillips curve
- Monetary policy
- Social security
- Money supply
- Expansionary monetary policy
- Interest rate
- Renewable resource
- Economic stability
- Quantity theory of money
- Velocity of money
- Environmental protection
- Equation of exchange
- Inflation rate
- Great Depression
- Inflation
- AD-AS model
- Monetary base
- Fannie Mae
- Mortgage loan

Visit Cram101.com for full Practice Exams

Chapter 14. Modern Macroeconomics and Monetary Policy
CHAPTER OUTLINE: KEY TERMS, PEOPLE, PLACES, CONCEPTS

| | Quantitative easing |

CHAPTER HIGHLIGHTS & NOTES: KEY TERMS, PEOPLE, PLACES, CONCEPTS

Phillips curve	In economics, the Phillips curve is a historical inverse relationship between the rate of unemployment and the rate of inflation in an economy. Stated simply, the lower the unemployment in an economy, the higher the rate of inflation. While it has been observed that there is a stable short run tradeoff between unemployment and inflation, this has not been observed in the long run.
Monetary policy	Monetary policy is the process by which the monetary authority of a country controls the supply of money, often targeting a rate of interest for the purpose of promoting economic growth and stability. The official goals usually include relatively stable prices and low unemployment. Monetary theory provides insight into how to craft optimal monetary policy.
Social security	Social security is a concept enshrined in Article 22 of the Universal Declaration of Human Rights which states that Everyone, as a member of society, has the right to social security and is entitled to realization, through national effort and international co-operation and in accordance with the organization and resources of each State, of the economic, social and cultural rights indispensable for his dignity and the free development of his personality. In simple term, this means that the signatories agree that society in which a person lives should help them to develop and to make the most of all the advantages (culture, work, social welfare) which are offered to them in the country. Social security may also refer to the action programs of government intended to promote the welfare of the population through assistance measures guaranteeing access to sufficient resources for food and shelter and to promote health and wellbeing for the population at large and potentially vulnerable segments such as children, the elderly, the sick and the unemployed.
Money supply	In economics, the money supply, is the total amount of money available in an economy at a specific time. There are several ways to define 'money,' but standard measures usually include currency in circulation and demand deposits (depositors' easily accessed assets on the books of financial institutions).

Chapter 14. Modern Macroeconomics and Monetary Policy

CHAPTER HIGHLIGHTS & NOTES: KEY TERMS, PEOPLE, PLACES, CONCEPTS

Expansionary monetary policy	In economics, expansionary policies are fiscal policies, like higher spending and tax cuts, that encourage economic growth. In turn, an expansionary monetary policy is monetary policy that seeks to increase the size of the money supply. In most nations, monetary policy is controlled by either a central bank or a finance ministry.
Interest rate	An interest rate is the rate at which interest is paid by a borrower for the use of money that they borrow from a lender. For example, a small company borrows capital from a bank to buy new assets for their business, and in return the lender receives interest at a predetermined interest rate for deferring the use of funds and instead lending it to the borrower. Interest rates are normally expressed as a percentage of the principal for a period of one year.
Renewable resource	A renewable resource is a natural resource with the ability to reproduce through biological or natural processes and replenished with the passage of time. Renewable resources are part of our natural environment and form our eco-system.

In 1962, within a report to the committee on natural resources which was forwarded to the President of the United States, Paul Weiss defined Renewable Resources as: 'The total range of living organisms providing man with food, fibers, drugs, etc...'. |
| Economic stability | Economic stability refers to an absence of excessive fluctuations in the macroeconomy. An economy with fairly constant output growth and low and stable inflation would be considered economically stable. |
| Quantity theory of money | In monetary economics, the quantity theory of money is the theory that money supply has a direct, proportional relationship with the price level.

The theory was challenged by Keynesian economics, but updated and reinvigorated by the monetarist school of economics. While mainstream economists agree that the quantity theory holds true in the long run, there is still disagreement about its applicability in the short run. |
| Velocity of money | The velocity of money is the average frequency with which a unit of money is spent on new goods and services produced domestically in a specific period of time. Velocity has to do with the amount of economic activity associated with a given money supply. When the period is understood, the velocity may be presented as a pure number; otherwise it should be given as a pure number over time. |
| Environmental protection | Environmental protection is a practice of protecting the environment, on individual, organizational or governmental levels, for the benefit of the natural environment and (or) humans. Due to the pressures of population and technology, the biophysical environment is being degraded, sometimes permanently. |

Visit Cram101.com for full Practice Exams

Chapter 14. Modern Macroeconomics and Monetary Policy

CHAPTER HIGHLIGHTS & NOTES: KEY TERMS, PEOPLE, PLACES, CONCEPTS

Equation of exchange	In economics, the equation of exchange is the relation: $M \cdot V = P \cdot Q$ where, for a given period, M is the total nominal amount of money in circulation on average in an economy. V is the velocity of money, that is the average frequency with which a unit of money is spent. P is the price level. Q is an index of real expenditures (on newly produced goods and services). Thus PQ is the level of nominal expenditures. This equation is a rearrangement of the definition of velocity: V = PQ / M. As such, without the introduction of any assumptions, it is a tautology. The quantity theory of money adds assumptions about the money supply, the price level, and the effect of interest rates on velocity to create a theory about the causes of inflation and the effects of monetary policy.
Inflation rate	In economics, the inflation rate is a measure of inflation, or the rate of increase of a price index such as the consumer price index. It is the percentage rate of change in price level over time, usually one year. The rate of decrease in the purchasing power of money is approximately equal.
Great Depression	The Great Depression was a severe worldwide economic depression in the decade preceding World War II. The timing of the Great Depression varied across nations, but in most countries it started in 1930 after the passage of the Smoot-Hawley Tariff bill (June 17), and lasted until the late 1930s or early 1940s. It was the longest, most widespread, and deepest depression of the 20th century. In the 21st century, the Great Depression is commonly used as an example of how far the world's economy can decline.
Inflation	In economics, inflation is a rise in the general level of prices of goods and services in an economy over a period of time. When the general price level rises, each unit of currency buys fewer goods and services. Consequently, inflation also reflects an erosion in the purchasing power of money - a loss of real value in the internal medium of exchange and unit of account in the economy.
AD-AS model	The AD-AS or Aggregate Demand-Aggregate Supply model is a macroeconomic model that explains price level and output through the relationship of aggregate demand and aggregate supply. It is based on the theory of John Maynard Keynes presented in his work The General Theory of Employment, Interest, and Money. It is one of the primary simplified representations in the modern field of macroeconomics, and is used by a broad array of economists, from libertarian, Monetarist supporters of laissez-faire, such as Milton Friedman to Post-Keynesian supporters of economic interventionism, such as Joan Robinson.

Chapter 14. Modern Macroeconomics and Monetary Policy

CHAPTER HIGHLIGHTS & NOTES: KEY TERMS, PEOPLE, PLACES, CONCEPTS

The conventional 'aggregate supply and demand' model is, in actuality, a Keynesian visualization that has come to be a widely accepted image of the theory. The Classical supply and demand model, which is largely based on Say's Law, or that supply creates its own demand, depicts the aggregate supply curve as being vertical at all times (not just in the long-run)Modeling

The AD/AS model is used to illustrate the Keynesian model of the business cycle. Movements of the two curves can be used to predict the effects that various exogenous events will have on two variables: real GDP and the price level. Furthermore, the model can be incorporated as a component in any of a variety of dynamic models (models of how variables like the price level and others evolve over time). The AD-AS model can be related to the Phillips curve model of wage or price inflation and unemployment.

Monetary base

In economics, the monetary base is a term relating to (but not being equivalent to) the money supply, the amount of money in the economy. The monetary base is highly liquid money that consists of coins, paper money, and commercial banks' reserves with the central bank. Measures of money are typically classified as levels of M, where the monetary base is smallest and lowest M-level: M0. Base money can be described as the most acceptable form of final payment.

Fannie Mae

The Federal National Mortgage Association (FNMA; OTCQB: FNMA), commonly known as Fannie Mae, was founded in 1938 during the Great Depression as part of the New Deal. It is a government-sponsored enterprise (GSE), though it has been a publicly traded company since 1968. The corporation's purpose is to expand the secondary mortgage market by securitizing mortgages in the form of mortgage-backed securities (MBS), allowing lenders to reinvest their assets into more lending and in effect increasing the number of lenders in the mortgage market by reducing the reliance on thrifts.

The Federal National Mortgage Association (FNMA), colloquially known as Fannie Mae, was established in 1938 by amendments to the National Housing Act after the Great Depression as part of Franklin Delano Roosevelt's New Deal.

Mortgage loan

A mortgage loan is a loan secured by real property through the use of a mortgage note which evidences the existence of the loan and the encumbrance of that realty through the granting of a mortgage which secures the loan. However, the word mortgage alone, in everyday usage, is most often used to mean mortgage loan.

The word mortgage is a Law French term meaning 'death contract,' meaning that the pledge ends (dies) when either the obligation is fulfilled or the property is taken through foreclosure.

Visit Cram101.com for full Practice Exams

Chapter 14. Modern Macroeconomics and Monetary Policy

CHAPTER HIGHLIGHTS & NOTES: KEY TERMS, PEOPLE, PLACES, CONCEPTS

| Quantitative easing | Quantitative easing is an unconventional monetary policy used by central banks to stimulate the national economy when conventional monetary policy has become ineffective. A central bank buys financial assets to inject a pre-determined quantity of money into the economy. This is distinguished from the more usual policy of buying or selling government bonds to keep market interest rates at a specified target value. |

CHAPTER QUIZ: KEY TERMS, PEOPLE, PLACES, CONCEPTS

1. In economics, _____ is a rise in the general level of prices of goods and services in an economy over a period of time. When the general price level rises, each unit of currency buys fewer goods and services. Consequently, _____ also reflects an erosion in the purchasing power of money - a loss of real value in the internal medium of exchange and unit of account in the economy.

    a. Academic inflation
    b. Agflation
    c. Anti-Inflation Act
    d. Inflation

2. The _____ was a severe worldwide economic depression in the decade preceding World War II. The timing of the _____ varied across nations, but in most countries it started in 1930 after the passage of the Smoot-Hawley Tariff bill (June 17), and lasted until the late 1930s or early 1940s. It was the longest, most widespread, and deepest depression of the 20th century.

    In the 21st century, the _____ is commonly used as an example of how far the world's economy can decline.

    a. Bank Night
    b. Battle of Ballantyne Pier
    c. Great Depression
    d. Bloody Sunday

3. In economics, the _____ is a measure of inflation, or the rate of increase of a price index such as the consumer price index. It is the percentage rate of change in price level over time, usually one year. The rate of decrease in the purchasing power of money is approximately equal.

    a. Inflation rate
    b. Inflation tax
    c. Inflation-indexed bond
    d. Inflationary gap

Visit Cram101.com for full Practice Exams

Chapter 14. Modern Macroeconomics and Monetary Policy

CHAPTER QUIZ: KEY TERMS, PEOPLE, PLACES, CONCEPTS

4. The AD-AS or Aggregate Demand-Aggregate Supply model is a macroeconomic model that explains price level and output through the relationship of aggregate demand and aggregate supply. It is based on the theory of John Maynard Keynes presented in his work The General Theory of Employment, Interest, and Money. It is one of the primary simplified representations in the modern field of macroeconomics, and is used by a broad array of economists, from libertarian, Monetarist supporters of laissez-faire, such as Milton Friedman to Post-Keynesian supporters of economic interventionism, such as Joan Robinson.

   The conventional 'aggregate supply and demand' model is, in actuality, a Keynesian visualization that has come to be a widely accepted image of the theory. The Classical supply and demand model, which is largely based on Say's Law, or that supply creates its own demand, depicts the aggregate supply curve as being vertical at all times (not just in the long-run)Modeling

   The AD/AS model is used to illustrate the Keynesian model of the business cycle. Movements of the two curves can be used to predict the effects that various exogenous events will have on two variables: real GDP and the price level. Furthermore, the model can be incorporated as a component in any of a variety of dynamic models (models of how variables like the price level and others evolve over time). The _____ can be related to the Phillips curve model of wage or price inflation and unemployment.

   a. AD-AS model
   b. AK model
   c. E2m.org
   d. Edgeworth box

5. _____ is the process by which the monetary authority of a country controls the supply of money, often targeting a rate of interest for the purpose of promoting economic growth and stability. The official goals usually include relatively stable prices and low unemployment. Monetary theory provides insight into how to craft optimal _____.

   a. Policy Ineffectiveness Proposition
   b. Monetary policy
   c. Structural unemployment
   d. Technological unemployment

ANSWER KEY
Chapter 14. Modern Macroeconomics and Monetary Policy

1. d
2. c
3. a
4. a
5. b

You can take the complete Chapter Practice Test

for Chapter 14. Modern Macroeconomics and Monetary Policy

on all key terms, persons, places, and concepts.

Online 99 Cents

http://www.epub40.13.20514.14.cram101.com/

Use www.Cram101.com for all your study needs

including Cram101's online interactive problem solving labs in

chemistry, statistics, mathematics, and more.

Chapter 15. Stabilization Policy, Output, and Employment

CHAPTER OUTLINE: KEY TERMS, PEOPLE, PLACES, CONCEPTS

_____ Economic stability

_____ Great Depression

_____ AD-AS model

_____ Federal Open Market Committee

_____ Home equity loan

_____ Open market

_____ Fiscal policy

_____ Economic indicator

_____ Business cycle

_____ Phillips curve

_____ Adaptive expectations

_____ Rational expectations

_____ Inflation rate

_____ Deadweight loss

_____ Recession

_____ Social security

_____ Debt crisis

_____ Troubled Asset Relief Program

_____ International trade

Visit Cram101.com for full Practice Exams

Chapter 15. Stabilization Policy, Output, and Employment

CHAPTER HIGHLIGHTS & NOTES: KEY TERMS, PEOPLE, PLACES, CONCEPTS

Economic stability	Economic stability refers to an absence of excessive fluctuations in the macroeconomy. An economy with fairly constant output growth and low and stable inflation would be considered economically stable.
Great Depression	The Great Depression was a severe worldwide economic depression in the decade preceding World War II. The timing of the Great Depression varied across nations, but in most countries it started in 1930 after the passage of the Smoot-Hawley Tariff bill (June 17), and lasted until the late 1930s or early 1940s. It was the longest, most widespread, and deepest depression of the 20th century. In the 21st century, the Great Depression is commonly used as an example of how far the world's economy can decline.
AD-AS model	The AD-AS or Aggregate Demand-Aggregate Supply model is a macroeconomic model that explains price level and output through the relationship of aggregate demand and aggregate supply. It is based on the theory of John Maynard Keynes presented in his work The General Theory of Employment, Interest, and Money. It is one of the primary simplified representations in the modern field of macroeconomics, and is used by a broad array of economists, from libertarian, Monetarist supporters of laissez-faire, such as Milton Friedman to Post-Keynesian supporters of economic interventionism, such as Joan Robinson. The conventional 'aggregate supply and demand' model is, in actuality, a Keynesian visualization that has come to be a widely accepted image of the theory. The Classical supply and demand model, which is largely based on Say's Law, or that supply creates its own demand, depicts the aggregate supply curve as being vertical at all times (not just in the long-run)Modeling The AD/AS model is used to illustrate the Keynesian model of the business cycle. Movements of the two curves can be used to predict the effects that various exogenous events will have on two variables: real GDP and the price level. Furthermore, the model can be incorporated as a component in any of a variety of dynamic models (models of how variables like the price level and others evolve over time). The AD-AS model can be related to the Phillips curve model of wage or price inflation and unemployment.
Federal Open Market Committee	The Federal Open Market Committee a committee within the Federal Reserve System, is charged under United States law with overseeing the nation's open market operations (i.e., the Fed's buying and selling of United States Treasury securities). It is the Federal Reserve committee that makes key decisions about interest rates and the growth of the United States money supply. It is the principal organ of United States national monetary policy.

Visit Cram101.com for full Practice Exams

Chapter 15. Stabilization Policy, Output, and Employment

CHAPTER HIGHLIGHTS & NOTES: KEY TERMS, PEOPLE, PLACES, CONCEPTS

Home equity loan	A home equity loan is a type of loan in which the borrower uses the equity in their home as collateral. Home equity loans are often used to finance major expenses such as home repairs, medical bills or college education. A home equity loan creates a lien against the borrower's house, and reduces actual home equity.
Open market	The term open market is used generally to refer to a situation close to free trade and in a more specific technical sense to interbank trade in securities. In a general sense used in economics and political economy, an open market refers to a market which is accessible to all economic actors. In an open market so defined, all economic actors have an equal opportunity of entry in that market.
Fiscal policy	In economics and political science, fiscal policy is the use of government revenue collection (taxation) and expenditure (spending) to influence the economy. The two main instruments of fiscal policy are government taxation and expenditure. Changes in the level and composition of taxation and government spending can impact the following variables in the economy:•Aggregate demand and the level of economic activity;•The pattern of resource allocation;•The distribution of income. Fiscal policy refers to the use of the government budget to influence economic activity.
Economic indicator	An economic indicator is a statistic about the economy. Economic indicators allow analysis of economic performance and predictions of future performance. One application of economic indicators is the study of business cycles.
Business cycle	The term business cycle refers to economy-wide fluctuations in production or economic activity over several months or years. These fluctuations occur around a long-term growth trend, and typically involve shifts over time between periods of relatively rapid economic growth (an expansion or boom), and periods of relative stagnation or decline (a contraction or recession). Business cycles are usually measured by considering the growth rate of real gross domestic product.
Phillips curve	In economics, the Phillips curve is a historical inverse relationship between the rate of unemployment and the rate of inflation in an economy. Stated simply, the lower the unemployment in an economy, the higher the rate of inflation. While it has been observed that there is a stable short run tradeoff between unemployment and inflation, this has not been observed in the long run.
Adaptive expectations	In economics, adaptive expectations means that people form their expectations about what will happen in the future based on what has happened in the past.

Chapter 15. Stabilization Policy, Output, and Employment

CHAPTER HIGHLIGHTS & NOTES: KEY TERMS, PEOPLE, PLACES, CONCEPTS

	For example, if inflation has been higher than expected in the past, people would revise expectations for the future.
	One simple version of adaptive expectations is stated in the following equation, where p^e is the next year's rate of inflation that is currently expected; p^e_{-1} is this year's rate of inflation that was expected last year; and p is this year's actual rate of inflation: $$p^e = p^e_{-1} + \lambda(p_{-1} - p^e_{-1})$$ where λ is between 0 and 1. This says that current expectations of future inflation reflect past expectations and an 'error-adjustment' term, in which current expectations are raised according to the gap between actual inflation and previous expectations.
Rational expectations	Rational expectations is a hypothesis in economics which states that agents' predictions of the future value of economically relevant variables are not systematically wrong in that all errors are random. Equivalently, this is to say that agents' expectations equal true statistical expected values. An alternative formulation is that rational expectations are model-consistent expectations, in that the agents inside the model assume the model's predictions are valid.
Inflation rate	In economics, the inflation rate is a measure of inflation, or the rate of increase of a price index such as the consumer price index. It is the percentage rate of change in price level over time, usually one year. The rate of decrease in the purchasing power of money is approximately equal.
Deadweight loss	In economics, a deadweight loss is a loss of economic efficiency that can occur when equilibrium for a good or service is not Pareto optimal. In other words, either people who would have more marginal benefit than marginal cost are not buying the product, or people who have more marginal cost than marginal benefit are buying the product. Causes of deadweight loss can include monopoly pricing (in the case of artificial scarcity), externalities, taxes or subsidies, and binding price ceilings or floors.
Recession	In economics, a recession is a business cycle contraction, a general slowdown in economic activity. Macroeconomic indicators such as GDP, employment, investment spending, capacity utilization, household income, business profits, and inflation fall, while bankruptcies and the unemployment rate rise. Recessions generally occur when there is a widespread drop in spending, often following an adverse supply shock or the bursting of an economic bubble.

Chapter 15. Stabilization Policy, Output, and Employment

CHAPTER HIGHLIGHTS & NOTES: KEY TERMS, PEOPLE, PLACES, CONCEPTS

Social security	Social security is a concept enshrined in Article 22 of the Universal Declaration of Human Rights which states that Everyone, as a member of society, has the right to social security and is entitled to realization, through national effort and international co-operation and in accordance with the organization and resources of each State, of the economic, social and cultural rights indispensable for his dignity and the free development of his personality. In simple term, this means that the signatories agree that society in which a person lives should help them to develop and to make the most of all the advantages (culture, work, social welfare) which are offered to them in the country. Social security may also refer to the action programs of government intended to promote the welfare of the population through assistance measures guaranteeing access to sufficient resources for food and shelter and to promote health and wellbeing for the population at large and potentially vulnerable segments such as children, the elderly, the sick and the unemployed.
Debt crisis	Debt crisis is the general term for a proliferation of massive public debt relative to tax revenues, especially in reference to Latin American countries during the 1980s, and the United States and the European Union since the mid-2000s. Europe •European sovereign debt crisis•Greek government debt crisis•Irish financial crisis•Portuguese economic crisisLatin America •Argentine debt restructuring•Latin American debt crisisNorth America •United States debt-ceiling crisis.
Troubled Asset Relief Program	The Troubled Asset Relief Program is a program of the United States government to purchase assets and equity from financial institutions to strengthen its financial sector that was signed into law by U.S. President George W. Bush on October 3, 2008. It was a component of the government's measures in 2008 to address the subprime mortgage crisis. The TARP program originally authorized expenditures of $700 billion and was expected to cost the U.S. taxpayers as much as $300 billion. The Dodd-Frank Wall Street Reform and Consumer Protection Act reduced the amount authorized to $475 billion.
International trade	International trade is the exchange of capital, goods, and services across international borders or territories. In most countries, such trade represents a significant share of gross domestic product (GDP). While international trade has been present throughout much of history, its economic, social, and political importance has been on the rise in recent centuries.

Chapter 15. Stabilization Policy, Output, and Employment

CHAPTER QUIZ: KEY TERMS, PEOPLE, PLACES, CONCEPTS

1. The _____ is a program of the United States government to purchase assets and equity from financial institutions to strengthen its financial sector that was signed into law by U.S. President George W. Bush on October 3, 2008. It was a component of the government's measures in 2008 to address the subprime mortgage crisis.

   The TARP program originally authorized expenditures of $700 billion and was expected to cost the U.S. taxpayers as much as $300 billion. The Dodd-Frank Wall Street Reform and Consumer Protection Act reduced the amount authorized to $475 billion.

   a. Capital Assistance Program
   b. Capital Purchase Program
   c. Troubled Asset Relief Program
   d. Public Law 110-343

2. The AD-AS or Aggregate Demand-Aggregate Supply model is a macroeconomic model that explains price level and output through the relationship of aggregate demand and aggregate supply. It is based on the theory of John Maynard Keynes presented in his work The General Theory of Employment, Interest, and Money. It is one of the primary simplified representations in the modern field of macroeconomics, and is used by a broad array of economists, from libertarian, Monetarist supporters of laissez-faire, such as Milton Friedman to Post-Keynesian supporters of economic interventionism, such as Joan Robinson.

   The conventional 'aggregate supply and demand' model is, in actuality, a Keynesian visualization that has come to be a widely accepted image of the theory. The Classical supply and demand model, which is largely based on Say's Law, or that supply creates its own demand, depicts the aggregate supply curve as being vertical at all times (not just in the long-run)Modeling

   The AD/AS model is used to illustrate the Keynesian model of the business cycle. Movements of the two curves can be used to predict the effects that various exogenous events will have on two variables: real GDP and the price level. Furthermore, the model can be incorporated as a component in any of a variety of dynamic models (models of how variables like the price level and others evolve over time). The _____ can be related to the Phillips curve model of wage or price inflation and unemployment.

   a. AD-IA model
   b. AK model
   c. E2m.org
   d. AD-AS model

3. In economics, the _____ is a historical inverse relationship between the rate of unemployment and the rate of inflation in an economy. Stated simply, the lower the unemployment in an economy, the higher the rate of inflation. While it has been observed that there is a stable short run tradeoff between unemployment and inflation, this has not been observed in the long run.

   a. Recession-proof job
   b. Reserve army of labour
   c. Structural unemployment

Visit Cram101.com for full Practice Exams

Chapter 15. Stabilization Policy, Output, and Employment

CHAPTER QUIZ: KEY TERMS, PEOPLE, PLACES, CONCEPTS

4. The term _____ refers to economy-wide fluctuations in production or economic activity over several months or years. These fluctuations occur around a long-term growth trend, and typically involve shifts over time between periods of relatively rapid economic growth (an expansion or boom), and periods of relative stagnation or decline (a contraction or recession).

   _____s are usually measured by considering the growth rate of real gross domestic product.

   a. Bank run
   b. Bull trap
   c. Conjuncture
   d. Business cycle

5. The term _____ is used generally to refer to a situation close to free trade and in a more specific technical sense to interbank trade in securities.

   In a general sense used in economics and political economy, an _____ refers to a market which is accessible to all economic actors. In an _____ so defined, all economic actors have an equal opportunity of entry in that market.

   a. Outside money
   b. Income protection insurance
   c. Index-linked Savings Certificates
   d. Open market

Visit Cram101.com for full Practice Exams

ANSWER KEY
Chapter 15. Stabilization Policy, Output, and Employment

1. c
2. d
3. d
4. d
5. d

You can take the complete Chapter Practice Test

for Chapter 15. Stabilization Policy, Output, and Employment

on all key terms, persons, places, and concepts.

Online 99 Cents

http://www.epub40.13.20514.15.cram101.com/

Use www.Cram101.com for all your study needs

including Cram101's online interactive problem solving labs in

chemistry, statistics, mathematics, and more.

Visit Cram101.com for full Practice Exams

Chapter 16. Creating an Environment for Growth and Prosperity

CHAPTER OUTLINE: KEY TERMS, PEOPLE, PLACES, CONCEPTS

	Economic growth
	Life expectancy
	Quality of life
	Standard of living
	Africa Source
	Gains from trade
	Income
	Mass production
	Total cost
	Entrepreneur
	Entrepreneurship
	Investment
	Phillips curve
	Barriers to entry
	Lehman Brothers
	Alternatives
	Rule of law
	Business cycle
	Monetary system

Visit Cram101.com for full Practice Exams

Chapter 16. Creating an Environment for Growth and Prosperity

CHAPTER OUTLINE: KEY TERMS, PEOPLE, PLACES, CONCEPTS

	Regulation
	Labor relations
	Natural resource
	Pollution
	Renewable resource
	Resource curse
	World Bank
	Economic freedom
	United Nations

CHAPTER HIGHLIGHTS & NOTES: KEY TERMS, PEOPLE, PLACES, CONCEPTS

Economic growth	Economic growth is the increase in the amount of the goods and services produced by an economy over time. It is conventionally measured as the percent rate of increase in real gross domestic product, or real GDP. Growth is usually calculated in real terms, i.e. inflation-adjusted terms, in order to net out the effect of inflation on the price of the goods and services produced. In economics, 'economic growth' or 'economic growth theory' typically refers to growth of potential output, i.e., production at 'full employment,' which is caused by growth in aggregate demand or observed output.
Life expectancy	Life expectancy is the expected (in the statistical sense) number of years of life remaining at a given age. It is denoted by e_x, which means the average number of subsequent years of life for someone now aged x, according to a particular mortality experience. (In technical literature, this symbol means the average number of complete years of life remaining, excluding fractions of a year.

Visit Cram101.com for full Practice Exams

Chapter 16. Creating an Environment for Growth and Prosperity

Quality of life	The term quality of life is used to evaluate the general well-being of individuals and societies. The term is used in a wide range of contexts, including the fields of international development, healthcare, and politics. Quality of life should not be confused with the concept of standard of living, which is based primarily on income.
Standard of living	Standard of living refers to the level of wealth, happiness, comfort, material goods and necessities available to a certain socioeconomic class in a certain geographic area. The standard of living includes factors such as income, quality and availability of employment, class disparity, poverty rate, quality and affordability of housing, hours of work required to purchase necessities, gross domestic product, inflation rate, number of vacation days per year, affordable access to quality healthcare, quality and availability of education, life expectancy, incidence of disease, cost of goods and services, infrastructure, national economic growth, economic and political stability, political and religious freedom, environmental quality, climate and safety. The standard of living is closely related to quality of life.
Africa Source	Africa Source is the name for a series of events, two of which have been held so far, in 2004 and 2006, at Namibia and Uganda respectively. These are held to promote the use of Free/Libre and Open Source Software (FLOSS) among non-profit and non-governmental organisations. Africa Source is part of the wider 'Source Camps' organised by Tactical Technology Collective (Tacticaltech.org) and its partners, and is also linked to the Asia Source and other parallel events held elsewhere in the 'developing' world.
Gains from trade	Gains from trade in economics refers to net benefits to agents from allowing an increase in voluntary trading with each other. In technical terms, it is the increase of consumer surplus plus producer surplus from lower tariffs or otherwise liberalizing trade. Gains from trade are commonly described as resulting from:•specialization in production from division of labor, economies of scale, scope, and agglomeration and relative availability of factor resources in types of output by farms, businesses, location and economies•a resulting increase in total output possibilities•trade through markets from sale of one type of output for other, more highly valued goods. Market incentives, such as reflected in prices of outputs and inputs, are theorized to attract factors of production, including labor, into activities according to comparative advantage, that is, for which they each have a low opportunity cost.
Income	Income is the consumption and savings opportunity gained by an entity within a specified time frame, which is generally expressed in monetary terms. However, for households and individuals, 'income is the sum of all the wages, salaries, profits, interests payments, rents and other forms of earnings received... in a given period of time.' For firms, income generally refers to net-profit: what remains of revenue after expenses have been subtracted.

Chapter 16. Creating an Environment for Growth and Prosperity

CHAPTER HIGHLIGHTS & NOTES: KEY TERMS, PEOPLE, PLACES, CONCEPTS

Mass production	Mass production is the production of large amounts of standardized products, including and especially on assembly lines.
Total cost	In economics, and cost accounting, total cost describes the total economic cost of production and is made up of variable costs, which vary according to the quantity of a good produced and include inputs such as labor and raw materials, plus fixed costs, which are independent of the quantity of a good produced and include inputs (capital) that cannot be varied in the short term, such as buildings and machinery. Total cost in economics includes the total opportunity cost of each factor of production as part of its fixed or variable costs. The rate at which total cost changes as the amount produced changes is called marginal cost.
Entrepreneur	An entrepreneur is an enterprising individual who builds capital through risk and/or initiative. The term was originally a loanword from French and was first defined by the Irish-French economist Richard Cantillon. Entrepreneur in English is a term applied to a person who is willing to help launch a new venture or enterprise and accept full responsibility for the outcome.
Entrepreneurship	Entrepreneurship is the act of being an entrepreneur or 'one who undertakes innovations, finance and business acumen in an effort to transform innovations into economic goods'. This may result in new organizations or may be part of revitalizing mature organizations in response to a perceived opportunity. The most obvious form of entrepreneurship is that of starting new businesses (referred as Startup Company); however, in recent years, the term has been extended to include social and political forms of entrepreneurial activity.
Investment	Investment has different meanings in finance and economics. Finance investment is putting money into something with the expectation of gain, that upon thorough analysis, has a high degree of security for the principal amount, as well as security of return, within an expected period of time. In contrast putting money into something with an expectation of gain without thorough analysis, without security of principal, and without security of return is speculation or gambling.
Phillips curve	In economics, the Phillips curve is a historical inverse relationship between the rate of unemployment and the rate of inflation in an economy. Stated simply, the lower the unemployment in an economy, the higher the rate of inflation. While it has been observed that there is a stable short run tradeoff between unemployment and inflation, this has not been observed in the long run.
Barriers to entry	In theories of competition in economics, barriers to entry, are obstacles that make it difficult to enter a given market.

Chapter 16. Creating an Environment for Growth and Prosperity

CHAPTER HIGHLIGHTS & NOTES: KEY TERMS, PEOPLE, PLACES, CONCEPTS

	The term can refer to hindrances a firm faces in trying to enter a market or industry - such as government regulation, or a large, established firm taking advantage of economies of scale - or those an individual faces in trying to gain entrance to a profession - such as education or licensing requirements.
	Because barriers to entry protect incumbent firms and restrict competition in a market, they can contribute to distortionary prices.
Lehman Brothers	Lehman Brothers Holdings Inc. (former NYSE ticker symbol LEH) ( ) was a global financial services firm. Before declaring bankruptcy in 2008, Lehman was the fourth largest investment bank in the USA (behind Goldman Sachs, Morgan Stanley, and Merrill Lynch), doing business in investment banking, equity and fixed-income sales and trading (especially U.S. Treasury securities), research, investment management, private equity, and private banking.
Alternatives	Founded in 1994, Alternatives, Action and Communication Network for International Development, is a non-governmental, international solidarity organization based in Montreal, Quebec, Canada.
	Alternatives works to promote justice and equality amongst individuals and communities worldwide. Active in over 35 countries, Alternatives supports local, community-based initiatives working towards the greater economic, social, and political rights of people and communities affected by poverty, discrimination, exploitation, and violence.
Rule of law	The rule of law is a legal maxim whereby governmental decisions are made by applying known legal principles. The phrase can be traced back to 17th century and was popularized in the 19th century by British jurist A. V. Dicey. The concept was familiar to ancient philosophers such as Aristotle, who wrote 'Law should govern'.
Business cycle	The term business cycle refers to economy-wide fluctuations in production or economic activity over several months or years. These fluctuations occur around a long-term growth trend, and typically involve shifts over time between periods of relatively rapid economic growth (an expansion or boom), and periods of relative stagnation or decline (a contraction or recession).
	Business cycles are usually measured by considering the growth rate of real gross domestic product.
Monetary system	A monetary system is anything that is accepted as a standard of value and measure of wealth in a particular region.
	However, the current trend is to use international trade and investment to alter the policy and legislation of individual governments.

Chapter 16. Creating an Environment for Growth and Prosperity

CHAPTER HIGHLIGHTS & NOTES: KEY TERMS, PEOPLE, PLACES, CONCEPTS

Regulation	Regulation is administrative legislation that constitutes or constrains rights and allocates responsibilities. It can be distinguished from primary legislation (by Parliament or elected legislative body) on the one hand and judge-made law on the other. Regulation can take many forms: legal restrictions promulgated by a government authority, self-regulation by an industry such as through a trade association, social regulation co-regulation, or market regulation.
Labor relations	Labor relations is the study and practice of managing unionized employment situations. In academia, labor relations is frequently a subarea within industrial relations, though scholars from many disciplines--including economics, sociology, history, law, and political science--also study labor unions and labor movements. In practice, labor relations is frequently a subarea within human resource management.
Natural resource	Natural resources occur naturally within environments that exist relatively undisturbed by mankind, in a natural form. A natural resource is often characterized by amounts of biodiversity and geodiversity existent in various ecosystems. Natural resources are derived from the environment.
Pollution	Pollution is the introduction of contaminants into a natural environment that causes instability, harm, or discomfort to the ecosystem i.e. physical systems or living organisms. Pollution can take the form of chemical substances or energy, such as noise, heat or light. Pollutants, the components of pollution, can be either foreign substances/energies or naturally occurring contaminants.
Renewable resource	A renewable resource is a natural resource with the ability to reproduce through biological or natural processes and replenished with the passage of time. Renewable resources are part of our natural environment and form our eco-system. In 1962, within a report to the committee on natural resources which was forwarded to the President of the United States, Paul Weiss defined Renewable Resources as: 'The total range of living organisms providing man with food, fibers, drugs, etc...'.
Resource curse	The resource curse refers to the paradox that countries and regions with an abundance of natural resources, specifically point-source non-renewable resources like minerals and fuels, tend to have less economic growth and worse development outcomes than countries with fewer natural resources. This is hypothesized to happen for many different reasons, including a decline in the competitiveness of other economic sectors (caused by appreciation of the real exchange rate as resource revenues enter an economy), volatility of revenues from the natural resource sector due to exposure to global commodity market swings, government mismanagement of resources, or weak, ineffectual, unstable or corrupt institutions (possibly due to the easily diverted actual or anticipated revenue stream from extractive activities). "

Chapter 16. Creating an Environment for Growth and Prosperity

CHAPTER HIGHLIGHTS & NOTES: KEY TERMS, PEOPLE, PLACES, CONCEPTS

World Bank	The World Bank is an international financial institution that provides loans to developing countries for capital programs. The World Bank's official goal is the reduction of poverty. According to the World Bank's Articles of Agreement (As amended effective 16 February 1989) all of its decisions must be guided by a commitment to promote foreign investment, international trade and facilitate capital investment.
Economic freedom	Economic freedom is a term used in economic and policy debates. As with freedom generally, there are various definitions, but no universally accepted concept of economic freedom. One major approach to economic freedom comes from classical liberal and libertarian traditions emphasizing free markets and private property, while another extends the welfare economics study of individual choice, with greater economic freedom coming from a 'larger' (in some technical sense) set of possible choices.
United Nations	The United Nations, is an international organization whose stated aims are facilitating cooperation in international law, international security, economic development, social progress, human rights, and achievement of world peace. The UN was founded in 1945 after World War II to replace the League of Nations, to stop wars between countries, and to provide a platform for dialogue. It contains multiple subsidiary organizations to carry out its missions.

CHAPTER QUIZ: KEY TERMS, PEOPLE, PLACES, CONCEPTS

1. _____ is the consumption and savings opportunity gained by an entity within a specified time frame, which is generally expressed in monetary terms. However, for households and individuals, '_____ is the sum of all the wages, salaries, profits, interests payments, rents and other forms of earnings received... in a given period of time.' For firms, _____ generally refers to net-profit: what remains of revenue after expenses have been subtracted. In the field of public economics, it may refer to the accumulation of both monetary and non-monetary consumption ability, the former being used as a proxy for total _____.

    a. Advance payment
    b. Income
    c. Aggregate income
    d. Average propensity to consume

2. . _____ in economics refers to net benefits to agents from allowing an increase in voluntary trading with each other. In technical terms, it is the increase of consumer surplus plus producer surplus from lower tariffs or otherwise liberalizing trade.

Chapter 16. Creating an Environment for Growth and Prosperity

CHAPTER QUIZ: KEY TERMS, PEOPLE, PLACES, CONCEPTS

_____ are commonly described as resulting from:•specialization in production from division of labor, economies of scale, scope, and agglomeration and relative availability of factor resources in types of output by farms, businesses, location and economies•a resulting increase in total output possibilities•trade through markets from sale of one type of output for other, more highly valued goods.

Market incentives, such as reflected in prices of outputs and inputs, are theorized to attract factors of production, including labor, into activities according to comparative advantage, that is, for which they each have a low opportunity cost.

a. Land use
b. Local Economic Development
c. MIG, Inc.
d. Gains from trade

3. An _____ is an enterprising individual who builds capital through risk and/or initiative. The term was originally a loanword from French and was first defined by the Irish-French economist Richard Cantillon. _____ in English is a term applied to a person who is willing to help launch a new venture or enterprise and accept full responsibility for the outcome.

a. Entrepreneur Walk of Fame
b. Entrepreneur
c. Entrepreneurial finance
d. Entrepreneurial Management Center

4. A _____ is anything that is accepted as a standard of value and measure of wealth in a particular region.

However, the current trend is to use international trade and investment to alter the policy and legislation of individual governments. The best recent example of this policy is the European Union's creation of the euro as a common currency for many of its individual states.

a. Money illusion
b. Money supply
c. Monetary system
d. Neutrality of money

5. . _____ is the increase in the amount of the goods and services produced by an economy over time. It is conventionally measured as the percent rate of increase in real gross domestic product, or real GDP. Growth is usually calculated in real terms, i.e. inflation-adjusted terms, in order to net out the effect of inflation on the price of the goods and services produced. In economics, '_____' or '_____ theory' typically refers to growth of potential output, i.e., production at 'full employment,' which is caused by growth in aggregate demand or observed output.

a. Edgeworth box
b. Equity
c. Equivalent variation

Visit Cram101.com for full Practice Exams

ANSWER KEY
Chapter 16. Creating an Environment for Growth and Prosperity

1. b
2. d
3. b
4. c
5. d

You can take the complete Chapter Practice Test

for Chapter 16. Creating an Environment for Growth and Prosperity
on all key terms, persons, places, and concepts.

Online 99 Cents

http://www.epub40.13.20514.16.cram101.com/

Use www.Cram101.com for all your study needs

including Cram101's online interactive problem solving labs in

chemistry, statistics, mathematics, and more.

Chapter 17. Institutions, Policies, and Cross-Country Differences in Income

CHAPTER OUTLINE: KEY TERMS, PEOPLE, PLACES, CONCEPTS

_____ Purchasing power

_____ Lehman Brothers

_____ Income

_____ Economic freedom

_____ Fiscal policy

_____ Monetary policy

_____ World Bank

_____ Phillips curve

_____ Poverty

_____ Economic growth

_____ Investment

_____ Open market

_____ Democratic Republic of the Congo

_____ Social security

_____ Decision making

Visit Cram101.com for full Practice Exams

Chapter 17. Institutions, Policies, and Cross-Country Differences in Income and Grow

CHAPTER HIGHLIGHTS & NOTES: KEY TERMS, PEOPLE, PLACES, CONCEPTS

Purchasing power	Purchasing power is the number of goods/services that can be purchased with a unit of currency. For example, if you had taken one dollar to a store in the 1950s, you would have been able to buy a greater number of items than you would today, indicating that you would have had a greater purchasing power in the 1950s. Currency can be either a commodity money, like gold or silver, or fiat currency, or free-floating market-valued currency like US dollars.
Lehman Brothers	Lehman Brothers Holdings Inc. (former NYSE ticker symbol LEH) ( ) was a global financial services firm. Before declaring bankruptcy in 2008, Lehman was the fourth largest investment bank in the USA (behind Goldman Sachs, Morgan Stanley, and Merrill Lynch), doing business in investment banking, equity and fixed-income sales and trading (especially U.S. Treasury securities), research, investment management, private equity, and private banking.
Income	Income is the consumption and savings opportunity gained by an entity within a specified time frame, which is generally expressed in monetary terms. However, for households and individuals, 'income is the sum of all the wages, salaries, profits, interests payments, rents and other forms of earnings received... in a given period of time.' For firms, income generally refers to net-profit: what remains of revenue after expenses have been subtracted. In the field of public economics, it may refer to the accumulation of both monetary and non-monetary consumption ability, the former being used as a proxy for total income.
Economic freedom	Economic freedom is a term used in economic and policy debates. As with freedom generally, there are various definitions, but no universally accepted concept of economic freedom. One major approach to economic freedom comes from classical liberal and libertarian traditions emphasizing free markets and private property, while another extends the welfare economics study of individual choice, with greater economic freedom coming from a 'larger' (in some technical sense) set of possible choices.
Fiscal policy	In economics and political science, fiscal policy is the use of government revenue collection (taxation) and expenditure (spending) to influence the economy. The two main instruments of fiscal policy are government taxation and expenditure. Changes in the level and composition of taxation and government spending can impact the following variables in the economy:•Aggregate demand and the level of economic activity;•The pattern of resource allocation;•The distribution of income. Fiscal policy refers to the use of the government budget to influence economic activity.
Monetary policy	Monetary policy is the process by which the monetary authority of a country controls the supply of money, often targeting a rate of interest for the purpose of promoting economic growth and stability. The official goals usually include relatively stable prices and low unemployment. Monetary theory provides insight into how to craft optimal monetary policy.

Chapter 17. Institutions, Policies, and Cross-Country Differences in Income and Grow

CHAPTER HIGHLIGHTS & NOTES: KEY TERMS, PEOPLE, PLACES, CONCEPTS

World Bank	The World Bank is an international financial institution that provides loans to developing countries for capital programs. The World Bank's official goal is the reduction of poverty. According to the World Bank's Articles of Agreement (As amended effective 16 February 1989) all of its decisions must be guided by a commitment to promote foreign investment, international trade and facilitate capital investment.
Phillips curve	In economics, the Phillips curve is a historical inverse relationship between the rate of unemployment and the rate of inflation in an economy. Stated simply, the lower the unemployment in an economy, the higher the rate of inflation. While it has been observed that there is a stable short run tradeoff between unemployment and inflation, this has not been observed in the long run.
Poverty	Poverty is the state of one who lacks a certain amount of material possessions or money. Absolute poverty or destitution refers to the one who lacks basic human needs, which commonly includes clean and fresh water, nutrition, health care, education, clothing and shelter. About 1.7 billion people are estimated to live in absolute poverty today.
Economic growth	Economic growth is the increase in the amount of the goods and services produced by an economy over time. It is conventionally measured as the percent rate of increase in real gross domestic product, or real GDP. Growth is usually calculated in real terms, i.e. inflation-adjusted terms, in order to net out the effect of inflation on the price of the goods and services produced. In economics, 'economic growth' or 'economic growth theory' typically refers to growth of potential output, i.e., production at 'full employment,' which is caused by growth in aggregate demand or observed output.
Investment	Investment has different meanings in finance and economics. Finance investment is putting money into something with the expectation of gain, that upon thorough analysis, has a high degree of security for the principal amount, as well as security of return, within an expected period of time. In contrast putting money into something with an expectation of gain without thorough analysis, without security of principal, and without security of return is speculation or gambling.
Open market	The term open market is used generally to refer to a situation close to free trade and in a more specific technical sense to interbank trade in securities. In a general sense used in economics and political economy, an open market refers to a market which is accessible to all economic actors. In an open market so defined, all economic actors have an equal opportunity of entry in that market.

Chapter 17. Institutions, Policies, and Cross-Country Differences in Income and Grow

CHAPTER HIGHLIGHTS & NOTES: KEY TERMS, PEOPLE, PLACES, CONCEPTS

Democratic Republic of the Congo	The Democratic Republic of the Congo, commonly referred to as DR Congo, Congo-Kinshasa or the DRC, is a country located in Central Africa. It is the second largest country in Africa by area since the accession of South Sudan as an independent country and the eleventh largest in the world. With a population of over 71 million, the Democratic Republic of the Congo is the nineteenth most populous nation in the world, the fourth most populous nation in Africa, as well as the most populous officially Francophone country. It borders the Central African Republic and South Sudan to the north; Uganda, Rwanda, and Burundi in the east; Zambia and Angola to the south; the Republic of the Congo, the Angolan exclave of Cabinda, and the Atlantic Ocean to the west; and is separated from Tanzania by Lake Tanganyika in the east.
Social security	Social security is a concept enshrined in Article 22 of the Universal Declaration of Human Rights which states that Everyone, as a member of society, has the right to social security and is entitled to realization, through national effort and international co-operation and in accordance with the organization and resources of each State, of the economic, social and cultural rights indispensable for his dignity and the free development of his personality. In simple term, this means that the signatories agree that society in which a person lives should help them to develop and to make the most of all the advantages (culture, work, social welfare) which are offered to them in the country. Social security may also refer to the action programs of government intended to promote the welfare of the population through assistance measures guaranteeing access to sufficient resources for food and shelter and to promote health and wellbeing for the population at large and potentially vulnerable segments such as children, the elderly, the sick and the unemployed.
Decision making	Decision making can be regarded as the mental processes (cognitive process) resulting in the selection of a course of action among several alternative scenarios. Every decision making process produces a final choice. The output can be an action or an opinion of choice.

Chapter 17. Institutions, Policies, and Cross-Country Differences in Income and Grov

CHAPTER QUIZ: KEY TERMS, PEOPLE, PLACES, CONCEPTS

1. _____ is the consumption and savings opportunity gained by an entity within a specified time frame, which is generally expressed in monetary terms. However, for households and individuals, '_____ is the sum of all the wages, salaries, profits, interests payments, rents and other forms of earnings received... in a given period of time.' For firms, _____ generally refers to net-profit: what remains of revenue after expenses have been subtracted. In the field of public economics, it may refer to the accumulation of both monetary and non-monetary consumption ability, the former being used as a proxy for total _____.

   a. Advance payment
   b. Aggregate expenditure
   c. Income
   d. Average propensity to consume

2. _____ is the number of goods/services that can be purchased with a unit of currency. For example, if you had taken one dollar to a store in the 1950s, you would have been able to buy a greater number of items than you would today, indicating that you would have had a greater _____ in the 1950s. Currency can be either a commodity money, like gold or silver, or fiat currency, or free-floating market-valued currency like US dollars.

   a. Quality of life
   b. Purchasing power
   c. Quality-of-life Index
   d. Receiver operating characteristic

3. _____ is a concept enshrined in Article 22 of the Universal Declaration of Human Rights which states that Everyone, as a member of society, has the right to _____ and is entitled to realization, through national effort and international co-operation and in accordance with the organization and resources of each State, of the economic, social and cultural rights indispensable for his dignity and the free development of his personality. In simple term, this means that the signatories agree that society in which a person lives should help them to develop and to make the most of all the advantages (culture, work, social welfare) which are offered to them in the country.

   _____ may also refer to the action programs of government intended to promote the welfare of the population through assistance measures guaranteeing access to sufficient resources for food and shelter and to promote health and wellbeing for the population at large and potentially vulnerable segments such as children, the elderly, the sick and the unemployed.

   a. Social Security Agency
   b. Social security
   c. Structural adjustment loan
   d. Suits index

4. . _____ Holdings Inc. (former NYSE ticker symbol LEH) ( ) was a global financial services firm. Before declaring bankruptcy in 2008, Lehman was the fourth largest investment bank in the USA (behind Goldman Sachs, Morgan Stanley, and Merrill Lynch), doing business in investment banking, equity and fixed-income sales and trading (especially U.S. Treasury securities), research, investment management, private equity, and private banking.

   a. 15th century

Chapter 17. Institutions, Policies, and Cross-Country Differences in Income and Growth

CHAPTER QUIZ: KEY TERMS, PEOPLE, PLACES, CONCEPTS

   b. Quality of working life
   c. Quality-of-life Index
   d. Lehman Brothers

5. _____ is a term used in economic and policy debates. As with freedom generally, there are various definitions, but no universally accepted concept of _____. One major approach to _____ comes from classical liberal and libertarian traditions emphasizing free markets and private property, while another extends the welfare economics study of individual choice, with greater _____ coming from a 'larger' (in some technical sense) set of possible choices.

   a. Economic ideology
   b. Economic interventionism
   c. Economic liberalization
   d. Economic freedom

ANSWER KEY
Chapter 17. Institutions, Policies, and Cross-Country Differences in Income and Growth

1. c
2. b
3. b
4. d
5. d

You can take the complete Chapter Practice Test

for Chapter 17. Institutions, Policies, and Cross-Country Differences in Income and Growth

on all key terms, persons, places, and concepts.

Online 99 Cents

http://www.epub40.13.20514.17.cram101.com/

Use www.Cram101.com for all your study needs

including Cram101's online interactive problem solving labs in

chemistry, statistics, mathematics, and more.

Visit Cram101.com for full Practice Exams

Chapter 18. Gaining from International Trade

CHAPTER OUTLINE: KEY TERMS, PEOPLE, PLACES, CONCEPTS

- International trade
- Total cost
- AD-AS model
- Kyoto Protocol
- Comparative advantage
- Gains from trade
- Renewable resource
- Absolute advantage
- Great Depression
- Opportunity cost
- Phillips curve
- Robert Sommer
- Social security
- Free trade
- Supply and demand
- Deadweight loss
- Import quota
- Quota
- Black market

Visit Cram101.com for full Practice Exams

Chapter 18. Gaining from International Trade
CHAPTER OUTLINE: KEY TERMS, PEOPLE, PLACES, CONCEPTS

_____	Openness
_____	Trade barrier
_____	World Trade Organization
_____	Lehman Brothers
_____	Price support

CHAPTER HIGHLIGHTS & NOTES: KEY TERMS, PEOPLE, PLACES, CONCEPTS

International trade	International trade is the exchange of capital, goods, and services across international borders or territories. In most countries, such trade represents a significant share of gross domestic product (GDP). While international trade has been present throughout much of history, its economic, social, and political importance has been on the rise in recent centuries.
Total cost	In economics, and cost accounting, total cost describes the total economic cost of production and is made up of variable costs, which vary according to the quantity of a good produced and include inputs such as labor and raw materials, plus fixed costs, which are independent of the quantity of a good produced and include inputs (capital) that cannot be varied in the short term, such as buildings and machinery. Total cost in economics includes the total opportunity cost of each factor of production as part of its fixed or variable costs. The rate at which total cost changes as the amount produced changes is called marginal cost.
AD-AS model	The AD-AS or Aggregate Demand-Aggregate Supply model is a macroeconomic model that explains price level and output through the relationship of aggregate demand and aggregate supply. It is based on the theory of John Maynard Keynes presented in his work The General Theory of Employment, Interest, and Money. It is one of the primary simplified representations in the modern field of macroeconomics, and is used by a broad array of economists, from libertarian, Monetarist supporters of laissez-faire, such as Milton Friedman to Post-Keynesian supporters of economic interventionism, such as Joan Robinson.

Chapter 18. Gaining from International Trade

CHAPTER HIGHLIGHTS & NOTES: KEY TERMS, PEOPLE, PLACES, CONCEPTS

	The conventional 'aggregate supply and demand' model is, in actuality, a Keynesian visualization that has come to be a widely accepted image of the theory. The Classical supply and demand model, which is largely based on Say's Law, or that supply creates its own demand, depicts the aggregate supply curve as being vertical at all times (not just in the long-run)Modeling
	The AD/AS model is used to illustrate the Keynesian model of the business cycle. Movements of the two curves can be used to predict the effects that various exogenous events will have on two variables: real GDP and the price level. Furthermore, the model can be incorporated as a component in any of a variety of dynamic models (models of how variables like the price level and others evolve over time). The AD-AS model can be related to the Phillips curve model of wage or price inflation and unemployment.
Kyoto Protocol	The Kyoto Protocol is a protocol to the United Nations Framework Convention on Climate Change (UNFCCC or FCCC), aimed at fighting global warming. The UNFCCC is an international environmental treaty with the goal of achieving the 'stabilisation of greenhouse gas concentrations in the atmosphere at a level that would prevent dangerous anthropogenic interference with the climate system.'
	The Protocol was initially adopted on 11 December 1997 in Kyoto, Japan, and entered into force on 16 February 2005. As of September 2011, 191 states have signed and ratified the protocol. The only remaining signatory not to have ratified the protocol is the United States.
Comparative advantage	In economics, the theory of comparative advantage refers to the ability of a person or a country to produce a particular good or service at a lower marginal and opportunity cost over another. Even if one country is more efficient in the production of all goods (absolute advantage in all goods) than the other, both countries will still gain by trading with each other, as long as they have different relative efficiencies.
	For example, if, using machinery, a worker in one country can produce both shoes and shirts at 6 per hour, and a worker in a country with less machinery can produce either 2 shoes or 4 shirts in an hour, each country can gain from trade because their internal trade-offs between shoes and shirts are different.
Gains from trade	Gains from trade in economics refers to net benefits to agents from allowing an increase in voluntary trading with each other. In technical terms, it is the increase of consumer surplus plus producer surplus from lower tariffs or otherwise liberalizing trade.

Visit Cram101.com for full Practice Exams

Chapter 18. Gaining from International Trade

CHAPTER HIGHLIGHTS & NOTES: KEY TERMS, PEOPLE, PLACES, CONCEPTS

	Gains from trade are commonly described as resulting from:•specialization in production from division of labor, economies of scale, scope, and agglomeration and relative availability of factor resources in types of output by farms, businesses, location and economies•a resulting increase in total output possibilities•trade through markets from sale of one type of output for other, more highly valued goods.
	Market incentives, such as reflected in prices of outputs and inputs, are theorized to attract factors of production, including labor, into activities according to comparative advantage, that is, for which they each have a low opportunity cost.
Renewable resource	A renewable resource is a natural resource with the ability to reproduce through biological or natural processes and replenished with the passage of time. Renewable resources are part of our natural environment and form our eco-system.
	In 1962, within a report to the committee on natural resources which was forwarded to the President of the United States, Paul Weiss defined Renewable Resources as: 'The total range of living organisms providing man with food, fibers, drugs, etc...'.
Absolute advantage	In economics, the principle of absolute advantage refers to the ability of a party (an individual, or firm, or country) to produce more of a good or service than competitors, using the same amount of resources. Adam Smith first described the principle of absolute advantage in the context of international trade, using labor as the only input.
	Since absolute advantage is determined by a simple comparison of labor productivities, it is possible for a party to have no absolute advantage in anything; in that case, according to the theory of absolute advantage, no trade will occur with the other party.
Great Depression	The Great Depression was a severe worldwide economic depression in the decade preceding World War II. The timing of the Great Depression varied across nations, but in most countries it started in 1930 after the passage of the Smoot-Hawley Tariff bill (June 17), and lasted until the late 1930s or early 1940s. It was the longest, most widespread, and deepest depression of the 20th century.
	In the 21st century, the Great Depression is commonly used as an example of how far the world's economy can decline.
Opportunity cost	Opportunity cost is the cost of any activity measured in terms of the value of the next best alternative forgone (that is not chosen). It is the sacrifice related to the second best choice available to someone, or group, who has picked among several mutually exclusive choices.

Chapter 18. Gaining from International Trade

CHAPTER HIGHLIGHTS & NOTES: KEY TERMS, PEOPLE, PLACES, CONCEPTS

Phillips curve	In economics, the Phillips curve is a historical inverse relationship between the rate of unemployment and the rate of inflation in an economy. Stated simply, the lower the unemployment in an economy, the higher the rate of inflation. While it has been observed that there is a stable short run tradeoff between unemployment and inflation, this has not been observed in the long run.
Robert Sommer	Robert Sommer is an internationally known Environmental Psychologist and currently holds the position of Distinguished Professor of Psychology Emeritus at the Univeity of California, Davis. Sommer has written 14 books and over 600 articles, he may be best known for his book Peonal Space: The Behavioral Basis of Design (1969), which discusses the influence of the environment on human activities. '[Man] will adapt to hydrocarbons in the air, detergents in the water, crime in the streets, and crowded recreational areas.
Social security	Social security is a concept enshrined in Article 22 of the Universal Declaration of Human Rights which states that Everyone, as a member of society, has the right to social security and is entitled to realization, through national effort and international co-operation and in accordance with the organization and resources of each State, of the economic, social and cultural rights indispensable for his dignity and the free development of his personality. In simple term, this means that the signatories agree that society in which a person lives should help them to develop and to make the most of all the advantages (culture, work, social welfare) which are offered to them in the country. Social security may also refer to the action programs of government intended to promote the welfare of the population through assistance measures guaranteeing access to sufficient resources for food and shelter and to promote health and wellbeing for the population at large and potentially vulnerable segments such as children, the elderly, the sick and the unemployed.
Free trade	Free trade is a policy by which a government does not discriminate against imports or interfere with exports by applying tariffs (to imports) or subsidies (to exports) or quotas. According to the law of comparative advantage the policy permits trading partners mutual gains from trade of goods and services. Under a free trade policy, prices emerge from supply and demand, and are the sole determinant of resource allocation.
Supply and demand	Supply and demand is an economic model of price determination in a market. It concludes that in a competitive market, the unit price for a particular good will vary until it settles at a point where the quantity demanded by consumers (at current price) will equal the quantity supplied by producers (at current price), resulting in an economic equilibrium of price and quantity.

Visit Cram101.com for full Practice Exams

Chapter 18. Gaining from International Trade

CHAPTER HIGHLIGHTS & NOTES: KEY TERMS, PEOPLE, PLACES, CONCEPTS

	The four basic laws of supply and demand are:•If demand increases and supply remains unchanged, then it leads to higher equilibrium price and higher quantity.•If demand decreases and supply remains unchanged, then it leads to lower equilibrium price and lower quantity.•If supply increases and demand remains unchanged, then it leads to lower equilibrium price and higher quantity.•If supply decreases and demand remains unchanged, then it leads to higher equilibrium price and lower quantity.Graphical representation of supply and demand
	Although it is normal to regard the quantity demanded and the quantity supplied as functions of the price of the good, the standard graphical representation, usually attributed to Alfred Marshall, has price on the vertical axis and quantity on the horizontal axis, the opposite of the standard convention for the representation of a mathematical function.
Deadweight loss	In economics, a deadweight loss is a loss of economic efficiency that can occur when equilibrium for a good or service is not Pareto optimal. In other words, either people who would have more marginal benefit than marginal cost are not buying the product, or people who have more marginal cost than marginal benefit are buying the product.
	Causes of deadweight loss can include monopoly pricing (in the case of artificial scarcity), externalities, taxes or subsidies, and binding price ceilings or floors.
Import quota	An import quota is a limit on the quantity of a good that can be produced abroad and sold domestically. It is a type of protectionist trade restriction that sets a physical limit on the quantity of a good that can be imported into a country in a given period of time. If a quota is put on a good, less of it is imported.
Quota	Quota! may refer to: numerical goals •Racial quota!•Reservation in India•Quota!s in PakistanCommerce •Import quota, a type of trade restriction•Poundage quota, a quantitative limit on the amount of a commodity that can be marketed•Production quota, a numerical goal for the production of a good•Sales quota, a minimum sales goal for a set time span•Tariff-rate quota, a type of trade restrictionComputing •Bandwidth cap, the quota for upload or download of data•Disk quotaElectoral systems •Droop quota!•Election threshold•Hagenbach-Bischoff quota•Hare quota•Imperiali quotaFishing •Catch share•Individual fishing quotaMilitary •Quota System (Royal Navy)Statistics •Quota samplingOther •Jewish quota, a limit on the number of Jews to be employed or admitted•Quota share, distribution of a quota amongst individual entities•Screen quotas, policy that enforces a minimum number of domestic films in the theater•Ticket quota, target outputs for police forces.
Black market	A black market is a market in goods or services which operates outside the formal one(s) supported by established state powerg. 'the black market in bush meat' or the state jurisdiction 'the black market in China'.

Chapter 18. Gaining from International Trade

CHAPTER HIGHLIGHTS & NOTES: KEY TERMS, PEOPLE, PLACES, CONCEPTS

Openness	Openness is the quality of being open. It sometimes refers to a very general philosophical position from which some individuals and organizations operate, often highlighted by a decision-making process recognizing communal management by distributed stakeholders (users/producers/contributors) rather than a centralized authority (owners, experts, boards of directors, etc). Openness could be a synonym of :•Open system : Openness to experience, wiki, direct democracy, open spirituality, respect for all other beings, etc.
Trade barrier	Trade barriers are government-induced restrictions on international trade. The barriers can take many forms, including the following:•Tariffs•Non-tariff barriers to trade •Import licenses•Export licenses•Import quotas•Subsidies•Voluntary Export Restraints•Local content requirements•Embargo•Currency devaluation•Trade restriction Most trade barriers work on the same principle: the imposition of some sort of cost on trade that raises the price of the traded products. If two or more nations repeatedly use trade barriers against each other, then a trade war results.
World Trade Organization	The World Trade Organization is an organization that intends to supervise and liberalize international trade. The organization officially commenced on January 1, 1995 under the Marrakech Agreement, replacing the General Agreement on Tariffs and Trade (GATT), which commenced in 1948. The organization deals with regulation of trade between participating countries; it provides a framework for negotiating and formalizing trade agreements, and a dispute resolution process aimed at enforcing participants' adherence to WTO agreements which are signed by representatives of member governments:[fol.9-10] and ratified by their parliaments. Most of the issues that the WTO focuses on derive from previous trade negotiations, especially from the Uruguay Round (1986-1994).
Lehman Brothers	Lehman Brothers Holdings Inc. (former NYSE ticker symbol LEH) ( ) was a global financial services firm. Before declaring bankruptcy in 2008, Lehman was the fourth largest investment bank in the USA (behind Goldman Sachs, Morgan Stanley, and Merrill Lynch), doing business in investment banking, equity and fixed-income sales and trading (especially U.S. Treasury securities), research, investment management, private equity, and private banking.
Price support	In economics, a price support may be either a subsidy or a price control, both with the intended effect of keeping the market price of a good higher than the competitive equilibrium level. In the case of a price control, a price support is the minimum legal price a seller may charge, typically placed above equilibrium. It is the support of certain price levels at or above market values by the government.

Chapter 18. Gaining from International Trade

CHAPTER QUIZ: KEY TERMS, PEOPLE, PLACES, CONCEPTS

1. _____ is the exchange of capital, goods, and services across international borders or territories. In most countries, such trade represents a significant share of gross domestic product (GDP). While _____ has been present throughout much of history, its economic, social, and political importance has been on the rise in recent centuries.

    a. Absolute advantage
    b. International trade
    c. Agency for International Trade Information and Cooperation
    d. Agreement on Agriculture

2. In economics, and cost accounting, _____ describes the total economic cost of production and is made up of variable costs, which vary according to the quantity of a good produced and include inputs such as labor and raw materials, plus fixed costs, which are independent of the quantity of a good produced and include inputs (capital) that cannot be varied in the short term, such as buildings and machinery. _____ in economics includes the total opportunity cost of each factor of production as part of its fixed or variable costs.

    The rate at which _____ changes as the amount produced changes is called marginal cost.

    a. Total cost of ownership
    b. Total cost
    c. Transaction cost
    d. Value

3. In economics, the theory of _____ refers to the ability of a person or a country to produce a particular good or service at a lower marginal and opportunity cost over another. Even if one country is more efficient in the production of all goods (absolute advantage in all goods) than the other, both countries will still gain by trading with each other, as long as they have different relative efficiencies.

    For example, if, using machinery, a worker in one country can produce both shoes and shirts at 6 per hour, and a worker in a country with less machinery can produce either 2 shoes or 4 shirts in an hour, each country can gain from trade because their internal trade-offs between shoes and shirts are different.

    a. Competitiveness Policy Council
    b. Concertina model
    c. Confirming house
    d. Comparative advantage

4. . _____ Holdings Inc. (former NYSE ticker symbol LEH) ( ) was a global financial services firm. Before declaring bankruptcy in 2008, Lehman was the fourth largest investment bank in the USA (behind Goldman Sachs, Morgan Stanley, and Merrill Lynch), doing business in investment banking, equity and fixed-income sales and trading (especially U.S. Treasury securities), research, investment management, private equity, and private banking.

    a. 15th century
    b. World government
    c. Lehman Brothers

Visit Cram101.com for full Practice Exams

Chapter 18. Gaining from International Trade

CHAPTER QUIZ: KEY TERMS, PEOPLE, PLACES, CONCEPTS

5. The AD-AS or Aggregate Demand-Aggregate Supply model is a macroeconomic model that explains price level and output through the relationship of aggregate demand and aggregate supply. It is based on the theory of John Maynard Keynes presented in his work The General Theory of Employment, Interest, and Money. It is one of the primary simplified representations in the modern field of macroeconomics, and is used by a broad array of economists, from libertarian, Monetarist supporters of laissez-faire, such as Milton Friedman to Post-Keynesian supporters of economic interventionism, such as Joan Robinson.

The conventional 'aggregate supply and demand' model is, in actuality, a Keynesian visualization that has come to be a widely accepted image of the theory. The Classical supply and demand model, which is largely based on Say's Law, or that supply creates its own demand, depicts the aggregate supply curve as being vertical at all times (not just in the long-run)Modeling

The AD/AS model is used to illustrate the Keynesian model of the business cycle. Movements of the two curves can be used to predict the effects that various exogenous events will have on two variables: real GDP and the price level. Furthermore, the model can be incorporated as a component in any of a variety of dynamic models (models of how variables like the price level and others evolve over time). The _____ can be related to the Phillips curve model of wage or price inflation and unemployment.

a. AD-IA model
b. AD-AS model
c. E2m.org
d. Edgeworth box

ANSWER KEY
Chapter 18. Gaining from International Trade

1. b
2. b
3. d
4. c
5. b

You can take the complete Chapter Practice Test

for Chapter 18. Gaining from International Trade
on all key terms, persons, places, and concepts.

Online 99 Cents

http://www.epub40.13.20514.18.cram101.com/

Use www.Cram101.com for all your study needs

including Cram101's online interactive problem solving labs in

chemistry, statistics, mathematics, and more.

Chapter 19. International Finance and the Foreign Exchange Market

CHAPTER OUTLINE: KEY TERMS, PEOPLE, PLACES, CONCEPTS

- International finance
- Great Depression
- Social security
- International trade
- Supply and demand
- Appreciation
- Depreciation
- Euro
- AD-AS model
- Environmental protection
- Income
- Interest rate
- European Central Bank
- Federal Reserve System
- Currency board
- Fixed exchange rate
- Gold standard
- Balance of payments
- Balance

Visit Cram101.com for full Practice Exams

Chapter 19. International Finance and the Foreign Exchange Market

CHAPTER OUTLINE: KEY TERMS, PEOPLE, PLACES, CONCEPTS

_____ Balance of trade

_____ Current account

_____ Total cost

_____ Capital account

_____ Renewable resource

_____ Labor relations

_____ Business cycle

_____ Business failure

_____ Failure rate

_____ Microeconomics

Visit Cram101.com for full Practice Exams

Chapter 19. International Finance and the Foreign Exchange Market

CHAPTER HIGHLIGHTS & NOTES: KEY TERMS, PEOPLE, PLACES, CONCEPTS

International finance	International finance is the branch of financial economics broadly concerned with monetary and macroeconomic interrelations between two or more countries. International finance examines the dynamics of the global financial system, international monetary systems, balance of payments, exchange rates, foreign direct investment, and how these topics relate to international trade.
	Sometimes referred to as multinational finance, international finance is additionally concerned with matters of international financial management.
Great Depression	The Great Depression was a severe worldwide economic depression in the decade preceding World War II. The timing of the Great Depression varied across nations, but in most countries it started in 1930 after the passage of the Smoot-Hawley Tariff bill (June 17), and lasted until the late 1930s or early 1940s. It was the longest, most widespread, and deepest depression of the 20th century.
	In the 21st century, the Great Depression is commonly used as an example of how far the world's economy can decline.
Social security	Social security is a concept enshrined in Article 22 of the Universal Declaration of Human Rights which states that Everyone, as a member of society, has the right to social security and is entitled to realization, through national effort and international co-operation and in accordance with the organization and resources of each State, of the economic, social and cultural rights indispensable for his dignity and the free development of his personality. In simple term, this means that the signatories agree that society in which a person lives should help them to develop and to make the most of all the advantages (culture, work, social welfare) which are offered to them in the country.
	Social security may also refer to the action programs of government intended to promote the welfare of the population through assistance measures guaranteeing access to sufficient resources for food and shelter and to promote health and wellbeing for the population at large and potentially vulnerable segments such as children, the elderly, the sick and the unemployed.
International trade	International trade is the exchange of capital, goods, and services across international borders or territories. In most countries, such trade represents a significant share of gross domestic product (GDP). While international trade has been present throughout much of history, its economic, social, and political importance has been on the rise in recent centuries.
Supply and demand	Supply and demand is an economic model of price determination in a market. It concludes that in a competitive market, the unit price for a particular good will vary until it settles at a point where the quantity demanded by consumers (at current price) will equal the quantity supplied by producers (at current price), resulting in an economic equilibrium of price and quantity.

Chapter 19. International Finance and the Foreign Exchange Market

CHAPTER HIGHLIGHTS & NOTES: KEY TERMS, PEOPLE, PLACES, CONCEPTS

	The four basic laws of supply and demand are:•If demand increases and supply remains unchanged, then it leads to higher equilibrium price and higher quantity.•If demand decreases and supply remains unchanged, then it leads to lower equilibrium price and lower quantity.•If supply increases and demand remains unchanged, then it leads to lower equilibrium price and higher quantity.•If supply decreases and demand remains unchanged, then it leads to higher equilibrium price and lower quantity.Graphical representation of supply and demand
	Although it is normal to regard the quantity demanded and the quantity supplied as functions of the price of the good, the standard graphical representation, usually attributed to Alfred Marshall, has price on the vertical axis and quantity on the horizontal axis, the opposite of the standard convention for the representation of a mathematical function.
Appreciation	In accounting, appreciation of an asset is an increase in its value. In this sense it is the reverse of depreciation, which measures the fall in value of assets over their normal life-time. Generally, the term is reserved for property or, more specifically, land and buildings.
Depreciation	In economics, depreciation is the gradual decrease in the economic value of the capital stock of a firm, nation or other entity, either through physical depreciation, obsolescence or changes in the demand for the services of the capital in question. If capital stock is C_0 at the beginning of a period, investment is I and depreciation D, the capital stock at the end of the period, C_1, is $C_0 + I - D$.
	In economics, the value of a capital asset may be modeled as the present value of the flow of services the asset will generate in future, appropriately adjusted for uncertainty.
Euro	The euro was established by the provisions in the 1992 Maastricht Treaty. To participate in the currency, member states are meant to meet strict criteria, such as a budget deficit of less than three per cent of their GDP, a debt ratio of less than sixty per cent of GDP (both of which were ultimately widely flouted after introduction), low inflation, and interest rates close to the EU average. In the Maastricht Treaty, the United Kingdom and Denmark were granted exemptions per their request from moving to the stage of monetary union which would result in the introduction of the euro.
AD-AS model	The AD-AS or Aggregate Demand-Aggregate Supply model is a macroeconomic model that explains price level and output through the relationship of aggregate demand and aggregate supply. It is based on the theory of John Maynard Keynes presented in his work The General Theory of Employment, Interest, and Money.

Visit Cram101.com for full Practice Exams

Chapter 19. International Finance and the Foreign Exchange Market

CHAPTER HIGHLIGHTS & NOTES: KEY TERMS, PEOPLE, PLACES, CONCEPTS

	It is one of the primary simplified representations in the modern field of macroeconomics, and is used by a broad array of economists, from libertarian, Monetarist supporters of laissez-faire, such as Milton Friedman to Post-Keynesian supporters of economic interventionism, such as Joan Robinson. The conventional 'aggregate supply and demand' model is, in actuality, a Keynesian visualization that has come to be a widely accepted image of the theory. The Classical supply and demand model, which is largely based on Say's Law, or that supply creates its own demand, depicts the aggregate supply curve as being vertical at all times (not just in the long-run)Modeling The AD/AS model is used to illustrate the Keynesian model of the business cycle. Movements of the two curves can be used to predict the effects that various exogenous events will have on two variables: real GDP and the price level. Furthermore, the model can be incorporated as a component in any of a variety of dynamic models (models of how variables like the price level and others evolve over time). The AD-AS model can be related to the Phillips curve model of wage or price inflation and unemployment.
Environmental protection	Environmental protection is a practice of protecting the environment, on individual, organizational or governmental levels, for the benefit of the natural environment and (or) humans. Due to the pressures of population and technology, the biophysical environment is being degraded, sometimes permanently. This has been recognized, and governments have begun placing restraints on activities that cause environmental degradation.
Income	Income is the consumption and savings opportunity gained by an entity within a specified time frame, which is generally expressed in monetary terms. However, for households and individuals, 'income is the sum of all the wages, salaries, profits, interests payments, rents and other forms of earnings received... in a given period of time.' For firms, income generally refers to net-profit: what remains of revenue after expenses have been subtracted. In the field of public economics, it may refer to the accumulation of both monetary and non-monetary consumption ability, the former being used as a proxy for total income.
Interest rate	An interest rate is the rate at which interest is paid by a borrower for the use of money that they borrow from a lender. For example, a small company borrows capital from a bank to buy new assets for their business, and in return the lender receives interest at a predetermined interest rate for deferring the use of funds and instead lending it to the borrower. Interest rates are normally expressed as a percentage of the principal for a period of one year.
European Central Bank	The European Central Bank is the institution of the European Union (EU) that administers the monetary policy of the 17 EU Eurozone member states. It is thus one of the world's most important central banks.

Visit Cram101.com for full Practice Exams

Chapter 19. International Finance and the Foreign Exchange Market

CHAPTER HIGHLIGHTS & NOTES: KEY TERMS, PEOPLE, PLACES, CONCEPTS

Federal Reserve System	The Federal Reserve System is the central banking system of the United States. It was created on December 23, 1913 with the enactment of the Federal Reserve Act, largely in response to a series of financial panics, particularly a severe panic in 1907. Over time, the roles and responsibilities of the Federal Reserve System have expanded and its structure has evolved. Events such as the Great Depression were major factors leading to changes in the system.
Currency board	A currency board is a monetary authority which is required to maintain a fixed exchange rate with a foreign currency. This policy objective requires the conventional objectives of a central bank to be subordinated to the exchange rate target. Features of 'orthodox' currency boards

The main qualities of an orthodox currency board are:•A currency board's foreign currency reserves must be sufficient to ensure that all holders of its notes and coins (and all banks creditor of a Reserve Account at the currency board) can convert them into the reserve currency (usually 110-115% of the monetary base M0).•A currency board maintains absolute, unlimited convertibility between its notes and coins and the currency against which they are pegged (the anchor currency), at a fixed rate of exchange, with no restrictions on current-account or capital-account transactions.•A currency board only earns profit from interests on foreign reserves (less the expense of note-issuing), and does not engage in forward-exchange transactions. |
| Fixed exchange rate | A fixed exchange rate, is also referred to as the Tag of particular Rate, which is a type of exchange rate regime wherein currency's value is matched to the value of another single currency or to a basket of other currencies, or to another measure of value, such as gold.

A fixed exchange rate is usually used to stabilize the value of a currency against the currency it is pegged to. This makes trade and investments between the two countries easier and more predictable and is especially useful for small economies in which external trade forms a large part of their GDP.

It can also be used as a means to control inflation. |
| Gold standard | The gold standard is a monetary system in which the standard economic unit of account is a fixed weight of gold. There are distinct kinds of gold standard. First, the gold specie standard is a system in which the monetary unit is associated with circulating gold coins, or with the unit of value defined in terms of one particular circulating gold coin in conjunction with subsidiary coinage made from a lesser valuable metal. |
| Balance of payments | Balance of payments accounts are an accounting record of all monetary transactions between a country and the rest of the world. These transactions include payments for the country's exports and imports of goods, services, financial capital, and financial transfers. |

Visit Cram101.com for full Practice Exams

Chapter 19. International Finance and the Foreign Exchange Market

CHAPTER HIGHLIGHTS & NOTES: KEY TERMS, PEOPLE, PLACES, CONCEPTS

Balance	In banking and accountancy, the outstanding balance is the amount of money owed that remains in a deposit account at a given date, after all past remittances, payments and withdrawal have been accounted for. It can be positive (then, in the balance sheet of a firm, it is an asset) or negative (a liability).
Balance of trade	The balance of trade is the difference between the monetary value of exports and imports of output in an economy over a certain period. It is the relationship between a nation's imports and exports. A positive balance is known as a trade surplus if it consists of exporting more than is imported; a negative balance is referred to as a trade deficit or, informally, a trade gap.
Current account	In economics, the current account is one of the two primary components of the balance of payments, the other being capital account. It is the sum of the balance of trade (net earnings on exports minus payments for imports), factor income (earnings on foreign investments minus payments made to foreign investors) and cash transfers. The current account balance is one of two major measures of the nature of a country's foreign trade (the other being the net capital outflow).
Total cost	In economics, and cost accounting, total cost describes the total economic cost of production and is made up of variable costs, which vary according to the quantity of a good produced and include inputs such as labor and raw materials, plus fixed costs, which are independent of the quantity of a good produced and include inputs (capital) that cannot be varied in the short term, such as buildings and machinery. Total cost in economics includes the total opportunity cost of each factor of production as part of its fixed or variable costs. The rate at which total cost changes as the amount produced changes is called marginal cost.
Capital account	In macroeconomics and international finance, the capital account is one of two primary components of the balance of payments, the other being the current account. Whereas the current account reflects a nation's net income, the capital account reflects net change in national ownership of assets. A surplus in the capital account means money is flowing into the country, but unlike a surplus in the current account, the inbound flows will effectively be borrowings or sales of assets rather than earnings.
Renewable resource	A renewable resource is a natural resource with the ability to reproduce through biological or natural processes and replenished with the passage of time. Renewable resources are part of our natural environment and form our eco-system.

Chapter 19. International Finance and the Foreign Exchange Market

CHAPTER HIGHLIGHTS & NOTES: KEY TERMS, PEOPLE, PLACES, CONCEPTS

Labor relations	Labor relations is the study and practice of managing unionized employment situations. In academia, labor relations is frequently a subarea within industrial relations, though scholars from many disciplines--including economics, sociology, history, law, and political science--also study labor unions and labor movements. In practice, labor relations is frequently a subarea within human resource management.
Business cycle	The term business cycle refers to economy-wide fluctuations in production or economic activity over several months or years. These fluctuations occur around a long-term growth trend, and typically involve shifts over time between periods of relatively rapid economic growth (an expansion or boom), and periods of relative stagnation or decline (a contraction or recession). Business cycles are usually measured by considering the growth rate of real gross domestic product.
Business failure	Business failure refers to a company ceasing operations following its inability to make a profit or to bring in enough revenue to cover its expenses. A profitable business can fail if it does not generate adequate cash flow to meet expenses. Businesses can fail as a result of wars, recessions, high taxation, high interest rates, excessive regulations, management decisions, insufficient marketing, inability to compete with other similar businesses, or a lack of interest from the public in the business's offerings.
Failure rate	Failure rate is the frequency with which an engineered system or component fails, expressed for example in failures per hour. It is often denoted by the Greek letter λ (lambda) and is important in reliability engineering. The failure rate of a system usually depends on time, with the rate varying over the life cycle of the system.
Microeconomics	Microeconomics is a branch of economics that studies the behavior of individual households and firms in making decisions on the allocation of limited resources. Typically, it applies to markets where goods or services are bought and sold. Microeconomics examines how these decisions and behaviors affect the supply and demand for goods and services, which determines prices, and how prices, in turn, determine the quantity supplied and quantity demanded of goods and services.

Chapter 19. International Finance and the Foreign Exchange Market

CHAPTER QUIZ: KEY TERMS, PEOPLE, PLACES, CONCEPTS

1. A _____, is also referred to as the Tag of particular Rate, which is a type of exchange rate regime wherein currency's value is matched to the value of another single currency or to a basket of other currencies, or to another measure of value, such as gold.

   A _____ is usually used to stabilize the value of a currency against the currency it is pegged to. This makes trade and investments between the two countries easier and more predictable and is especially useful for small economies in which external trade forms a large part of their GDP.

   It can also be used as a means to control inflation.

   a. Flag of convenience
   b. Fixed exchange rate
   c. Foreign Exchange Committee
   d. Free trade

2. The _____ was established by the provisions in the 1992 Maastricht Treaty. To participate in the currency, member states are meant to meet strict criteria, such as a budget deficit of less than three per cent of their GDP, a debt ratio of less than sixty per cent of GDP (both of which were ultimately widely flouted after introduction), low inflation, and interest rates close to the EU average. In the Maastricht Treaty, the United Kingdom and Denmark were granted exemptions per their request from moving to the stage of monetary union which would result in the introduction of the _____.

   a. Euro calculator
   b. Euro
   c. Euro Group
   d. Euro Interbank Offered Rate

3. In banking and accountancy, the outstanding balance is the amount of money owed that remains in a deposit account at a given date, after all past remittances, payments and withdrawal have been accounted for. It can be positive (then, in the _____ sheet of a firm, it is an asset) or negative (a liability).

   a. Balance
   b. Bill and hold
   c. Capital appreciation
   d. Capital expenditure

4. _____ is the branch of financial economics broadly concerned with monetary and macroeconomic interrelations between two or more countries. _____ examines the dynamics of the global financial system, international monetary systems, balance of payments, exchange rates, foreign direct investment, and how these topics relate to international trade.

   Sometimes referred to as multinational finance, _____ is additionally concerned with matters of international financial management.

   a. International Fisher effect
   b. Inward investment

Chapter 19. International Finance and the Foreign Exchange Market

c. International finance
d. Arbitrista

5. The _____ was a severe worldwide economic depression in the decade preceding World War II. The timing of the _____ varied across nations, but in most countries it started in 1930 after the passage of the Smoot-Hawley Tariff bill (June 17), and lasted until the late 1930s or early 1940s. It was the longest, most widespread, and deepest depression of the 20th century.

    In the 21st century, the _____ is commonly used as an example of how far the world's economy can decline.

    a. Bank Night
    b. Battle of Ballantyne Pier
    c. Great Depression
    d. Bloody Sunday

ANSWER KEY
Chapter 19. International Finance and the Foreign Exchange Market

1. b
2. b
3. a
4. c
5. c

You can take the complete Chapter Practice Test

for Chapter 19. International Finance and the Foreign Exchange Market

on all key terms, persons, places, and concepts.

Online 99 Cents

http://www.epub40.13.20514.19.cram101.com/

Use www.Cram101.com for all your study needs

including Cram101's online interactive problem solving labs in

chemistry, statistics, mathematics, and more.

Chapter 20. Consumer Choice and Elasticity

CHAPTER OUTLINE: KEY TERMS, PEOPLE, PLACES, CONCEPTS

_____ Consumer choice

_____ Social security

_____ Consumer

_____ Income

_____ Law of demand

_____ Scarcity

_____ Utility

_____ Demand curve

_____ Marginal utility

_____ Price elasticity of demand

_____ AD-AS model

_____ Environmental protection

_____ Great Depression

_____ Normal good

_____ Inferior good

_____ Price elasticity of supply

Visit Cram101.com for full Practice Exams

Chapter 20. Consumer Choice and Elasticity

CHAPTER HIGHLIGHTS & NOTES: KEY TERMS, PEOPLE, PLACES, CONCEPTS

Consumer choice	Consumer choice is a theory of microeconomics that relates preferences for consumption goods and services to consumption expenditures and ultimately to consumer demand curves. The link between personal preferences, consumption, and the demand curve is one of the most closely studied relations in economics. Consumer choice theory is a way of analyzing how consumers may achieve equilibrium between preferences and expenditures by maximizing utility as subject to consumer budget constraints.
Social security	Social security is a concept enshrined in Article 22 of the Universal Declaration of Human Rights which states that Everyone, as a member of society, has the right to social security and is entitled to realization, through national effort and international co-operation and in accordance with the organization and resources of each State, of the economic, social and cultural rights indispensable for his dignity and the free development of his personality. In simple term, this means that the signatories agree that society in which a person lives should help them to develop and to make the most of all the advantages (culture, work, social welfare) which are offered to them in the country. Social security may also refer to the action programs of government intended to promote the welfare of the population through assistance measures guaranteeing access to sufficient resources for food and shelter and to promote health and wellbeing for the population at large and potentially vulnerable segments such as children, the elderly, the sick and the unemployed.
Consumer	A consumer is a person or group of people that are the final users of products and or services generated within a social system. A consumer may be a person or group, such as a household. The concept of a consumer may vary significantly by context.
Income	Income is the consumption and savings opportunity gained by an entity within a specified time frame, which is generally expressed in monetary terms. However, for households and individuals, 'income is the sum of all the wages, salaries, profits, interests payments, rents and other forms of earnings received... in a given period of time.' For firms, income generally refers to net-profit: what remains of revenue after expenses have been subtracted. In the field of public economics, it may refer to the accumulation of both monetary and non-monetary consumption ability, the former being used as a proxy for total income.
Law of demand	In economics, the law of demand is an economic law, which states that consumers buy more of a good when its price decreases and less when its price increases (ceteris paribus). The greater the amount to be sold, the smaller the price at which it is offered must be, in order for it to find purchasers.

Visit Cram101.com for full Practice Exams

Chapter 20. Consumer Choice and Elasticity

CHAPTER HIGHLIGHTS & NOTES: KEY TERMS, PEOPLE, PLACES, CONCEPTS

Scarcity	Scarcity is the fundamental economic problem of having humans who have wants and needs in a world of limited resources. It states that society has insufficient productive resources to fulfill all human wants and needs. Alternatively, scarcity implies that not all of society's goals can be pursued at the same time; trade-offs are made of one good against others.
Utility	In economics, utility is a representation of preferences over some set of goods and services. Preferences have a utility representation so long as they are transitive, complete, and continuous. Utility is usually applied by economists in such constructs as the indifference curve, which plot the combination of commodities that an individual or a society would accept to maintain a given level of satisfaction.
Demand curve	In economics, the demand curve is the graph depicting the relationship between the price of a certain commodity and the amount of it that consumers are willing and able to purchase at that given price. It is a graphic representation of a demand schedule. The demand curve for all consumers together follows from the demand curve of every individual consumer: the individual demands at each price are added together.
Marginal utility	In economics, the marginal utility of a good or service is the gain from an increase in the consumption of that good or service. Economists sometimes speak of a law of diminishing marginal utility, meaning that the first unit of consumption of a good or service yields more utility than the second and subsequent units. The concept of marginal utility played a crucial role in the marginal revolution of the late 19th century, and led to the replacement of the labor theory of value by neoclassical value theory in which the relative prices of goods and services are simultaneously determined by marginal rates of substitution in consumption and marginal rates of transformation in production, which are equal in economic equilibrium.
Price elasticity of demand	Price elasticity of demand is a measure used in economics to show the responsiveness, or elasticity, of the quantity demanded of a good or service to a change in its price. More precisely, it gives the percentage change in quantity demanded in response to a one percent change in price (holding constant all the other determinants of demand, such as income). It was devised by Alfred Marshall.
AD-AS model	The AD-AS or Aggregate Demand-Aggregate Supply model is a macroeconomic model that explains price level and output through the relationship of aggregate demand and aggregate supply. It is based on the theory of John Maynard Keynes presented in his work The General Theory of Employment, Interest, and Money.

Chapter 20. Consumer Choice and Elasticity

CHAPTER HIGHLIGHTS & NOTES: KEY TERMS, PEOPLE, PLACES, CONCEPTS

	It is one of the primary simplified representations in the modern field of macroeconomics, and is used by a broad array of economists, from libertarian, Monetarist supporters of laissez-faire, such as Milton Friedman to Post-Keynesian supporters of economic interventionism, such as Joan Robinson.
	The conventional 'aggregate supply and demand' model is, in actuality, a Keynesian visualization that has come to be a widely accepted image of the theory. The Classical supply and demand model, which is largely based on Say's Law, or that supply creates its own demand, depicts the aggregate supply curve as being vertical at all times (not just in the long-run)Modeling
	The AD/AS model is used to illustrate the Keynesian model of the business cycle. Movements of the two curves can be used to predict the effects that various exogenous events will have on two variables: real GDP and the price level. Furthermore, the model can be incorporated as a component in any of a variety of dynamic models (models of how variables like the price level and others evolve over time). The AD-AS model can be related to the Phillips curve model of wage or price inflation and unemployment.
Environmental protection	Environmental protection is a practice of protecting the environment, on individual, organizational or governmental levels, for the benefit of the natural environment and (or) humans. Due to the pressures of population and technology, the biophysical environment is being degraded, sometimes permanently. This has been recognized, and governments have begun placing restraints on activities that cause environmental degradation.
Great Depression	The Great Depression was a severe worldwide economic depression in the decade preceding World War II. The timing of the Great Depression varied across nations, but in most countries it started in 1930 after the passage of the Smoot-Hawley Tariff bill (June 17), and lasted until the late 1930s or early 1940s. It was the longest, most widespread, and deepest depression of the 20th century.
	In the 21st century, the Great Depression is commonly used as an example of how far the world's economy can decline.
Normal good	In economics, normal goods are any goods for which demand increases when income increases and falls when income decreases but price remains constant, i.e. with a positive income elasticity of demand. The term does not necessarily refer to the quality of the good, but an abnormal good would clearly not be in demand, except for possibly lower socioeconomic groups.

Chapter 20. Consumer Choice and Elasticity

CHAPTER HIGHLIGHTS & NOTES: KEY TERMS, PEOPLE, PLACES, CONCEPTS

Inferior good	In consumer theory, an inferior good is a good that decreases in demand when consumer income rises, unlike normal goods, for which the opposite is observed. Normal goods are those for which consumers' demand increases when their income increases. This would be the opposite of a superior good, one that is often associated with wealth and the wealthy, whereas an inferior good is often associated with lower socio-economic groups.
Price elasticity of supply	Price elasticity of supply is a measure used in economics to show the responsiveness, or elasticity, of the quantity supplied of a good or service to a change in its price. When the coefficient is less than one, the st good can be described as inelastic; when the coefficient is greater than one, the supply can be described as elastic. An elasticity of zero indicates that quantity supplied does not respond to a price change: it is 'fixed' in supply.

CHAPTER QUIZ: KEY TERMS, PEOPLE, PLACES, CONCEPTS

1. A _____ is a person or group of people that are the final users of products and or services generated within a social system. A _____ may be a person or group, such as a household. The concept of a _____ may vary significantly by context.

    a. Consumer complaint
    b. Consumer unit
    c. Cost of poor quality
    d. Consumer

2. _____ is a theory of microeconomics that relates preferences for consumption goods and services to consumption expenditures and ultimately to consumer demand curves. The link between personal preferences, consumption, and the demand curve is one of the most closely studied relations in economics. _____ theory is a way of analyzing how consumers may achieve equilibrium between preferences and expenditures by maximizing utility as subject to consumer budget constraints.

    a. Consumer choice
    b. Contour set
    c. Corner solution
    d. Customer equity

3. . _____ is a measure used in economics to show the responsiveness, or elasticity, of the quantity supplied of a good or service to a change in its price.

    When the coefficient is less than one, the st good can be described as inelastic; when the coefficient is greater than one, the supply can be described as elastic.

Visit Cram101.com for full Practice Exams

Chapter 20. Consumer Choice and Elasticity

CHAPTER QUIZ: KEY TERMS, PEOPLE, PLACES, CONCEPTS

An elasticity of zero indicates that quantity supplied does not respond to a price change: it is 'fixed' in supply.

- a. Price elasticity of supply
- b. Total revenue test
- c. Yield elasticity of bond value
- d. Public good

4. In economics, the _____ is the graph depicting the relationship between the price of a certain commodity and the amount of it that consumers are willing and able to purchase at that given price. It is a graphic representation of a demand schedule. The _____ for all consumers together follows from the _____ of every individual consumer: the individual demands at each price are added together.

- a. Hubbert curve
- b. J curve
- c. Kuznets curve
- d. Demand curve

5. In economics, the _____ is an economic law, which states that consumers buy more of a good when its price decreases and less when its price increases (ceteris paribus).

The greater the amount to be sold, the smaller the price at which it is offered must be, in order for it to find purchasers.

_____ states that the amount demanded of a commodity and its price are inversely related, other things remaining constant.

- a. Lerner index
- b. Law of demand
- c. Loyalty program
- d. Marginal cost

Visit Cram101.com for full Practice Exams

ANSWER KEY
Chapter 20. Consumer Choice and Elasticity

1. d
2. a
3. a
4. d
5. b

You can take the complete Chapter Practice Test

for Chapter 20. Consumer Choice and Elasticity
on all key terms, persons, places, and concepts.

Online 99 Cents

http://www.epub40.13.20514.20.cram101.com/

Use www.Cram101.com for all your study needs including Cram101's online interactive problem solving labs in chemistry, statistics, mathematics, and more.

Chapter 21. Costs and the Supply of Goods

CHAPTER OUTLINE: KEY TERMS, PEOPLE, PLACES, CONCEPTS

- _____ Business cycle
- _____ Renewable resource
- _____ Residual claimant
- _____ Great Depression
- _____ Income tax
- _____ Tax credit
- _____ Phillips curve
- _____ Explicit cost
- _____ Implicit cost
- _____ Opportunity cost
- _____ Product market
- _____ Total cost
- _____ Absolute advantage
- _____ Average fixed cost
- _____ Average variable cost
- _____ Fixed cost
- _____ Marginal cost
- _____ Variable cost
- _____ Diminishing returns

Visit Cram101.com for full Practice Exams

Chapter 21. Costs and the Supply of Goods

CHAPTER OUTLINE: KEY TERMS, PEOPLE, PLACES, CONCEPTS

	Marginal product
	Cost curve
	Economies of scale
	Mass production
	Sunk costs

CHAPTER HIGHLIGHTS & NOTES: KEY TERMS, PEOPLE, PLACES, CONCEPTS

Business cycle	The term business cycle refers to economy-wide fluctuations in production or economic activity over several months or years. These fluctuations occur around a long-term growth trend, and typically involve shifts over time between periods of relatively rapid economic growth (an expansion or boom), and periods of relative stagnation or decline (a contraction or recession). Business cycles are usually measured by considering the growth rate of real gross domestic product.
Renewable resource	A renewable resource is a natural resource with the ability to reproduce through biological or natural processes and replenished with the passage of time. Renewable resources are part of our natural environment and form our eco-system. In 1962, within a report to the committee on natural resources which was forwarded to the President of the United States, Paul Weiss defined Renewable Resources as: 'The total range of living organisms providing man with food, fibers, drugs, etc...'.
Residual claimant	In economics, the residual claimant is the agent who receives the net income (income after deducting all costs). Residual claimancy is generally required in order for there to be moral hazard, which is a problem typical of information asymmetry.

Visit Cram101.com for full Practice Exams

Chapter 21. Costs and the Supply of Goods

CHAPTER HIGHLIGHTS & NOTES: KEY TERMS, PEOPLE, PLACES, CONCEPTS

Great Depression	The Great Depression was a severe worldwide economic depression in the decade preceding World War II. The timing of the Great Depression varied across nations, but in most countries it started in 1930 after the passage of the Smoot-Hawley Tariff bill (June 17), and lasted until the late 1930s or early 1940s. It was the longest, most widespread, and deepest depression of the 20th century. In the 21st century, the Great Depression is commonly used as an example of how far the world's economy can decline.
Income tax	An income tax is a tax levied on the income of individuals or businesses (corporations or other legal entities). Various income tax systems exist, with varying degrees of tax incidence. Income taxation can be progressive, proportional, or regressive.
Tax credit	A tax credit is a sum deducted from the total amount a taxpayer owes to the state. A tax credit may be granted for various types of taxes, such as an income tax, property tax, or VAT. It may be granted in recognition of taxes already paid, as a subsidy, or to encourage investment or other behaviors. In some systems tax credits are 'refundable' to the extent they exceed the relevant tax.
Phillips curve	In economics, the Phillips curve is a historical inverse relationship between the rate of unemployment and the rate of inflation in an economy. Stated simply, the lower the unemployment in an economy, the higher the rate of inflation. While it has been observed that there is a stable short run tradeoff between unemployment and inflation, this has not been observed in the long run.
Explicit cost	An explicit cost is a direct payment made to others in the course of running a business, such as wage, rent and materials, as opposed to implicit costs, which are those where no actual payment is made. It is possible still to underestimate these costs, however: for example, pension contributions and other 'perks' must be taken into account when considering the cost of labour. Explicit costs are taken into account along with implicit ones when considering economic profit.
Implicit cost	In economics, an implicit cost, implied cost, or notional cost, is the opportunity cost equal to what a firm must give up in order to use factors which it neither purchases nor hires. It is the opposite of an explicit cost, which is borne directly. In other words, an implicit cost is any cost that results from using an asset instead of renting, selling, or lending it.
Opportunity cost	Opportunity cost is the cost of any activity measured in terms of the value of the next best alternative forgone (that is not chosen). It is the sacrifice related to the second best choice available to someone, or group, who has picked among several mutually exclusive choices.

Chapter 21. Costs and the Supply of Goods

CHAPTER HIGHLIGHTS & NOTES: KEY TERMS, PEOPLE, PLACES, CONCEPTS

Product market	Product market is a mechanism that allows people to easily buy and sell products. Services are often included in the scope of the term. Product market regulation is an economic term that describes restrictions in the market.
Total cost	In economics, and cost accounting, total cost describes the total economic cost of production and is made up of variable costs, which vary according to the quantity of a good produced and include inputs such as labor and raw materials, plus fixed costs, which are independent of the quantity of a good produced and include inputs (capital) that cannot be varied in the short term, such as buildings and machinery. Total cost in economics includes the total opportunity cost of each factor of production as part of its fixed or variable costs. The rate at which total cost changes as the amount produced changes is called marginal cost.
Absolute advantage	In economics, the principle of absolute advantage refers to the ability of a party (an individual, or firm, or country) to produce more of a good or service than competitors, using the same amount of resources. Adam Smith first described the principle of absolute advantage in the context of international trade, using labor as the only input. Since absolute advantage is determined by a simple comparison of labor productivities, it is possible for a party to have no absolute advantage in anything; in that case, according to the theory of absolute advantage, no trade will occur with the other party.
Average fixed cost	Average fixed cost is an economics term that refers to fixed costs of production (FC) divided by the quantity (Q) of output produced. $$AFC = \frac{FC}{Q}$$ Average fixed cost is a per-unit-of-output measure of fixed costs. As the total number of goods produced increases, the average fixed cost decreases because the same amount of fixed costs is being spread over a larger number of units of output.
Average variable cost	Average variable cost is an economics term that refers to a firm's variable costs (labor, electricity, etc). divided by the quantity (Q) of output produced. Variable costs are those costs which vary with output.
Fixed cost	In economics, fixed costs are business expenses that are not dependent on the level of goods or services produced by the business. They tend to be time-related, such as salaries or rents being paid per month, and are often referred to as overhead costs.

Chapter 21. Costs and the Supply of Goods

CHAPTER HIGHLIGHTS & NOTES: KEY TERMS, PEOPLE, PLACES, CONCEPTS

Marginal cost	In economics and finance, marginal cost is the change in total cost that arises when the quantity produced changes by one unit. That is, it is the cost of producing one more unit of a good. If the good being produced is infinitely divisible, so the size of a marginal cost will change with volume, as a non-linear and non-proportional cost function includes the following:•variable terms dependent to volume,•constant terms independent to volume and occurring with the respective lot size,•jump fix cost increase or decrease dependent to steps of volume increase. In practice the above definition of marginal cost as the change in total cost as a result of an increase in output of one unit is inconsistent with the calculation of marginal cost as MC=dTC/dQ for virtually all non-linear functions.
Variable cost	Variable costs are expenses that change in proportion to the activity of a business. Variable cost is the sum of marginal costs over all units produced. It can also be considered normal costs.
Diminishing returns	In economics, diminishing returns is the decrease in the marginal (per-unit) output of a production process as the amount of a single factor of production is increased, while the amounts of all other factors of production stay constant. The law of diminishing returns states that in all productive processes, adding more of one factor of production, while holding all others constant, will at some point yield lower per-unit returns. The law of diminishing returns does not imply that adding more of a factor will decrease the total production, a condition known as negative returns, though in fact this is common.
Marginal product	In economics and in particular neoclassical economics, the marginal product is the extra output that can be produced by using one more unit of the input (for instance, the difference in output when a firm's labor usage is increased from five to six units), assuming that the quantities of no other inputs to production change. The marginal product of a given input can be expressed as $$MP = \frac{\Delta Y}{\Delta X}$$ where ΔX is the change in the firm's use of the input (conventionally a one-unit change) and ΔY is the change in quantity of output produced. Note that the quantity Y of the 'product' is typically defined ignoring external costs and benefits.
Cost curve	In economics, a cost curve is a graph of the costs of production as a function of total quantity produced. In a free market economy, productively efficient firms use these curves to find the optimal point of production (minimising cost), and profit maximizing firms can use them to decide output quantities to achieve those aims.

Visit Cram101.com for full Practice Exams

Chapter 21. Costs and the Supply of Goods

CHAPTER HIGHLIGHTS & NOTES: KEY TERMS, PEOPLE, PLACES, CONCEPTS

Economies of scale	In microeconomics, economies of scale refers to the cost advantages that an enterprise obtains due to expansion. There are factors that cause a producer's average cost per unit to fall as the scale of output is increased. 'Economies of scale' is a long run concept and refers to reductions in unit cost as the size of a facility and the usage levels of other inputs increase.
Mass production	Mass production is the production of large amounts of standardized products, including and especially on assembly lines.
Sunk costs	In economics and business decision-making, sunk costs are retrospective (past) costs that have already been incurred and cannot be recovered. Sunk costs are sometimes contrasted with prospective costs, which are future costs that may be incurred or changed if an action is taken. Both retrospective and prospective costs may be either fixed (continuous for as long as the business is in operation and unaffected by output volume) or variable (dependent on volume) costs.

CHAPTER QUIZ: KEY TERMS, PEOPLE, PLACES, CONCEPTS

1. _____ is the production of large amounts of standardized products, including and especially on assembly lines.

    a. Mechanization
    b. Mass production
    c. Modelling of particle breakage
    d. North American Industry Classification System

2. In economics, the _____ is a historical inverse relationship between the rate of unemployment and the rate of inflation in an economy. Stated simply, the lower the unemployment in an economy, the higher the rate of inflation. While it has been observed that there is a stable short run tradeoff between unemployment and inflation, this has not been observed in the long run.

    a. Recession-proof job
    b. Reserve army of labour
    c. Phillips curve
    d. Technological unemployment

3. . A _____ is a natural resource with the ability to reproduce through biological or natural processes and replenished with the passage of time. _____s are part of our natural environment and form our eco-system.

    In 1962, within a report to the committee on natural resources which was forwarded to the President of the United States, Paul Weiss defined _____s as: 'The total range of living organisms providing man with food, fibers, drugs, etc...'.

    a. Sustainable yield

Visit Cram101.com for full Practice Exams

Chapter 21. Costs and the Supply of Goods

CHAPTER QUIZ: KEY TERMS, PEOPLE, PLACES, CONCEPTS

   b. Renewable resource
   c. Virginia school of political economy
   d. Missing square puzzle

4. In economics and finance, _____ is the change in total cost that arises when the quantity produced changes by one unit. That is, it is the cost of producing one more unit of a good. If the good being produced is infinitely divisible, so the size of a _____ will change with volume, as a non-linear and non-proportional cost function includes the following:•variable terms dependent to volume,•constant terms independent to volume and occurring with the respective lot size,•jump fix cost increase or decrease dependent to steps of volume increase.

    In practice the above definition of _____ as the change in total cost as a result of an increase in output of one unit is inconsistent with the calculation of _____ as MC=dTC/dQ for virtually all non-linear functions.

   a. Marginal product
   b. Marginal product of labor
   c. Marginal rate of technical substitution
   d. Marginal cost

5. An _____ is a tax levied on the income of individuals or businesses (corporations or other legal entities). Various _____ systems exist, with varying degrees of tax incidence. Income taxation can be progressive, proportional, or regressive.

   a. Income tax audit
   b. Income tax
   c. Inflation tax
   d. Installment sale

Visit Cram101.com for full Practice Exams

ANSWER KEY
Chapter 21. Costs and the Supply of Goods

1. b
2. c
3. b
4. d
5. b

You can take the complete Chapter Practice Test

for Chapter 21. Costs and the Supply of Goods
on all key terms, persons, places, and concepts.

Online 99 Cents

http://www.epub40.13.20514.21.cram101.com/

Use www.Cram101.com for all your study needs

including Cram101's online interactive problem solving labs in

chemistry, statistics, mathematics, and more.

Chapter 22. Price Takers and the Competitive Process

CHAPTER OUTLINE: KEY TERMS, PEOPLE, PLACES, CONCEPTS

- Great Depression
- Social security
- Demand curve
- Profit maximization
- Business cycle
- Phillips curve
- Experimental economics

CHAPTER HIGHLIGHTS & NOTES: KEY TERMS, PEOPLE, PLACES, CONCEPTS

Great Depression	The Great Depression was a severe worldwide economic depression in the decade preceding World War II. The timing of the Great Depression varied across nations, but in most countries it started in 1930 after the passage of the Smoot-Hawley Tariff bill (June 17), and lasted until the late 1930s or early 1940s. It was the longest, most widespread, and deepest depression of the 20th century. In the 21st century, the Great Depression is commonly used as an example of how far the world's economy can decline.
Social security	Social security is a concept enshrined in Article 22 of the Universal Declaration of Human Rights which states that Everyone, as a member of society, has the right to social security and is entitled to realization, through national effort and international co-operation and in accordance with the organization and resources of each State, of the economic, social and cultural rights indispensable for his dignity and the free development of his personality. In simple term, this means that the signatories agree that society in which a person lives should help them to develop and to make the most of all the advantages (culture, work, social welfare) which are offered to them in the country.

Chapter 22. Price Takers and the Competitive Process

CHAPTER HIGHLIGHTS & NOTES: KEY TERMS, PEOPLE, PLACES, CONCEPTS

Demand curve	In economics, the demand curve is the graph depicting the relationship between the price of a certain commodity and the amount of it that consumers are willing and able to purchase at that given price. It is a graphic representation of a demand schedule. The demand curve for all consumers together follows from the demand curve of every individual consumer: the individual demands at each price are added together.
Profit maximization	In economics, profit maximization is the short run or long run process by which a firm determines the price and output level that returns the greatest profit. There are several approaches to this problem. The total revenue-total cost perspective relies on the fact that profit equals revenue minus cost and focuses on minimizing this difference, and the marginal revenue-marginal cost perspective is based on the fact that total profit reaches its maximum point where marginal revenue equals marginal cost.
Business cycle	The term business cycle refers to economy-wide fluctuations in production or economic activity over several months or years. These fluctuations occur around a long-term growth trend, and typically involve shifts over time between periods of relatively rapid economic growth (an expansion or boom), and periods of relative stagnation or decline (a contraction or recession). Business cycles are usually measured by considering the growth rate of real gross domestic product.
Phillips curve	In economics, the Phillips curve is a historical inverse relationship between the rate of unemployment and the rate of inflation in an economy. Stated simply, the lower the unemployment in an economy, the higher the rate of inflation. While it has been observed that there is a stable short run tradeoff between unemployment and inflation, this has not been observed in the long run.
Experimental economics	Experimental economics is the application of experimental methods to study economic questions. Data collected in experiments are used to estimate effect size, test the validity of economic theories, and illuminate market mechanisms. Economic experiments usually use cash to motivate subjects, in order to mimic real-world incentives.

Chapter 22. Price Takers and the Competitive Process

CHAPTER QUIZ: KEY TERMS, PEOPLE, PLACES, CONCEPTS

1. _____ is the application of experimental methods to study economic questions. Data collected in experiments are used to estimate effect size, test the validity of economic theories, and illuminate market mechanisms. Economic experiments usually use cash to motivate subjects, in order to mimic real-world incentives.

    a. 15th century
    b. Reserve army of labour
    c. Structural unemployment
    d. Experimental economics

2. The _____ was a severe worldwide economic depression in the decade preceding World War II. The timing of the _____ varied across nations, but in most countries it started in 1930 after the passage of the Smoot-Hawley Tariff bill (June 17), and lasted until the late 1930s or early 1940s. It was the longest, most widespread, and deepest depression of the 20th century.

    In the 21st century, the _____ is commonly used as an example of how far the world's economy can decline.

    a. Bank Night
    b. Battle of Ballantyne Pier
    c. Great Depression
    d. Bloody Sunday

3. _____ is a concept enshrined in Article 22 of the Universal Declaration of Human Rights which states that Everyone, as a member of society, has the right to _____ and is entitled to realization, through national effort and international co-operation and in accordance with the organization and resources of each State, of the economic, social and cultural rights indispensable for his dignity and the free development of his personality. In simple term, this means that the signatories agree that society in which a person lives should help them to develop and to make the most of all the advantages (culture, work, social welfare) which are offered to them in the country.

    _____ may also refer to the action programs of government intended to promote the welfare of the population through assistance measures guaranteeing access to sufficient resources for food and shelter and to promote health and wellbeing for the population at large and potentially vulnerable segments such as children, the elderly, the sick and the unemployed.

    a. Social Security Agency
    b. Social security
    c. Structural adjustment loan
    d. Suits index

4. . In economics, the _____ is the graph depicting the relationship between the price of a certain commodity and the amount of it that consumers are willing and able to purchase at that given price. It is a graphic representation of a demand schedule. The _____ for all consumers together follows from the _____ of every individual consumer: the individual demands at each price are added together.

    a. Demand curve
    b. J curve

Visit Cram101.com for full Practice Exams

Chapter 22. Price Takers and the Competitive Process

CHAPTER QUIZ: KEY TERMS, PEOPLE, PLACES, CONCEPTS

    c. Kuznets curve
    d. Laffer curve

5. In economics, _____ is the short run or long run process by which a firm determines the price and output level that returns the greatest profit. There are several approaches to this problem. The total revenue-total cost perspective relies on the fact that profit equals revenue minus cost and focuses on minimizing this difference, and the marginal revenue-marginal cost perspective is based on the fact that total profit reaches its maximum point where marginal revenue equals marginal cost.

    a. Profit sharing
    b. Profitect
    c. Profit maximization
    d. Rate of profit

ANSWER KEY
Chapter 22. Price Takers and the Competitive Process

1. d
2. c
3. b
4. a
5. c

You can take the complete Chapter Practice Test

for Chapter 22. Price Takers and the Competitive Process
on all key terms, persons, places, and concepts.

Online 99 Cents

http://www.epub40.13.20514.22.cram101.com/

Use www.Cram101.com for all your study needs

including Cram101's online interactive problem solving labs in

chemistry, statistics, mathematics, and more.

Visit Cram101.com for full Practice Exams

Chapter 23. Price-Searcher Markets with Low Entry Barriers

CHAPTER OUTLINE: KEY TERMS, PEOPLE, PLACES, CONCEPTS

- Great Depression
- Monopolistic competition
- Renewable resource
- Marginal cost
- Contestable market
- Phillips curve
- Social security
- AD-AS model
- Advertising
- Price discrimination
- Entrepreneur
- Entrepreneurship
- Incentive
- Business cycle
- Business failure
- Free trade
- PayPal

Visit Cram101.com for full Practice Exams

Chapter 23. Price-Searcher Markets with Low Entry Barriers

CHAPTER HIGHLIGHTS & NOTES: KEY TERMS, PEOPLE, PLACES, CONCEPTS

Great Depression	The Great Depression was a severe worldwide economic depression in the decade preceding World War II. The timing of the Great Depression varied across nations, but in most countries it started in 1930 after the passage of the Smoot-Hawley Tariff bill (June 17), and lasted until the late 1930s or early 1940s. It was the longest, most widespread, and deepest depression of the 20th century. In the 21st century, the Great Depression is commonly used as an example of how far the world's economy can decline.
Monopolistic competition	Monopolistic competition is a type of imperfect competition such that one or two producers sell products that are differentiated from one another as goods but not perfect substitutes (such as from branding, quality, or location). In monopolistic competition, a firm takes the prices charged by its rivals as given and ignores the impact of its own prices on the prices of other firms. In a monopolistically competitive market, firms can behave like monopolies in the short run, including by using market power to generate profit.
Renewable resource	A renewable resource is a natural resource with the ability to reproduce through biological or natural processes and replenished with the passage of time. Renewable resources are part of our natural environment and form our eco-system. In 1962, within a report to the committee on natural resources which was forwarded to the President of the United States, Paul Weiss defined Renewable Resources as: 'The total range of living organisms providing man with food, fibers, drugs, etc...'.
Marginal cost	In economics and finance, marginal cost is the change in total cost that arises when the quantity produced changes by one unit. That is, it is the cost of producing one more unit of a good. If the good being produced is infinitely divisible, so the size of a marginal cost will change with volume, as a non-linear and non-proportional cost function includes the following:•variable terms dependent to volume,•constant terms independent to volume and occurring with the respective lot size,•jump fix cost increase or decrease dependent to steps of volume increase. In practice the above definition of marginal cost as the change in total cost as a result of an increase in output of one unit is inconsistent with the calculation of marginal cost as MC=dTC/dQ for virtually all non-linear functions.
Contestable market	In economics, the theory of contestable markets, associated primarily with its 1982 proponent William J. Baumol, holds that there exist markets served by a small number of firms, which are nevertheless characterized by competitive equilibria (and therefore desirable welfare outcomes) because of the existence of potential short-term entrants.

Chapter 23. Price-Searcher Markets with Low Entry Barriers

CHAPTER HIGHLIGHTS & NOTES: KEY TERMS, PEOPLE, PLACES, CONCEPTS

	A perfectly contestable market has three main features. It is a market that has -•No entry or exit barriers•No sunk costs•Access to the same level of technology (to incumbent firms and new entrants)
	Although, a perfectly contestable market is not possible in real life, therefore we talk about the degree of contestability of a market.
Phillips curve	In economics, the Phillips curve is a historical inverse relationship between the rate of unemployment and the rate of inflation in an economy. Stated simply, the lower the unemployment in an economy, the higher the rate of inflation. While it has been observed that there is a stable short run tradeoff between unemployment and inflation, this has not been observed in the long run.
Social security	Social security is a concept enshrined in Article 22 of the Universal Declaration of Human Rights which states that Everyone, as a member of society, has the right to social security and is entitled to realization, through national effort and international co-operation and in accordance with the organization and resources of each State, of the economic, social and cultural rights indispensable for his dignity and the free development of his personality. In simple term, this means that the signatories agree that society in which a person lives should help them to develop and to make the most of all the advantages (culture, work, social welfare) which are offered to them in the country.
	Social security may also refer to the action programs of government intended to promote the welfare of the population through assistance measures guaranteeing access to sufficient resources for food and shelter and to promote health and wellbeing for the population at large and potentially vulnerable segments such as children, the elderly, the sick and the unemployed.
AD-AS model	The AD-AS or Aggregate Demand-Aggregate Supply model is a macroeconomic model that explains price level and output through the relationship of aggregate demand and aggregate supply. It is based on the theory of John Maynard Keynes presented in his work The General Theory of Employment, Interest, and Money. It is one of the primary simplified representations in the modern field of macroeconomics, and is used by a broad array of economists, from libertarian, Monetarist supporters of laissez-faire, such as Milton Friedman to Post-Keynesian supporters of economic interventionism, such as Joan Robinson.
	The conventional 'aggregate supply and demand' model is, in actuality, a Keynesian visualization that has come to be a widely accepted image of the theory. The Classical supply and demand model, which is largely based on Say's Law, or that supply creates its own demand, depicts the aggregate supply curve as being vertical at all times (not just in the long-run)Modeling

Chapter 23. Price-Searcher Markets with Low Entry Barriers

CHAPTER HIGHLIGHTS & NOTES: KEY TERMS, PEOPLE, PLACES, CONCEPTS

	The AD/AS model is used to illustrate the Keynesian model of the business cycle. Movements of the two curves can be used to predict the effects that various exogenous events will have on two variables: real GDP and the price level. Furthermore, the model can be incorporated as a component in any of a variety of dynamic models (models of how variables like the price level and others evolve over time). The AD-AS model can be related to the Phillips curve model of wage or price inflation and unemployment.
Advertising	Advertising is a form of communication used to encourage or persuade an audience (viewers, readers or listeners. Sometimes a specific group of people). to continue or take some new action.
Price discrimination	Price discrimination are transacted at different prices from the same provider. In a theoretical market with perfect information, perfect substitutes, and no transaction costs or prohibition on secondary exchange to prevent arbitrage, price discrimination can only be a feature of monopolistic and oligopolistic markets, where market power can be exercised. Otherwise, the moment the seller tries to sell the same good at different prices, the buyer at the lower price can arbitrage by selling to the consumer buying at the higher price but with a tiny discount.
Entrepreneur	An entrepreneur is an enterprising individual who builds capital through risk and/or initiative. The term was originally a loanword from French and was first defined by the Irish-French economist Richard Cantillon. Entrepreneur in English is a term applied to a person who is willing to help launch a new venture or enterprise and accept full responsibility for the outcome.
Entrepreneurship	Entrepreneurship is the act of being an entrepreneur or 'one who undertakes innovations, finance and business acumen in an effort to transform innovations into economic goods'. This may result in new organizations or may be part of revitalizing mature organizations in response to a perceived opportunity. The most obvious form of entrepreneurship is that of starting new businesses (referred as Startup Company); however, in recent years, the term has been extended to include social and political forms of entrepreneurial activity.
Incentive	Since human beings are purposeful creatures, the study of incentive structures is central to the study of all economic activity (both in terms of individual decision-making and in terms of co-operation and competition within a larger institutional structure). Economic analysis, then, of the differences between societies (and between different organizations within a society) largely amounts to characterizing the differences in incentive structures faced by individuals involved in these collective efforts. Ultimately, incentives aim to provide value for money and contribute to organizational success.
Business cycle	The term business cycle refers to economy-wide fluctuations in production or economic activity over several months or years.

Chapter 23. Price-Searcher Markets with Low Entry Barriers

CHAPTER HIGHLIGHTS & NOTES: KEY TERMS, PEOPLE, PLACES, CONCEPTS

	These fluctuations occur around a long-term growth trend, and typically involve shifts over time between periods of relatively rapid economic growth (an expansion or boom), and periods of relative stagnation or decline (a contraction or recession).
	Business cycles are usually measured by considering the growth rate of real gross domestic product.
Business failure	Business failure refers to a company ceasing operations following its inability to make a profit or to bring in enough revenue to cover its expenses. A profitable business can fail if it does not generate adequate cash flow to meet expenses.
	Businesses can fail as a result of wars, recessions, high taxation, high interest rates, excessive regulations, management decisions, insufficient marketing, inability to compete with other similar businesses, or a lack of interest from the public in the business's offerings.
Free trade	Free trade is a policy by which a government does not discriminate against imports or interfere with exports by applying tariffs (to imports) or subsidies (to exports) or quotas. According to the law of comparative advantage the policy permits trading partners mutual gains from trade of goods and services.
	Under a free trade policy, prices emerge from supply and demand, and are the sole determinant of resource allocation.
PayPal	PayPal Inc.
	PayPal is a global e-commerce business allowing payments and money transfers to be made through the Internet. Online money transfers serve as electronic alternatives to paying with traditional paper methods, such as checks and money orders.
	Originally, a PayPal account could be funded with an electronic debit from a bank account or by a credit card at the payer's choice.

Visit Cram101.com for full Practice Exams

Chapter 23. Price-Searcher Markets with Low Entry Barriers

CHAPTER QUIZ: KEY TERMS, PEOPLE, PLACES, CONCEPTS

1. Since human beings are purposeful creatures, the study of _____ structures is central to the study of all economic activity (both in terms of individual decision-making and in terms of co-operation and competition within a larger institutional structure). Economic analysis, then, of the differences between societies (and between different organizations within a society) largely amounts to characterizing the differences in _____ structures faced by individuals involved in these collective efforts. Ultimately, _____s aim to provide value for money and contribute to organizational success.

    a. Incentive
    b. Indifference curve
    c. Isocost
    d. Isoelastic utility

2. _____ refers to a company ceasing operations following its inability to make a profit or to bring in enough revenue to cover its expenses. A profitable business can fail if it does not generate adequate cash flow to meet expenses.

    Businesses can fail as a result of wars, recessions, high taxation, high interest rates, excessive regulations, management decisions, insufficient marketing, inability to compete with other similar businesses, or a lack of interest from the public in the business's offerings.

    a. Business information
    b. Business license
    c. Business failure
    d. Business networking

3. In economics, the _____ is a historical inverse relationship between the rate of unemployment and the rate of inflation in an economy. Stated simply, the lower the unemployment in an economy, the higher the rate of inflation. While it has been observed that there is a stable short run tradeoff between unemployment and inflation, this has not been observed in the long run.

    a. Recession-proof job
    b. Reserve army of labour
    c. Phillips curve
    d. Technological unemployment

4. . In economics, the theory of _____s, associated primarily with its 1982 proponent William J. Baumol, holds that there exist markets served by a small number of firms, which are nevertheless characterized by competitive equilibria (and therefore desirable welfare outcomes) because of the existence of potential short-term entrants.

    A perfectly _____ has three main features. It is a market that has -•No entry or exit barriers•No sunk costs•Access to the same level of technology (to incumbent firms and new entrants)

    Although, a perfectly _____ is not possible in real life, therefore we talk about the degree of contestability of a market.

    a. Copyright law of the European Union
    b. Contestable market

c. De facto monopoly

Chapter 23. Price-Searcher Markets with Low Entry Barriers

CHAPTER QUIZ: KEY TERMS, PEOPLE, PLACES, CONCEPTS

5. A _____ is a natural resource with the ability to reproduce through biological or natural processes and replenished with the passage of time. _____s are part of our natural environment and form our eco-system.

   In 1962, within a report to the committee on natural resources which was forwarded to the President of the United States, Paul Weiss defined _____s as: 'The total range of living organisms providing man with food, fibers, drugs, etc...'.

   a. Renewable resource
   b. Private finance initiative
   c. Privatization
   d. Rule of three

ANSWER KEY
Chapter 23. Price-Searcher Markets with Low Entry Barriers

1. a
2. c
3. c
4. b
5. a

You can take the complete Chapter Practice Test

for Chapter 23. Price-Searcher Markets with Low Entry Barriers
on all key terms, persons, places, and concepts.

Online 99 Cents

http://www.epub40.13.20514.23.cram101.com/

Use www.Cram101.com for all your study needs

including Cram101's online interactive problem solving labs in

chemistry, statistics, mathematics, and more.

Chapter 24. Price-Searcher Markets with High Entry Barriers

CHAPTER OUTLINE: KEY TERMS, PEOPLE, PLACES, CONCEPTS

- Great Depression
- Affordable housing
- Economies of scale
- Alternatives
- Monopoly
- Renewable resource
- AD-AS model
- Profit maximization
- Interdependence
- Oligopoly
- Collusion
- Incentive
- Obstacle
- Government
- Uncertainty
- Social security
- Game theory
- Criticism
- Market power

Visit Cram101.com for full Practice Exams

Chapter 24. Price-Searcher Markets with High Entry Barriers

CHAPTER OUTLINE: KEY TERMS, PEOPLE, PLACES, CONCEPTS

- Rent-seeking
- Federal Trade Commission Act
- Labor relations
- Sherman Antitrust Act
- Natural monopoly
- Competitiveness

CHAPTER HIGHLIGHTS & NOTES: KEY TERMS, PEOPLE, PLACES, CONCEPTS

Great Depression	The Great Depression was a severe worldwide economic depression in the decade preceding World War II. The timing of the Great Depression varied across nations, but in most countries it started in 1930 after the passage of the Smoot-Hawley Tariff bill (June 17), and lasted until the late 1930s or early 1940s. It was the longest, most widespread, and deepest depression of the 20th century. In the 21st century, the Great Depression is commonly used as an example of how far the world's economy can decline.
Affordable housing	Affordable housing is a term used to describe dwelling units whose total housing costs for either rented or purchased unit, are deemed affordable to those that have a median household income. In Australia, the National Affordable Housing Summit Group developed their definition of affordable housing as housing which is 'reasonably adequate in standard and location for lower or middle income households and does not cost so much that a household is unlikely to be able to meet other basic needs on a sustainable basis.' In the United Kingdom affordable housing includes 'social rented and intermediate housing, provided to specified eligible households whose needs are not met by the market.' Most of the literature on affordable housing refers to a number of forms that exist along a continuum - from emergency shelters, to transitional housing, to non-market rental (also known as social or subsidized housing), to formal and informal rental, indigenous housing and ending with affordable home ownership.

Visit Cram101.com for full Practice Exams

Chapter 24. Price-Searcher Markets with High Entry Barriers

CHAPTER HIGHLIGHTS & NOTES: KEY TERMS, PEOPLE, PLACES, CONCEPTS

	The usage of the term housing affordability became widespread in the 1980s in Europe and North America. A growing body of literature found the term problematic.
Economies of scale	In microeconomics, economies of scale refers to the cost advantages that an enterprise obtains due to expansion. There are factors that cause a producer's average cost per unit to fall as the scale of output is increased. 'Economies of scale' is a long run concept and refers to reductions in unit cost as the size of a facility and the usage levels of other inputs increase.
Alternatives	Founded in 1994, Alternatives, Action and Communication Network for International Development, is a non-governmental, international solidarity organization based in Montreal, Quebec, Canada. Alternatives works to promote justice and equality amongst individuals and communities worldwide. Active in over 35 countries, Alternatives supports local, community-based initiatives working towards the greater economic, social, and political rights of people and communities affected by poverty, discrimination, exploitation, and violence.
Monopoly	A monopoly (from Greek monos μ?νος (alone or single) + polein πωλε?ν (to sell)) exists when a specific person or enterprise is the only supplier of a particular commodity (this contrasts with a monopsony which relates to a single entity's control of a market to purchase a good or service, and with oligopoly which consists of a few entities dominating an industry). Monopolies are thus characterized by a lack of economic competition to produce the good or service and a lack of viable substitute goods. The verb 'monopolize' refers to the process by which a company gains the ability to raise prices or exclude competitors.
Renewable resource	A renewable resource is a natural resource with the ability to reproduce through biological or natural processes and replenished with the passage of time. Renewable resources are part of our natural environment and form our eco-system. In 1962, within a report to the committee on natural resources which was forwarded to the President of the United States, Paul Weiss defined Renewable Resources as: 'The total range of living organisms providing man with food, fibers, drugs, etc...'.
AD-AS model	The AD-AS or Aggregate Demand-Aggregate Supply model is a macroeconomic model that explains price level and output through the relationship of aggregate demand and aggregate supply. It is based on the theory of John Maynard Keynes presented in his work The General Theory of Employment, Interest, and Money. It is one of the primary simplified representations in the modern field of macroeconomics, and is used by a broad array of economists, from libertarian, Monetarist supporters of laissez-faire, such as Milton Friedman to Post-Keynesian supporters of economic interventionism, such as Joan Robinson.

Chapter 24. Price-Searcher Markets with High Entry Barriers

CHAPTER HIGHLIGHTS & NOTES: KEY TERMS, PEOPLE, PLACES, CONCEPTS

	The conventional 'aggregate supply and demand' model is, in actuality, a Keynesian visualization that has come to be a widely accepted image of the theory. The Classical supply and demand model, which is largely based on Say's Law, or that supply creates its own demand, depicts the aggregate supply curve as being vertical at all times (not just in the long-run)Modeling
	The AD/AS model is used to illustrate the Keynesian model of the business cycle. Movements of the two curves can be used to predict the effects that various exogenous events will have on two variables: real GDP and the price level. Furthermore, the model can be incorporated as a component in any of a variety of dynamic models (models of how variables like the price level and others evolve over time). The AD-AS model can be related to the Phillips curve model of wage or price inflation and unemployment.
Profit maximization	In economics, profit maximization is the short run or long run process by which a firm determines the price and output level that returns the greatest profit. There are several approaches to this problem. The total revenue-total cost perspective relies on the fact that profit equals revenue minus cost and focuses on minimizing this difference, and the marginal revenue-marginal cost perspective is based on the fact that total profit reaches its maximum point where marginal revenue equals marginal cost.
Interdependence	Interdependence is a relationship in which each member is mutually dependent on the others. This concept differs from a dependence relationship, where some members are dependent and some are not.
	In an interdependent relationship, participants may be emotionally, economically, ecologically and/or morally reliant on and responsible to each other.
Oligopoly	An oligopoly is a market form in which a market or industry is dominated by a small number of sellers (oligopolists). Because there are few sellers, each oligopolist is likely to be aware of the actions of the others. The decisions of one firm influence, and are influenced by, the decisions of other firms.
Collusion	Collusion is an agreement between two or more persons, sometimes illegal and therefore secretive, to limit open competition by deceiving, misleading, or defrauding others of their legal rights, or to obtain an objective forbidden by law typically by defrauding or gaining an unfair advantage. It is an agreement among firms to divide the market, set prices, or limit production. It can involve 'wage fixing, kickbacks, or misrepresenting the independence of the relationship between the colluding parties'.

Chapter 24. Price-Searcher Markets with High Entry Barriers

CHAPTER HIGHLIGHTS & NOTES: KEY TERMS, PEOPLE, PLACES, CONCEPTS

Incentive	Since human beings are purposeful creatures, the study of incentive structures is central to the study of all economic activity (both in terms of individual decision-making and in terms of co-operation and competition within a larger institutional structure). Economic analysis, then, of the differences between societies (and between different organizations within a society) largely amounts to characterizing the differences in incentive structures faced by individuals involved in these collective efforts. Ultimately, incentives aim to provide value for money and contribute to organizational success.
Obstacle	An obstacle is an object, thing, action or situation that causes an obstruction. There are, therefore, different types of obstacles, which can be physical, economic, biopsychosocial, cultural, political, technological or even military. As physical obstacles, we can enumerate all those physical barriers that block the action and prevent the progress or the achievement of a concrete goal.
Government	Government, refers to the legislators, administrators, and arbitrators in the administrative bureaucracy who control a state at a given time, and to the system of government by which they are organized (Referred : More to govern than control). Government is the means by which state policy is enforced, as well as the mechanism for determining the policy of the state. A form of government, or form of state governance, refers to the set of political institutions by which a government of a state is organized.
Uncertainty	Uncertainty is a term used in subtly different ways in a number of fields, including physics, philosophy, statistics, economics, finance, insurance, psychology, sociology, engineering, and information science. It applies to predictions of future events, to physical measurements already made, or to the unknown. Although the terms are used in various ways among the general public, many specialists in decision theory, statistics and other quantitative fields have defined uncertainty, risk, and their measurement as:•Uncertainty: The lack of certainty, A state of having limited knowledge where it is impossible to exactly describe the existing state, a future outcome, or more than one possible outcome.•Measurement of Uncertainty: A set of possible states or outcomes where probabilities are assigned to each possible state or outcome - this also includes the application of a probability density function to continuous variables•Risk: A state of uncertainty where some possible outcomes have an undesired effect or significant loss.•Measurement of Risk: A set of measured uncertainties where some possible outcomes are losses, and the magnitudes of those losses - this also includes loss functions over continuous variables. Knightian uncertainty.

Visit Cram101.com for full Practice Exams

Chapter 24. Price-Searcher Markets with High Entry Barriers

CHAPTER HIGHLIGHTS & NOTES: KEY TERMS, PEOPLE, PLACES, CONCEPTS

Social security	Social security is a concept enshrined in Article 22 of the Universal Declaration of Human Rights which states that Everyone, as a member of society, has the right to social security and is entitled to realization, through national effort and international co-operation and in accordance with the organization and resources of each State, of the economic, social and cultural rights indispensable for his dignity and the free development of his personality. In simple term, this means that the signatories agree that society in which a person lives should help them to develop and to make the most of all the advantages (culture, work, social welfare) which are offered to them in the country. Social security may also refer to the action programs of government intended to promote the welfare of the population through assistance measures guaranteeing access to sufficient resources for food and shelter and to promote health and wellbeing for the population at large and potentially vulnerable segments such as children, the elderly, the sick and the unemployed.
Game theory	Game theory is the study of strategic decision making. More formally, it is 'the study of mathematical models of conflict and cooperation between intelligent rational decision-makers.' An alternative term suggested 'as a more descriptive name for the discipline' is interactive decision theory. Game theory is mainly used in economics, political science, and psychology, as well as logic and biology.
Criticism	Criticism is the practice of judging the merits and faults of something or someone in an intelligible way. •The judger is called 'the critic'.•To engage in criticism is 'to criticize'.•One specific item of criticism is called 'a criticism'. Criticism can be:•directed toward a person or an animal; at a group, authority or organization; at a specific behaviour; or at an object of some kind (an idea, a relationship, a condition, a process, or a thing).•personal (delivered directly from one person to another, in a personal capacity), or impersonal (expressing the view of an organization, and not aimed at anyone personally).•highly specific and detailed, or very abstract and general.•verbal (expressed in language) or non-verbal (expressed symbolically, or expressed through an action or a way of behaving).•explicit (the criticism is clearly stated) or implicit (a criticism is implied by what is being said, but it is not stated openly).•the result of critical thinking or spontaneous impulse. To criticize does not necessarily imply 'to find fault', but the word is often taken to mean the simple expression of an objection against prejudice, or a disapproval. Often criticism involves active disagreement, but it may only mean 'taking sides'.
Market power	In economics, market power is the ability of a firm to profitably raise the market price of a good or service over marginal cost. In perfectly competitive markets, market participants have no market power. A firm with market power can raise prices without losing its customers to competitors.

Chapter 24. Price-Searcher Markets with High Entry Barriers

CHAPTER HIGHLIGHTS & NOTES: KEY TERMS, PEOPLE, PLACES, CONCEPTS

Rent-seeking	In economics, rent-seeking is an attempt to obtain economic rent by manipulating the social or political environment in which economic activities occur, rather than by creating new wealth, for example, spending money on political lobbying in order to be given a share of wealth that has already been created. A famous example of rent-seeking is the limiting of access to lucrative occupations, as by medieval guilds or modern state certifications and licensures. People accused of rent seeking typically argue that they are indeed creating new wealth by improving quality controls, guaranteeing that charlatans do not prey on a gullible public, and preventing bubbles.
Federal Trade Commission Act	The Federal Trade Commission Act of 1914 (15 U.S.C §§ 41-58, as amended) started the Federal Trade Commission (FTC), a bipartisan body of five members appointed by the president of the United States for seven-year terms. This commission was authorized to issue 'cease and desist' orders to large corporations to curb unfair trade practices. This Act also gave more flexibility to the U.S. Congress for judicial matters.
Labor relations	Labor relations is the study and practice of managing unionized employment situations. In academia, labor relations is frequently a subarea within industrial relations, though scholars from many disciplines--including economics, sociology, history, law, and political science--also study labor unions and labor movements. In practice, labor relations is frequently a subarea within human resource management.
Sherman Antitrust Act	The Sherman Antitrust Act is a landmark federal statute on competition law passed by Congress in 1890. It prohibits certain business activities that reduce competition in the marketplace, and requires the United States federal government to investigate and pursue trusts, companies, and organizations suspected of being in violation. It was the first Federal statute to limit cartels and monopolies, and today still forms the basis for most antitrust litigation by the United States federal government. However, for the most part, politicians were unwilling to refer to the law until Theodore Roosevelt's presidency (1901-1909).
Natural monopoly	A monopoly describes a situation where all sales in a market are undertaken by a single firm. A natural monopoly by contrast is a condition on the cost-technology of an industry whereby it is most efficient (involving the lowest long-run average cost) for production to be concentrated in a single firm. In some cases, this gives the largest supplier in an industry, often the first supplier in a market, an overwhelming cost advantage over other actual and potential competitors.
Competitiveness	Competitiveness is a comparative concept of the ability and performance of a firm, sub-sector or country to sell and supply goods and services in a given market. The term may also be applied to markets, where it is used to refer to the extent to which the market structure may be regarded as perfectly competitive.

Chapter 24. Price-Searcher Markets with High Entry Barriers

CHAPTER QUIZ: KEY TERMS, PEOPLE, PLACES, CONCEPTS

1. The AD-AS or Aggregate Demand-Aggregate Supply model is a macroeconomic model that explains price level and output through the relationship of aggregate demand and aggregate supply. It is based on the theory of John Maynard Keynes presented in his work The General Theory of Employment, Interest, and Money. It is one of the primary simplified representations in the modern field of macroeconomics, and is used by a broad array of economists, from libertarian, Monetarist supporters of laissez-faire, such as Milton Friedman to Post-Keynesian supporters of economic interventionism, such as Joan Robinson.

    The conventional 'aggregate supply and demand' model is, in actuality, a Keynesian visualization that has come to be a widely accepted image of the theory. The Classical supply and demand model, which is largely based on Say's Law, or that supply creates its own demand, depicts the aggregate supply curve as being vertical at all times (not just in the long-run)Modeling

    The AD/AS model is used to illustrate the Keynesian model of the business cycle. Movements of the two curves can be used to predict the effects that various exogenous events will have on two variables: real GDP and the price level. Furthermore, the model can be incorporated as a component in any of a variety of dynamic models (models of how variables like the price level and others evolve over time). The _____ can be related to the Phillips curve model of wage or price inflation and unemployment.

    a. AD-IA model
    b. AK model
    c. E2m.org
    d. AD-AS model

2. The _____ was a severe worldwide economic depression in the decade preceding World War II. The timing of the _____ varied across nations, but in most countries it started in 1930 after the passage of the Smoot-Hawley Tariff bill (June 17), and lasted until the late 1930s or early 1940s. It was the longest, most widespread, and deepest depression of the 20th century.

    In the 21st century, the _____ is commonly used as an example of how far the world's economy can decline.

    a. Bank Night
    b. Great Depression
    c. Bennett buggy
    d. Bloody Sunday

3. . The _____ is a landmark federal statute on competition law passed by Congress in 1890. It prohibits certain business activities that reduce competition in the marketplace, and requires the United States federal government to investigate and pursue trusts, companies, and organizations suspected of being in violation. It was the first Federal statute to limit cartels and monopolies, and today still forms the basis for most antitrust litigation by the United States federal government. However, for the most part, politicians were unwilling to refer to the law until Theodore Roosevelt's presidency (1901-1909).

    a. Special 301 Report
    b. State monopoly capitalism
    c. Supracompetitive pricing

Chapter 24. Price-Searcher Markets with High Entry Barriers

CHAPTER QUIZ: KEY TERMS, PEOPLE, PLACES, CONCEPTS

4. _____ is the practice of judging the merits and faults of something or someone in an intelligible way. •The judger is called 'the critic'.•To engage in _____ is 'to criticize'.•One specific item of _____ is called 'a _____'.

    _____ can be:•directed toward a person or an animal; at a group, authority or organization; at a specific behaviour; or at an object of some kind (an idea, a relationship, a condition, a process, or a thing).•personal (delivered directly from one person to another, in a personal capacity), or impersonal (expressing the view of an organization, and not aimed at anyone personally).•highly specific and detailed, or very abstract and general.•verbal (expressed in language) or non-verbal (expressed symbolically, or expressed through an action or a way of behaving).•explicit (the _____ is clearly stated) or implicit (a _____ is implied by what is being said, but it is not stated openly).•the result of critical thinking or spontaneous impulse.

    To criticize does not necessarily imply 'to find fault', but the word is often taken to mean the simple expression of an objection against prejudice, or a disapproval. Often _____ involves active disagreement, but it may only mean 'taking sides'.

    a. Cross-cultural psychology
    b. Crowdsourcing
    c. Cultural jet lag
    d. Criticism

5. Founded in 1994, _____, Action and Communication Network for International Development, is a non-governmental, international solidarity organization based in Montreal, Quebec, Canada.

    _____ works to promote justice and equality amongst individuals and communities worldwide. Active in over 35 countries, _____ supports local, community-based initiatives working towards the greater economic, social, and political rights of people and communities affected by poverty, discrimination, exploitation, and violence.

    a. Alternatives
    b. UK Collaborative on Development Sciences
    c. Industrial production index
    d. Isocost

Visit Cram101.com for full Practice Exams

ANSWER KEY
Chapter 24. Price-Searcher Markets with High Entry Barriers

1. d
2. b
3. d
4. d
5. a

You can take the complete Chapter Practice Test

for Chapter 24. Price-Searcher Markets with High Entry Barriers

on all key terms, persons, places, and concepts.

Online 99 Cents

http://www.epub40.13.20514.24.cram101.com/

Use www.Cram101.com for all your study needs

including Cram101's online interactive problem solving labs in

chemistry, statistics, mathematics, and more.

Chapter 25. The Supply of and Demand for Productive Resources

CHAPTER OUTLINE: KEY TERMS, PEOPLE, PLACES, CONCEPTS

- _____ Renewable resource
- _____ Supply and demand
- _____ Product market
- _____ Great Depression
- _____ Human capital
- _____ Social security
- _____ Derived demand
- _____ Marginal product
- _____ Marginal revenue
- _____ AD-AS model

Visit Cram101.com for full Practice Exams

Chapter 25. The Supply of and Demand for Productive Resources

CHAPTER HIGHLIGHTS & NOTES: KEY TERMS, PEOPLE, PLACES, CONCEPTS

Renewable resource	A renewable resource is a natural resource with the ability to reproduce through biological or natural processes and replenished with the passage of time. Renewable resources are part of our natural environment and form our eco-system.
	In 1962, within a report to the committee on natural resources which was forwarded to the President of the United States, Paul Weiss defined Renewable Resources as: 'The total range of living organisms providing man with food, fibers, drugs, etc...'.
Supply and demand	Supply and demand is an economic model of price determination in a market. It concludes that in a competitive market, the unit price for a particular good will vary until it settles at a point where the quantity demanded by consumers (at current price) will equal the quantity supplied by producers (at current price), resulting in an economic equilibrium of price and quantity.
	The four basic laws of supply and demand are:•If demand increases and supply remains unchanged, then it leads to higher equilibrium price and higher quantity.•If demand decreases and supply remains unchanged, then it leads to lower equilibrium price and lower quantity.•If supply increases and demand remains unchanged, then it leads to lower equilibrium price and higher quantity.•If supply decreases and demand remains unchanged, then it leads to higher equilibrium price and lower quantity.Graphical representation of supply and demand
	Although it is normal to regard the quantity demanded and the quantity supplied as functions of the price of the good, the standard graphical representation, usually attributed to Alfred Marshall, has price on the vertical axis and quantity on the horizontal axis, the opposite of the standard convention for the representation of a mathematical function.
Product market	Product market is a mechanism that allows people to easily buy and sell products. Services are often included in the scope of the term. Product market regulation is an economic term that describes restrictions in the market.
Great Depression	The Great Depression was a severe worldwide economic depression in the decade preceding World War II. The timing of the Great Depression varied across nations, but in most countries it started in 1930 after the passage of the Smoot-Hawley Tariff bill (June 17), and lasted until the late 1930s or early 1940s. It was the longest, most widespread, and deepest depression of the 20th century.
	In the 21st century, the Great Depression is commonly used as an example of how far the world's economy can decline.
Human capital	Human capital is the stock of competencies, knowledge, social and personality attributes, including creativity, embodied in the ability to perform labor so as to produce economic value.

Visit Cram101.com for full Practice Exams

Chapter 25. The Supply of and Demand for Productive Resources

CHAPTER HIGHLIGHTS & NOTES: KEY TERMS, PEOPLE, PLACES, CONCEPTS

	It is an aggregate economic view of the human being acting within economies, which is an attempt to capture the social, biological, cultural and psychological complexity as they interact in explicit and/or economic transactions.
	It was assumed in early economic theories, reflecting the context in which the secondary sector of the economy was producing much more than the tertiary sector was able to produce at the time in most countries - to be a fungible resource, homogeneous, and easily interchangeable, and it was referred to simply as workforce or labor, one of three factors of production (the others being land, and assumed-interchangeable assets of money and physical equipment).
Social security	Social security is a concept enshrined in Article 22 of the Universal Declaration of Human Rights which states that Everyone, as a member of society, has the right to social security and is entitled to realization, through national effort and international co-operation and in accordance with the organization and resources of each State, of the economic, social and cultural rights indispensable for his dignity and the free development of his personality. In simple term, this means that the signatories agree that society in which a person lives should help them to develop and to make the most of all the advantages (culture, work, social welfare) which are offered to them in the country.
	Social security may also refer to the action programs of government intended to promote the welfare of the population through assistance measures guaranteeing access to sufficient resources for food and shelter and to promote health and wellbeing for the population at large and potentially vulnerable segments such as children, the elderly, the sick and the unemployed.
Derived demand	Derived demand is a term in economics, where demand for one good or service occurs as a result of the demand for another intermediate/ final good or service. This may occur as the former is a part of production of the second. For example, demand for coal leads to derived demand for mining, as coal must be mined for coal to be consumed.
Marginal product	In economics and in particular neoclassical economics, the marginal product is the extra output that can be produced by using one more unit of the input (for instance, the difference in output when a firm's labor usage is increased from five to six units), assuming that the quantities of no other inputs to production change. The marginal product of a given input can be expressed as $$MP = \frac{\Delta Y}{\Delta X}$$ where ΔX is the change in the firm's use of the input (conventionally a one-unit change) and ΔY is the change in quantity of output produced. Note that the quantity Y of the 'product' is typically defined ignoring external costs and benefits.

Chapter 25. The Supply of and Demand for Productive Resources

CHAPTER HIGHLIGHTS & NOTES: KEY TERMS, PEOPLE, PLACES, CONCEPTS

Marginal revenue	In microeconomics, marginal revenue is the additional revenue that will be generated by increasing product sales by 1 unit. It can also be described as the Unit Revenue the last item sold has generated for the firm. In a perfectly competitive market, the additional revenue generated by selling an additional unit of a good is equal to price the firm is able to charge the buyer of the good.
AD-AS model	The AD-AS or Aggregate Demand-Aggregate Supply model is a macroeconomic model that explains price level and output through the relationship of aggregate demand and aggregate supply. It is based on the theory of John Maynard Keynes presented in his work The General Theory of Employment, Interest, and Money. It is one of the primary simplified representations in the modern field of macroeconomics, and is used by a broad array of economists, from libertarian, Monetarist supporters of laissez-faire, such as Milton Friedman to Post-Keynesian supporters of economic interventionism, such as Joan Robinson. The conventional 'aggregate supply and demand' model is, in actuality, a Keynesian visualization that has come to be a widely accepted image of the theory. The Classical supply and demand model, which is largely based on Say's Law, or that supply creates its own demand, depicts the aggregate supply curve as being vertical at all times (not just in the long-run)Modeling The AD/AS model is used to illustrate the Keynesian model of the business cycle. Movements of the two curves can be used to predict the effects that various exogenous events will have on two variables: real GDP and the price level. Furthermore, the model can be incorporated as a component in any of a variety of dynamic models (models of how variables like the price level and others evolve over time). The AD-AS model can be related to the Phillips curve model of wage or price inflation and unemployment.

Chapter 25. The Supply of and Demand for Productive Resources

CHAPTER QUIZ: KEY TERMS, PEOPLE, PLACES, CONCEPTS

1. _____ is an economic model of price determination in a market. It concludes that in a competitive market, the unit price for a particular good will vary until it settles at a point where the quantity demanded by consumers (at current price) will equal the quantity supplied by producers (at current price), resulting in an economic equilibrium of price and quantity.

   The four basic laws of _____ are:•If demand increases and supply remains unchanged, then it leads to higher equilibrium price and higher quantity.•If demand decreases and supply remains unchanged, then it leads to lower equilibrium price and lower quantity.•If supply increases and demand remains unchanged, then it leads to lower equilibrium price and higher quantity.•If supply decreases and demand remains unchanged, then it leads to higher equilibrium price and lower quantity.Graphical representation of _____

   Although it is normal to regard the quantity demanded and the quantity supplied as functions of the price of the good, the standard graphical representation, usually attributed to Alfred Marshall, has price on the vertical axis and quantity on the horizontal axis, the opposite of the standard convention for the representation of a mathematical function.

   a. 15th century
   b. Supply and demand
   c. Great Horde
   d. Muradiye Complex

2. In economics and in particular neoclassical economics, the _____ is the extra output that can be produced by using one more unit of the input (for instance, the difference in output when a firm's labor usage is increased from five to six units), assuming that the quantities of no other inputs to production change. The _____ of a given input can be expressed as $MP = \dfrac{\Delta Y}{\Delta X}$

   where ΔX is the change in the firm's use of the input (conventionally a one-unit change) and ΔY is the change in quantity of output produced. Note that the quantity Y of the 'product' is typically defined ignoring external costs and benefits.

   a. Marginal product
   b. Marginal rate of technical substitution
   c. Means of production
   d. Multifactor productivity

3. . The _____ was a severe worldwide economic depression in the decade preceding World War II. The timing of the _____ varied across nations, but in most countries it started in 1930 after the passage of the Smoot-Hawley Tariff bill (June 17), and lasted until the late 1930s or early 1940s. It was the longest, most widespread, and deepest depression of the 20th century.

   In the 21st century, the _____ is commonly used as an example of how far the world's economy can decline.

   a. Bank Night
   b. Great Depression
   c. Bennett buggy

Chapter 25. The Supply of and Demand for Productive Resources

CHAPTER QUIZ: KEY TERMS, PEOPLE, PLACES, CONCEPTS

4. The AD-AS or Aggregate Demand-Aggregate Supply model is a macroeconomic model that explains price level and output through the relationship of aggregate demand and aggregate supply. It is based on the theory of John Maynard Keynes presented in his work The General Theory of Employment, Interest, and Money. It is one of the primary simplified representations in the modern field of macroeconomics, and is used by a broad array of economists, from libertarian, Monetarist supporters of laissez-faire, such as Milton Friedman to Post-Keynesian supporters of economic interventionism, such as Joan Robinson.

The conventional 'aggregate supply and demand' model is, in actuality, a Keynesian visualization that has come to be a widely accepted image of the theory. The Classical supply and demand model, which is largely based on Say's Law, or that supply creates its own demand, depicts the aggregate supply curve as being vertical at all times (not just in the long-run)Modeling

The AD/AS model is used to illustrate the Keynesian model of the business cycle. Movements of the two curves can be used to predict the effects that various exogenous events will have on two variables: real GDP and the price level. Furthermore, the model can be incorporated as a component in any of a variety of dynamic models (models of how variables like the price level and others evolve over time). The _____ can be related to the Phillips curve model of wage or price inflation and unemployment.

   a. AD-IA model
   b. AK model
   c. AD-AS model
   d. Edgeworth box

5. _____ is a concept enshrined in Article 22 of the Universal Declaration of Human Rights which states that Everyone, as a member of society, has the right to _____ and is entitled to realization, through national effort and international co-operation and in accordance with the organization and resources of each State, of the economic, social and cultural rights indispensable for his dignity and the free development of his personality. In simple term, this means that the signatories agree that society in which a person lives should help them to develop and to make the most of all the advantages (culture, work, social welfare) which are offered to them in the country.

_____ may also refer to the action programs of government intended to promote the welfare of the population through assistance measures guaranteeing access to sufficient resources for food and shelter and to promote health and wellbeing for the population at large and potentially vulnerable segments such as children, the elderly, the sick and the unemployed.

   a. Social security
   b. Social welfare function
   c. Structural adjustment loan
   d. Suits index

ANSWER KEY
Chapter 25. The Supply of and Demand for Productive Resources

1. b
2. a
3. b
4. c
5. a

You can take the complete Chapter Practice Test

for Chapter 25. The Supply of and Demand for Productive Resources

on all key terms, persons, places, and concepts.

Online 99 Cents

http://www.epub40.13.20514.25.cram101.com/

Use www.Cram101.com for all your study needs

including Cram101's online interactive problem solving labs in

chemistry, statistics, mathematics, and more.

Visit Cram101.com for full Practice Exams

Chapter 26. Earnings, Productivity, and the Job Market

CHAPTER OUTLINE: KEY TERMS, PEOPLE, PLACES, CONCEPTS

- Income tax
- Kyoto Protocol
- Tax credit
- Social security
- Human capital
- GDP deflator
- Employment discrimination
- Total cost
- Wage
- Productivity
- Automation

Visit Cram101.com for full Practice Exams

Chapter 26. Earnings, Productivity, and the Job Market

CHAPTER HIGHLIGHTS & NOTES: KEY TERMS, PEOPLE, PLACES, CONCEPTS

Income tax	An income tax is a tax levied on the income of individuals or businesses (corporations or other legal entities). Various income tax systems exist, with varying degrees of tax incidence. Income taxation can be progressive, proportional, or regressive.
Kyoto Protocol	The Kyoto Protocol is a protocol to the United Nations Framework Convention on Climate Change (UNFCCC or FCCC), aimed at fighting global warming. The UNFCCC is an international environmental treaty with the goal of achieving the 'stabilisation of greenhouse gas concentrations in the atmosphere at a level that would prevent dangerous anthropogenic interference with the climate system.' The Protocol was initially adopted on 11 December 1997 in Kyoto, Japan, and entered into force on 16 February 2005. As of September 2011, 191 states have signed and ratified the protocol. The only remaining signatory not to have ratified the protocol is the United States.
Tax credit	A tax credit is a sum deducted from the total amount a taxpayer owes to the state. A tax credit may be granted for various types of taxes, such as an income tax, property tax, or VAT. It may be granted in recognition of taxes already paid, as a subsidy, or to encourage investment or other behaviors. In some systems tax credits are 'refundable' to the extent they exceed the relevant tax.
Social security	Social security is a concept enshrined in Article 22 of the Universal Declaration of Human Rights which states that Everyone, as a member of society, has the right to social security and is entitled to realization, through national effort and international co-operation and in accordance with the organization and resources of each State, of the economic, social and cultural rights indispensable for his dignity and the free development of his personality. In simple term, this means that the signatories agree that society in which a person lives should help them to develop and to make the most of all the advantages (culture, work, social welfare) which are offered to them in the country. Social security may also refer to the action programs of government intended to promote the welfare of the population through assistance measures guaranteeing access to sufficient resources for food and shelter and to promote health and wellbeing for the population at large and potentially vulnerable segments such as children, the elderly, the sick and the unemployed.
Human capital	Human capital is the stock of competencies, knowledge, social and personality attributes, including creativity, embodied in the ability to perform labor so as to produce economic value. It is an aggregate economic view of the human being acting within economies, which is an attempt to capture the social, biological, cultural and psychological complexity as they interact in explicit and/or economic transactions.

Visit Cram101.com for full Practice Exams

Chapter 26. Earnings, Productivity, and the Job Market

CHAPTER HIGHLIGHTS & NOTES: KEY TERMS, PEOPLE, PLACES, CONCEPTS

GDP deflator	In economics, the GDP deflator is a measure of the level of prices of all new, domestically produced, final goods and services in an economy. GDP stands for gross domestic product, the total value of all final goods and services produced within that economy during a specified period. Measurement in national accounts
	In most systems of national accounts the GDP deflator measures the ratio of nominal GDP to the real measure of GDP. The formula used to calculate the deflator is: $$\text{GDP deflator} = \frac{\text{Nominal GDP}}{\text{Real GDP}} \times 100$$
	Dividing the nominal GDP by the GDP deflator and multiplying it by 100 would then give the figure for real GDP, hence deflating the nominal GDP into a real measure.
Employment discrimination	Employment discrimination is discrimination in hiring, promotion, job assignment, termination, and compensation. It includes various types of harassment.
	Many jurisdictions prohibit some types of employment discrimination, often by forbidding discrimination based on certain traits ('protected categories').
Total cost	In economics, and cost accounting, total cost describes the total economic cost of production and is made up of variable costs, which vary according to the quantity of a good produced and include inputs such as labor and raw materials, plus fixed costs, which are independent of the quantity of a good produced and include inputs (capital) that cannot be varied in the short term, such as buildings and machinery. Total cost in economics includes the total opportunity cost of each factor of production as part of its fixed or variable costs.
	The rate at which total cost changes as the amount produced changes is called marginal cost.
Wage	A wage is a compensation, usually financial, received by workers in exchange for their labor.
	Compensation in terms of wages is given to workers and compensation in terms of salary is given to employees. Compensation is a monetary benefit given to employees in return for the services provided by them.
Productivity	Productivity is a measure of the efficiency of production. Productivity is a ratio of production output to what is required to produce it (inputs). The measure of productivity is defined as a total output per one unit of a total input.
Automation	Automation is the use of control systems and information technologies to reduce the need for human work in the production of goods and services.

Chapter 26. Earnings, Productivity, and the Job Market

CHAPTER HIGHLIGHTS & NOTES: KEY TERMS, PEOPLE, PLACES, CONCEPTS

In the scope of industrialisation, automation is a step beyond mechanisation. Whereas mechanisation provides human operators with machinery to assist them with the muscular requirements of work, automation greatly decreases the need for human sensory and mental requirements as well.

CHAPTER QUIZ: KEY TERMS, PEOPLE, PLACES, CONCEPTS

1. A _____ is a sum deducted from the total amount a taxpayer owes to the state. A _____ may be granted for various types of taxes, such as an income tax, property tax, or VAT. It may be granted in recognition of taxes already paid, as a subsidy, or to encourage investment or other behaviors. In some systems _____s are 'refundable' to the extent they exceed the relevant tax.

   a. Tax cut
   b. Tax credit
   c. Tax deferral
   d. Tax expense

2. An _____ is a tax levied on the income of individuals or businesses (corporations or other legal entities). Various _____ systems exist, with varying degrees of tax incidence. Income taxation can be progressive, proportional, or regressive.

   a. Income tax audit
   b. Indirect tax
   c. Income tax
   d. Installment sale

3. _____ is a measure of the efficiency of production. _____ is a ratio of production output to what is required to produce it (inputs). The measure of _____ is defined as a total output per one unit of a total input.

   a. Productivity Alpha
   b. Productivity
   c. Productivity model
   d. Productivity world

4. . The _____ is a protocol to the United Nations Framework Convention on Climate Change (UNFCCC or FCCC), aimed at fighting global warming. The UNFCCC is an international environmental treaty with the goal of achieving the 'stabilisation of greenhouse gas concentrations in the atmosphere at a level that would prevent dangerous anthropogenic interference with the climate system.'

The Protocol was initially adopted on 11 December 1997 in Kyoto, Japan, and entered into force on 16 February 2005. As of September 2011, 191 states have signed and ratified the protocol.

Chapter 26. Earnings, Productivity, and the Job Market

Visit Cram101.com for full Practice Exams

The only remaining signatory not to have ratified the protocol is the United States.

a. The London Accord
b. Marginal abatement cost
c. Kyoto Protocol
d. Reducing Emissions from Deforestation and Forest Degradation

5. _____ is a concept enshrined in Article 22 of the Universal Declaration of Human Rights which states that Everyone, as a member of society, has the right to _____ and is entitled to realization, through national effort and international co-operation and in accordance with the organization and resources of each State, of the economic, social and cultural rights indispensable for his dignity and the free development of his personality. In simple term, this means that the signatories agree that society in which a person lives should help them to develop and to make the most of all the advantages (culture, work, social welfare) which are offered to them in the country.

_____ may also refer to the action programs of government intended to promote the welfare of the population through assistance measures guaranteeing access to sufficient resources for food and shelter and to promote health and wellbeing for the population at large and potentially vulnerable segments such as children, the elderly, the sick and the unemployed.

a. Social Security Agency
b. Social welfare function
c. Social security
d. Suits index

ANSWER KEY
Chapter 26. Earnings, Productivity, and the Job Market

1. b
2. c
3. b
4. c
5. c

You can take the complete Chapter Practice Test

for Chapter 26. Earnings, Productivity, and the Job Market
on all key terms, persons, places, and concepts.

Online 99 Cents

http://www.epub40.13.20514.26.cram101.com/

Use www.Cram101.com for all your study needs including Cram101's online interactive problem solving labs in chemistry, statistics, mathematics, and more.

Visit Cram101.com for full Practice Exams

Chapter 27. Investment, the Capital Market, and the Wealth of Nations

CHAPTER OUTLINE: KEY TERMS, PEOPLE, PLACES, CONCEPTS

- Capital market
- Investment
- Phillips curve
- Interest rate
- Time preference
- Inflation
- Inflation rate
- Real interest rate
- Discounting
- Present value
- Income tax
- Tax credit
- Human capital
- Africa Source
- Entrepreneurship
- Product market
- Profit
- Uncertainty
- Uncertainty principle

Visit Cram101.com for full Practice Exams

Chapter 27. Investment, the Capital Market, and the Wealth of Nations

CHAPTER OUTLINE: KEY TERMS, PEOPLE, PLACES, CONCEPTS

	Economic growth
	Investor
	Fannie Mae
	Crony capitalism
	Mortgage loan
	Regulation

CHAPTER HIGHLIGHTS & NOTES: KEY TERMS, PEOPLE, PLACES, CONCEPTS

Capital market	A capital market is a market for securities (debt or equity), where business enterprises (companies) and governments can raise long-term funds. It is defined as a market in which money is provided for periods longer than a year,Sullivan, arthur; Steven M. Sheffrin (2003). Economics: Principles in action.
Investment	Investment has different meanings in finance and economics. Finance investment is putting money into something with the expectation of gain, that upon thorough analysis, has a high degree of security for the principal amount, as well as security of return, within an expected period of time. In contrast putting money into something with an expectation of gain without thorough analysis, without security of principal, and without security of return is speculation or gambling.
Phillips curve	In economics, the Phillips curve is a historical inverse relationship between the rate of unemployment and the rate of inflation in an economy. Stated simply, the lower the unemployment in an economy, the higher the rate of inflation. While it has been observed that there is a stable short run tradeoff between unemployment and inflation, this has not been observed in the long run.
Interest rate	An interest rate is the rate at which interest is paid by a borrower for the use of money that they borrow from a lender.

Visit Cram101.com for full Practice Exams

Chapter 27. Investment, the Capital Market, and the Wealth of Nations

CHAPTER HIGHLIGHTS & NOTES: KEY TERMS, PEOPLE, PLACES, CONCEPTS

	For example, a small company borrows capital from a bank to buy new assets for their business, and in return the lender receives interest at a predetermined interest rate for deferring the use of funds and instead lending it to the borrower. Interest rates are normally expressed as a percentage of the principal for a period of one year.
Time preference	In economics, time preference pertains to how large a premium a consumer places on enjoyment nearer in time over more remote enjoyment. There is no absolute distinction that separates 'high' and 'low' time preference, only comparisons with others either individually or in aggregate. Someone with a high time preference is focused substantially on his well-being in the present and the immediate future relative to the average person, while someone with low time preference places more emphasis than average on their well-being in the further future.
Inflation	In economics, inflation is a rise in the general level of prices of goods and services in an economy over a period of time. When the general price level rises, each unit of currency buys fewer goods and services. Consequently, inflation also reflects an erosion in the purchasing power of money - a loss of real value in the internal medium of exchange and unit of account in the economy.
Inflation rate	In economics, the inflation rate is a measure of inflation, or the rate of increase of a price index such as the consumer price index. It is the percentage rate of change in price level over time, usually one year. The rate of decrease in the purchasing power of money is approximately equal.
Real interest rate	The 'real interest rate' is the rate of interest an investor expects to receive after allowing for inflation. It can be described more formally by the Fisher equation, which states that the real interest rate is approximately the nominal interest rate minus the inflation rate. If, for example, an investor were able to lock in a 5% interest rate for the coming year and anticipated a 2% rise in prices, he would expect to earn a real interest rate of 3%.
Discounting	Discounting is a financial mechanism in which a debtor obtains the right to delay payments to a creditor, for a defined period of time, in exchange for a charge or fee. Essentially, the party that owes money in the present purchases the right to delay the payment until some future date. The discount, or charge, is simply the difference between the original amount owed in the present and the amount that has to be paid in the future to settle the debt.
Present value	Present value, is the value on a given date of a payment or series of payments made at other times. If the payments are in the future, they are discounted to reflect the time value of money and other factors such as investment risk.

Visit Cram101.com for full Practice Exams

Chapter 27. Investment, the Capital Market, and the Wealth of Nations

CHAPTER HIGHLIGHTS & NOTES: KEY TERMS, PEOPLE, PLACES, CONCEPTS

Income tax	An income tax is a tax levied on the income of individuals or businesses (corporations or other legal entities). Various income tax systems exist, with varying degrees of tax incidence. Income taxation can be progressive, proportional, or regressive.
Tax credit	A tax credit is a sum deducted from the total amount a taxpayer owes to the state. A tax credit may be granted for various types of taxes, such as an income tax, property tax, or VAT. It may be granted in recognition of taxes already paid, as a subsidy, or to encourage investment or other behaviors. In some systems tax credits are 'refundable' to the extent they exceed the relevant tax.
Human capital	Human capital is the stock of competencies, knowledge, social and personality attributes, including creativity, embodied in the ability to perform labor so as to produce economic value. It is an aggregate economic view of the human being acting within economies, which is an attempt to capture the social, biological, cultural and psychological complexity as they interact in explicit and/or economic transactions. It was assumed in early economic theories, reflecting the context in which the secondary sector of the economy was producing much more than the tertiary sector was able to produce at the time in most countries - to be a fungible resource, homogeneous, and easily interchangeable, and it was referred to simply as workforce or labor, one of three factors of production (the others being land, and assumed-interchangeable assets of money and physical equipment).
Africa Source	Africa Source is the name for a series of events, two of which have been held so far, in 2004 and 2006, at Namibia and Uganda respectively. These are held to promote the use of Free/Libre and Open Source Software (FLOSS) among non-profit and non-governmental organisations. Africa Source is part of the wider 'Source Camps' organised by Tactical Technology Collective (Tacticaltech.org) and its partners, and is also linked to the Asia Source and other parallel events held elsewhere in the 'developing' world.
Entrepreneurship	Entrepreneurship is the act of being an entrepreneur or 'one who undertakes innovations, finance and business acumen in an effort to transform innovations into economic goods'. This may result in new organizations or may be part of revitalizing mature organizations in response to a perceived opportunity. The most obvious form of entrepreneurship is that of starting new businesses (referred as Startup Company); however, in recent years, the term has been extended to include social and political forms of entrepreneurial activity.
Product market	Product market is a mechanism that allows people to easily buy and sell products. Services are often included in the scope of the term. Product market regulation is an economic term that describes restrictions in the market.
Profit	In neoclassical microeconomic theory, the term profit has two related but distinct meanings.

Chapter 27. Investment, the Capital Market, and the Wealth of Nations

CHAPTER HIGHLIGHTS & NOTES: KEY TERMS, PEOPLE, PLACES, CONCEPTS

	Normal profit represents the total opportunity costs (both explicit and implicit) of a venture to an investor, whilst economic profit (also abnormal, pure, supernormal or excess profit, as the case may be monopoly or oligopoly profit) is, at least in the neoclassical microeconomic theory which dominates modern economics, the difference between a firm's total revenue and all costs (including normal profit). A related concept, sometimes considered synonymous in certain contexts, is that of economic rent.
Uncertainty	Uncertainty is a term used in subtly different ways in a number of fields, including physics, philosophy, statistics, economics, finance, insurance, psychology, sociology, engineering, and information science. It applies to predictions of future events, to physical measurements already made, or to the unknown.
	Although the terms are used in various ways among the general public, many specialists in decision theory, statistics and other quantitative fields have defined uncertainty, risk, and their measurement as:•Uncertainty: The lack of certainty, A state of having limited knowledge where it is impossible to exactly describe the existing state, a future outcome, or more than one possible outcome.•Measurement of Uncertainty: A set of possible states or outcomes where probabilities are assigned to each possible state or outcome - this also includes the application of a probability density function to continuous variables•Risk: A state of uncertainty where some possible outcomes have an undesired effect or significant loss.•Measurement of Risk: A set of measured uncertainties where some possible outcomes are losses, and the magnitudes of those losses - this also includes loss functions over continuous variables.
	Knightian uncertainty.
Uncertainty principle	In quantum mechanics, the uncertainty principle is any of a variety of mathematical inequalities asserting a fundamental limit on the precision with which certain pairs of physical properties of a particle, such as position x and momentum p, can be simultaneously known. The more precisely the position of some particle is determined, the less precisely its momentum can be known, and vice versa. The original heuristic argument that such a limit should exist was given by Werner Heisenberg in 1927. A more formal inequality relating the standard deviation of position σ_x and the standard deviation of momentum σ_p was derived by Kennard later that year (and independently by Weyl in 1928), $$\sigma_x \sigma_p \geq \frac{\hbar}{2}.$$ where h is the reduced Planck constant.
Economic growth	Economic growth is the increase in the amount of the goods and services produced by an economy over time. It is conventionally measured as the percent rate of increase in real gross domestic product, or real GDP. Growth is usually calculated in real terms, i.e.

Chapter 27. Investment, the Capital Market, and the Wealth of Nations

CHAPTER HIGHLIGHTS & NOTES: KEY TERMS, PEOPLE, PLACES, CONCEPTS

	inflation-adjusted terms, in order to net out the effect of inflation on the price of the goods and services produced. In economics, 'economic growth' or 'economic growth theory' typically refers to growth of potential output, i.e., production at 'full employment,' which is caused by growth in aggregate demand or observed output.
Investor	An investor is a party that makes an investment into one or more categories of assets --- equity, debt securities, real estate, currency, commodity, derivatives such as put and call options, etc. --- with the objective of making a profit. This definition makes no distinction between those in the primary and secondary markets.
Fannie Mae	The Federal National Mortgage Association (FNMA; OTCQB: FNMA), commonly known as Fannie Mae, was founded in 1938 during the Great Depression as part of the New Deal. It is a government-sponsored enterprise (GSE), though it has been a publicly traded company since 1968. The corporation's purpose is to expand the secondary mortgage market by securitizing mortgages in the form of mortgage-backed securities (MBS), allowing lenders to reinvest their assets into more lending and in effect increasing the number of lenders in the mortgage market by reducing the reliance on thrifts. The Federal National Mortgage Association (FNMA), colloquially known as Fannie Mae, was established in 1938 by amendments to the National Housing Act after the Great Depression as part of Franklin Delano Roosevelt's New Deal.
Crony capitalism	Crony capitalism is a term describing an economy in which success in business depends on close relationships between business people and government officials. It may be exhibited by favoritism in the distribution of legal permits, government grants, special tax breaks, and so forth. Crony capitalism is believed to arise when political cronyism spills over into the business world; self-serving friendships and family ties between businessmen and the government influence the economy and society to the extent that it corrupts public-serving economic and political ideals.
Mortgage loan	A mortgage loan is a loan secured by real property through the use of a mortgage note which evidences the existence of the loan and the encumbrance of that realty through the granting of a mortgage which secures the loan. However, the word mortgage alone, in everyday usage, is most often used to mean mortgage loan. The word mortgage is a Law French term meaning 'death contract,' meaning that the pledge ends (dies) when either the obligation is fulfilled or the property is taken through foreclosure.

Chapter 27. Investment, the Capital Market, and the Wealth of Nations

CHAPTER HIGHLIGHTS & NOTES: KEY TERMS, PEOPLE, PLACES, CONCEPTS

Regulation	Regulation is administrative legislation that constitutes or constrains rights and allocates responsibilities. It can be distinguished from primary legislation (by Parliament or elected legislative body) on the one hand and judge-made law on the other. Regulation can take many forms: legal restrictions promulgated by a government authority, self-regulation by an industry such as through a trade association, social regulation co-regulation, or market regulation.

CHAPTER QUIZ: KEY TERMS, PEOPLE, PLACES, CONCEPTS

1. A _____ is a market for securities (debt or equity), where business enterprises (companies) and governments can raise long-term funds. It is defined as a market in which money is provided for periods longer than a year,Sullivan, arthur; Steven M. Sheffrin (2003). Economics: Principles in action.

   a. Center for Audit Quality
   b. Central Counterparty Clearing
   c. Capital market
   d. Clearing balance requirement

2. _____, is the value on a given date of a payment or series of payments made at other times.

   If the payments are in the future, they are discounted to reflect the time value of money and other factors such as investment risk. If they are in the past, their value is correspondingly enhanced to reflect that those payments have been earning interest in the intervening time.

   a. Present value
   b. Quantitative investing
   c. QuantLib
   d. Quantum finance

3. In quantum mechanics, the _____ is any of a variety of mathematical inequalities asserting a fundamental limit on the precision with which certain pairs of physical properties of a particle, such as position x and momentum p, can be simultaneously known. The more precisely the position of some particle is determined, the less precisely its momentum can be known, and vice versa. The original heuristic argument that such a limit should exist was given by Werner Heisenberg in 1927. A more formal inequality relating the standard deviation of position σ_x and the standard deviation of momentum σ_p was derived by Kennard later that year (and independently by Weyl in 1928),

$$\sigma_x \sigma_p \geq \frac{\hbar}{2},$$

   where h is the reduced Planck constant.

   a. Arbitrista

b. Stack Exchange Network
c. Stack Overflow
d. Uncertainty principle

4. In economics, _____ is a rise in the general level of prices of goods and services in an economy over a period of time. When the general price level rises, each unit of currency buys fewer goods and services. Consequently, _____ also reflects an erosion in the purchasing power of money - a loss of real value in the internal medium of exchange and unit of account in the economy.

   a. Academic inflation
   b. Agflation
   c. Anti-Inflation Act
   d. Inflation

5. An _____ is a party that makes an investment into one or more categories of assets --- equity, debt securities, real estate, currency, commodity, derivatives such as put and call options, etc. --- with the objective of making a profit. This definition makes no distinction between those in the primary and secondary markets.

   a. Iraq Relief and Reconstruction Fund
   b. Open-ended investment company
   c. Investor
   d. Umbrella fund

ANSWER KEY
Chapter 27. Investment, the Capital Market, and the Wealth of Nations

1. c
2. a
3. d
4. d
5. c

You can take the complete Chapter Practice Test

for Chapter 27. Investment, the Capital Market, and the Wealth of Nations

on all key terms, persons, places, and concepts.

Online 99 Cents

http://www.epub40.13.20514.27.cram101.com/

Use www.Cram101.com for all your study needs

including Cram101's online interactive problem solving labs in

chemistry, statistics, mathematics, and more.

Chapter 28. Income, Inequaltiy and Poverty

CHAPTER OUTLINE: KEY TERMS, PEOPLE, PLACES, CONCEPTS

- _____ Transfer payment
- _____ GDP deflator
- _____ Lehman Brothers
- _____ Income tax
- _____ Tax credit
- _____ Tax rate
- _____ Phillips curve
- _____ Poverty
- _____ Poverty threshold
- _____ Great Depression
- _____ Earned income tax credit
- _____ Social security
- _____ Progressive tax
- _____ Human capital
- _____ Government revenue
- _____ Government spending
- _____ Payroll
- _____ Tax cut
- _____ Public good

Visit Cram101.com for full Practice Exams

Chapter 28. Income, Inequaltiy and Poverty
CHAPTER OUTLINE: KEY TERMS, PEOPLE, PLACES, CONCEPTS

_____ Debt crisis

_____ Payroll tax

_____ Social Security Trust Fund

_____ Baby boomer

_____ Redistribution of wealth

_____ Black market

_____ Incentive

_____ Stock market

_____ Business cycle

_____ Primary market

_____ Secondary market

_____ Future value

_____ Interest rate

_____ Mutual fund

_____ Random walk

_____ Deadweight loss

_____ Keynesian economics

_____ Fiscal policy

_____ Malinvestment

Visit Cram101.com for full Practice Exams

Chapter 28. Income, Inequaltiy and Poverty

CHAPTER OUTLINE: KEY TERMS, PEOPLE, PLACES, CONCEPTS

| Invisible hand

| Monetary policy

| Renewable resource

| Resource allocation

| International trade

| Foreclosure

| Securities lending

| Affordable housing

| Basis point

| Mortgage loan

| Secondary mortgage market

| Fannie Mae

| AD-AS model

| Structural unemployment

| Subprime mortgage

| Bear Stearns

| Securities and Exchange Commission

| Debt-to-capital ratio

| Tax deduction

Visit Cram101.com for full Practice Exams

Chapter 28. Income, Inequaltiy and Poverty
CHAPTER OUTLINE: KEY TERMS, PEOPLE, PLACES, CONCEPTS

	Roaring Twenties
	Money supply
	Bank reserves
	Trade barrier
	Kyoto Protocol
	Labor relations
	Minimum wage
	Unemployment
	Inflation
	Budget crisis
	Debt-to-GDP ratio
	External debt
	Government debt
	Capital formation
	Balanced budget
	Political economy
	Health insurance
	Competitiveness
	Consumer Price Index

Visit Cram101.com for full Practice Exams

Chapter 28. Income, Inequaltiy and Poverty

CHAPTER OUTLINE: KEY TERMS, PEOPLE, PLACES, CONCEPTS

_____ | Price index
_____ | Regulation
_____ | Health savings account
_____ | Savings account
_____ | Property tax
_____ | School choice
_____ | Employment discrimination
_____ | Labor force
_____ | Bargaining power
_____ | Right-to-work law
_____ | Wage
_____ | Union
_____ | Roger A. Sedjo
_____ | Land management
_____ | Land use
_____ | Environmental protection
_____ | Global warming
_____ | Open market
_____ | Total cost

Visit Cram101.com for full Practice Exams

Chapter 28. Income, Inequaltiy and Poverty
CHAPTER OUTLINE: KEY TERMS, PEOPLE, PLACES, CONCEPTS

	The commons
	Tragedy of the commons
	Stock market crash
	Free trade

CHAPTER HIGHLIGHTS & NOTES: KEY TERMS, PEOPLE, PLACES, CONCEPTS

Transfer payment	In economics, a transfer payment is a redistribution of income in the market system. These payments are considered to be exhaustive because they do not directly absorb resources or create output. Examples of certain transfer payments include welfare (financial aid), social security, and government making subsidies for certain businesses (firms).
GDP deflator	In economics, the GDP deflator is a measure of the level of prices of all new, domestically produced, final goods and services in an economy. GDP stands for gross domestic product, the total value of all final goods and services produced within that economy during a specified period. Measurement in national accounts In most systems of national accounts the GDP deflator measures the ratio of nominal GDP to the real measure of GDP. The formula used to calculate the deflator is: $$\text{GDP deflator} = \frac{\text{Nominal GDP}}{\text{Real GDP}} \times 100$$ Dividing the nominal GDP by the GDP deflator and multiplying it by 100 would then give the figure for real GDP, hence deflating the nominal GDP into a real measure.
Lehman Brothers	Lehman Brothers Holdings Inc. (former NYSE ticker symbol LEH) ( ) was a global financial services firm. Before declaring bankruptcy in 2008, Lehman was the fourth largest investment bank in the USA (behind Goldman Sachs, Morgan Stanley, and Merrill Lynch), doing business in investment banking, equity and fixed-income sales and trading (especially U.S. Treasury securities), research, investment management, private equity, and private banking.

Chapter 28. Income, Inequaltiy and Poverty

CHAPTER HIGHLIGHTS & NOTES: KEY TERMS, PEOPLE, PLACES, CONCEPTS

Income tax	An income tax is a tax levied on the income of individuals or businesses (corporations or other legal entities). Various income tax systems exist, with varying degrees of tax incidence. Income taxation can be progressive, proportional, or regressive.
Tax credit	A tax credit is a sum deducted from the total amount a taxpayer owes to the state. A tax credit may be granted for various types of taxes, such as an income tax, property tax, or VAT. It may be granted in recognition of taxes already paid, as a subsidy, or to encourage investment or other behaviors. In some systems tax credits are 'refundable' to the extent they exceed the relevant tax.
Tax rate	In a tax system and in economics, the tax rate describes the burden ratio (usually expressed as a percentage) at which a business or person is taxed. There are several methods used to present a tax rate: statutory, average, marginal, and effective. These rates can also be presented using different definitions applied to a tax base: inclusive and exclusive.
Phillips curve	In economics, the Phillips curve is a historical inverse relationship between the rate of unemployment and the rate of inflation in an economy. Stated simply, the lower the unemployment in an economy, the higher the rate of inflation. While it has been observed that there is a stable short run tradeoff between unemployment and inflation, this has not been observed in the long run.
Poverty	Poverty is the state of one who lacks a certain amount of material possessions or money. Absolute poverty or destitution refers to the one who lacks basic human needs, which commonly includes clean and fresh water, nutrition, health care, education, clothing and shelter. About 1.7 billion people are estimated to live in absolute poverty today.
Poverty threshold	The poverty threshold, is the minimum level of income deemed adequate in a given country. In practice, like the definition of poverty, the official or common understanding of the poverty line is significantly higher in developed countries than in developing countries. The common international poverty line has in the past been roughly $1 a day.
Great Depression	The Great Depression was a severe worldwide economic depression in the decade preceding World War II. The timing of the Great Depression varied across nations, but in most countries it started in 1930 after the passage of the Smoot-Hawley Tariff bill (June 17), and lasted until the late 1930s or early 1940s. It was the longest, most widespread, and deepest depression of the 20th century. In the 21st century, the Great Depression is commonly used as an example of how far the world's economy can decline.

Chapter 28. Income, Inequaltiy and Poverty

CHAPTER HIGHLIGHTS & NOTES: KEY TERMS, PEOPLE, PLACES, CONCEPTS

Earned income tax credit	The United States federal earned income tax credit is a refundable tax credit for low- and medium-income individuals and couples, primarily for those who have qualifying children. When the credit exceeds the amount of taxes owed, it results in a tax refund to those who qualify and claim the credit. That is, this credit is refundable.
Social security	Social security is a concept enshrined in Article 22 of the Universal Declaration of Human Rights which states that Everyone, as a member of society, has the right to social security and is entitled to realization, through national effort and international co-operation and in accordance with the organization and resources of each State, of the economic, social and cultural rights indispensable for his dignity and the free development of his personality. In simple term, this means that the signatories agree that society in which a person lives should help them to develop and to make the most of all the advantages (culture, work, social welfare) which are offered to them in the country. Social security may also refer to the action programs of government intended to promote the welfare of the population through assistance measures guaranteeing access to sufficient resources for food and shelter and to promote health and wellbeing for the population at large and potentially vulnerable segments such as children, the elderly, the sick and the unemployed.
Progressive tax	A progressive tax is a tax by which the tax rate increases as the taxable base amount increases. 'Progressive' describes a distribution effect on income or expenditure, referring to the way the rate progresses from low to high, where the average tax rate is less than the marginal tax rate. It can be applied to individual taxes or to a tax system as a whole; a year, multi-year, or lifetime.
Human capital	Human capital is the stock of competencies, knowledge, social and personality attributes, including creativity, embodied in the ability to perform labor so as to produce economic value. It is an aggregate economic view of the human being acting within economies, which is an attempt to capture the social, biological, cultural and psychological complexity as they interact in explicit and/or economic transactions. It was assumed in early economic theories, reflecting the context in which the secondary sector of the economy was producing much more than the tertiary sector was able to produce at the time in most countries - to be a fungible resource, homogeneous, and easily interchangeable, and it was referred to simply as workforce or labor, one of three factors of production (the others being land, and assumed-interchangeable assets of money and physical equipment).
Government revenue	Government revenue is revenue received by a government. Its opposite is government spending. Yet, governments coin money.Government revenue is an important part of fiscal policy.
Government spending	Government spending includes all government consumption, investment but excludes transfer payments made by a state.

Chapter 28. Income, Inequaltiy and Poverty

CHAPTER HIGHLIGHTS & NOTES: KEY TERMS, PEOPLE, PLACES, CONCEPTS

	Government acquisition of goods and services for current use to directly satisfy individual or collective needs of the members of the community is classed as government final consumption expenditure.
	Government acquisition of goods and services intended to create future benefits, such as infrastructure investment or research spending, is classed as government investment (gross fixed capital formation), which usually is the largest part of the government gross capital formation.
Payroll	In a company, payroll is the sum of all financial records of salaries for an employee, wages, bonuses and deductions. In accounting, payroll refers to the amount paid to employees for services they provided during a certain period of time. Payroll plays a major role in a company for several reasons.
Tax cut	A tax cut is a reduction in taxes. The immediate effects of a tax cut are a decrease in the real income of the government and an increase in the real income of those whose tax rate has been lowered. Due to the perceived benefit in growing real incomes among tax payers politicians have sought to claim their proposed tax credits as tax cuts.
Public good	In economics, a public good is a good that is both non-excludable and non-rivalrous in that individuals can not be effectively excluded from use and where use by one individual does not reduce availability to others. Examples of public goods include fresh air, clean water, knowledge, lighthouses, open source software, radio and television broadcasts, roads, street lighting. Public goods that are available everywhere are sometimes referred to as global public goods.
Debt crisis	Debt crisis is the general term for a proliferation of massive public debt relative to tax revenues, especially in reference to Latin American countries during the 1980s, and the United States and the European Union since the mid-2000s. Europe •European sovereign debt crisis•Greek government debt crisis•Irish financial crisis•Portuguese economic crisisLatin America •Argentine debt restructuring•Latin American debt crisisNorth America •United States debt-ceiling crisis.
Payroll tax	Payroll tax generally refers to two different kinds of similar taxes. The first kind is a tax that employers are required to withhold from employees' wages, also known as withholding tax, pay-as-you-earn tax (PAYE), or pay-as-you-go tax (PAYG) and often covering advance payment of income tax and social security contributions. The second kind is a tax that is paid from the employer's own funds and that is directly related to employing a worker, which can consist of a fixed charge or be proportionally linked to an employee's pay.

Visit Cram101.com for full Practice Exams

Chapter 28. Income, Inequaltiy and Poverty

CHAPTER HIGHLIGHTS & NOTES: KEY TERMS, PEOPLE, PLACES, CONCEPTS

Social Security Trust Fund	In the United States, the Social Security Trust Fund is a fund operated by the Social Security Administration into which are paid payroll tax contributions from workers and employers under the Social Security system and out of which benefit payments are made to retirees, survivors, and the disabled, and for general administrative expenses. The fund also earns interest. There technically are two component funds, the Old-Age and Survivors Insurance (OASI) and Disability Insurance (DI) Trust Funds, referred to collectively as the OASDI funds.
Baby boomer	A baby boomer is a person who was born during the demographic Post-World War II baby boom and who grew up during the period between 1946 and 1964. The term 'baby boomer' is sometimes used in a cultural context. Therefore, it is impossible to achieve broad consensus of a precise definition, even within a given territory. Different groups, organizations, individuals, and scholars may have widely varying opinions on what constitutes a baby boomer, both technically and culturally.
Redistribution of wealth	Redistribution of wealth is the transfer of income, wealth or property from some individuals to others caused by a social mechanism such as taxation, monetary policies, welfare, nationalization, charity, divorce or tort law. Most often it refers to progressive redistribution, from the rich to the poor, although it may also refer to regressive redistribution, from the poor to the rich. The desirability and effects of redistribution are actively debated on ethical and economic grounds.
Black market	A black market is a market in goods or services which operates outside the formal one(s) supported by established state powerg. 'the black market in bush meat' or the state jurisdiction 'the black market in China'. It is distinct from the grey market, in which commodities are distributed through channels which, while legal, are unofficial, unauthorized, or unintended by the original manufacturer, and the white market, the legal market for goods and services.
Incentive	Since human beings are purposeful creatures, the study of incentive structures is central to the study of all economic activity (both in terms of individual decision-making and in terms of co-operation and competition within a larger institutional structure). Economic analysis, then, of the differences between societies (and between different organizations within a society) largely amounts to characterizing the differences in incentive structures faced by individuals involved in these collective efforts. Ultimately, incentives aim to provide value for money and contribute to organizational success.
Stock market	A stock market is a public entity (a loose network of economic transactions, not a physical facility or discrete entity) for the trading of company stock (shares) and derivatives at an agreed price; these are securities listed on a stock exchange as well as those only traded privately.

Chapter 28. Income, Inequaltiy and Poverty

CHAPTER HIGHLIGHTS & NOTES: KEY TERMS, PEOPLE, PLACES, CONCEPTS

	The size of the world stock market was estimated at about $36.6 trillion at the beginning of October 2008. The total world derivatives market has been estimated at about $791 trillion face or nominal value, 11 times the size of the entire world economy. The value of the derivatives market, because it is stated in terms of notional values, cannot be directly compared to a stock or a fixed income security, which traditionally refers to an actual value.
Business cycle	The term business cycle refers to economy-wide fluctuations in production or economic activity over several months or years. These fluctuations occur around a long-term growth trend, and typically involve shifts over time between periods of relatively rapid economic growth (an expansion or boom), and periods of relative stagnation or decline (a contraction or recession).
	Business cycles are usually measured by considering the growth rate of real gross domestic product.
Primary market	The primary market is that part of the capital markets that deals with the issuance of new securities. Companies, governments or public sector institutions can obtain funding through the sale of a new stock or bond issue. This is typically done through a syndicate of securities dealers.
Secondary market	The secondary market, is the financial market in which previously issued financial instruments such as stock, bonds, options, and futures are bought and sold. Another frequent usage of 'secondary market' is to refer to loans which are sold by a mortgage bank to investors such as Fannie Mae and Freddie Mac.
	The term 'secondary market' is also used to refer to the market for any used goods or assets, or an alternative use for an existing product or asset where the customer base is the second market (for example, corn has been traditionally used primarily for food production and feedstock, but a 'second' or 'third' market has developed for use in ethanol production).
Future value	Future value is the value of an asset at a specific date. It measures the nominal future sum of money that a given sum of money is 'worth' at a specified time in the future assuming a certain interest rate, or more generally, rate of return; it is the present value multiplied by the accumulation function. The value does not include corrections for inflation or other factors that affect the true value of money in the future.
Interest rate	An interest rate is the rate at which interest is paid by a borrower for the use of money that they borrow from a lender. For example, a small company borrows capital from a bank to buy new assets for their business, and in return the lender receives interest at a predetermined interest rate for deferring the use of funds and instead lending it to the borrower.

Visit Cram101.com for full Practice Exams

Chapter 28. Income, Inequaltiy and Poverty

CHAPTER HIGHLIGHTS & NOTES: KEY TERMS, PEOPLE, PLACES, CONCEPTS

Mutual fund	A mutual fund is a type of professionally-managed collective investment scheme that pools money from many investors to purchase securities. While there is no legal definition of mutual fund, the term is most commonly applied only to those collective investment schemes that are regulated, available to the general public and open-ended in nature. Hedge funds are not considered a type of mutual fund.
Random walk	A random walk is a mathematical formalisation of a trajectory that consists of taking successive random steps. For example, the path traced by a molecule as it travels in a liquid or a gas, the search path of a foraging animal, the price of a fluctuating stock and the financial status of a gambler can all be modeled as random walks. The term random walk was first introduced by Karl Pearson in 1905. Random walks have been used in many fields: ecology, economics, psychology, computer science, physics, chemistry, and biology.
Deadweight loss	In economics, a deadweight loss is a loss of economic efficiency that can occur when equilibrium for a good or service is not Pareto optimal. In other words, either people who would have more marginal benefit than marginal cost are not buying the product, or people who have more marginal cost than marginal benefit are buying the product. Causes of deadweight loss can include monopoly pricing (in the case of artificial scarcity), externalities, taxes or subsidies, and binding price ceilings or floors.
Keynesian economics	Keynesian economics are the group of macroeconomic schools of thought based on the ideas of 20th-century economist John Maynard Keynes. Advocates of Keynesian economics argue that private sector decisions sometimes lead to inefficient macroeconomic outcomes which require active policy responses by the public sector, particularly monetary policy actions by the central bank and fiscal policy actions by the government to stabilize output over the business cycle. The theories forming the basis of Keynesian economics were first presented in The General Theory of Employment, Interest and Money, published in 1936. The interpretations of Keynes are contentious and several schools of thought claim his legacy.
Fiscal policy	In economics and political science, fiscal policy is the use of government revenue collection (taxation) and expenditure (spending) to influence the economy. The two main instruments of fiscal policy are government taxation and expenditure. Changes in the level and composition of taxation and government spending can impact the following variables in the economy:•Aggregate demand and the level of economic activity;•The pattern of resource allocation;•The distribution of income. Fiscal policy refers to the use of the government budget to influence economic activity.

Chapter 28. Income, Inequaltiy and Poverty

CHAPTER HIGHLIGHTS & NOTES: KEY TERMS, PEOPLE, PLACES, CONCEPTS

Malinvestment	Malinvestment is a concept developed by the Austrian School of economic thought, that refers to investments of firms being badly allocated due to what they assert to be an artificially low cost of credit and an unsustainable increase in money supply, often blamed on a central bank. This concept is central to the Austrian business cycle theory. Austrian economists such as Nobel laureate F. A. Hayek largely advocate the idea that malinvestment occurs due to the combination of fractional reserve banking and artificially low interest rates misleading relative price signals which eventually necessitate a corrective contraction--a boom followed by a bust.
Invisible hand	In economics, invisible hand is the term economists use to describe the self-regulating nature of the marketplace. This is a metaphor first coined by the economist Adam Smith. The exact phrase is used just three times in his writings, but has come to capture his important claim that by trying to maximize their own gains in a free market, individual ambition benefits society, even if the ambitious have no benevolent intentions.
Monetary policy	Monetary policy is the process by which the monetary authority of a country controls the supply of money, often targeting a rate of interest for the purpose of promoting economic growth and stability. The official goals usually include relatively stable prices and low unemployment. Monetary theory provides insight into how to craft optimal monetary policy.
Renewable resource	A renewable resource is a natural resource with the ability to reproduce through biological or natural processes and replenished with the passage of time. Renewable resources are part of our natural environment and form our eco-system. In 1962, within a report to the committee on natural resources which was forwarded to the President of the United States, Paul Weiss defined Renewable Resources as: 'The total range of living organisms providing man with food, fibers, drugs, etc...'.
Resource allocation	Resource allocation is used to assign the available resources in an economic way. It is part of resource management. In project management, resource allocation is the scheduling of activities and the resources required by those activities while taking into consideration both the resource availability and the project time.
International trade	International trade is the exchange of capital, goods, and services across international borders or territories. In most countries, such trade represents a significant share of gross domestic product (GDP). While international trade has been present throughout much of history, its economic, social, and political importance has been on the rise in recent centuries.
Foreclosure	Foreclosure is a specific legal process in which a lender attempts to recover the balance of a loan from a borrower who has stopped making payments to the lender by forcing the sale of the asset used as the collateral for the loan.

Chapter 28. Income, Inequaltiy and Poverty

CHAPTER HIGHLIGHTS & NOTES: KEY TERMS, PEOPLE, PLACES, CONCEPTS

	Formally, a mortgage lender (mortgagee), or other lien holder, obtains a termination of a mortgage borrower (mortgagor)'s equitable right of redemption, either by court order or by operation of law (after following a specific statutory procedure). Usually a lender obtains a security interest from a borrower who mortgages or pledges an asset like a house to secure the loan.
Securities lending	In finance, securities lending or stock lending refers to the lending of securities by one party to another. The terms of the loan will be governed by a 'Securities Lending Agreement', which requires that the borrower provides the lender with collateral, in the form of cash, government securities, or a Letter of Credit of value equal to or greater than the loaned securities. The agreement is a contract enforceable under relevant law, which is often specified in the agreement.
Affordable housing	Affordable housing is a term used to describe dwelling units whose total housing costs for either rented or purchased unit, are deemed affordable to those that have a median household income. In Australia, the National Affordable Housing Summit Group developed their definition of affordable housing as housing which is 'reasonably adequate in standard and location for lower or middle income households and does not cost so much that a household is unlikely to be able to meet other basic needs on a sustainable basis.' In the United Kingdom affordable housing includes 'social rented and intermediate housing, provided to specified eligible households whose needs are not met by the market.' Most of the literature on affordable housing refers to a number of forms that exist along a continuum - from emergency shelters, to transitional housing, to non-market rental (also known as social or subsidized housing), to formal and informal rental, indigenous housing and ending with affordable home ownership. The usage of the term housing affordability became widespread in the 1980s in Europe and North America. A growing body of literature found the term problematic.
Basis point	Book · Category · A basis point is a unit equal to 1/100 of a percentage point or one part per ten thousand. The same unit is also (rarely) called a permyriad (literally meaning 'for (every) myriad (ten thousand)'), and in that context is written with U+2031 ? per ten thousand sign (HTML:) which looks like a percent sign (%) with two extra zeroes at the end (like a stylized form of the four zeros in the denominator, although it originates as a natural extension of the percent (%) and permille (‰) signs). A basis point is defined as:1 basis point = 1 permyriad = one one-hundredth percent1 bp = 1? = 0.01% = 0.1‰ = 10^{-4} = $1/10000$ = 0.00011% = 100 bp = 100?

Chapter 28. Income, Inequaltiy and Poverty

CHAPTER HIGHLIGHTS & NOTES: KEY TERMS, PEOPLE, PLACES, CONCEPTS

Mortgage loan	A mortgage loan is a loan secured by real property through the use of a mortgage note which evidences the existence of the loan and the encumbrance of that realty through the granting of a mortgage which secures the loan. However, the word mortgage alone, in everyday usage, is most often used to mean mortgage loan. The word mortgage is a Law French term meaning 'death contract,' meaning that the pledge ends (dies) when either the obligation is fulfilled or the property is taken through foreclosure.
Secondary mortgage market	The secondary mortgage market is the market for the sale of securities or bonds collateralized by the value of mortgage loans. The mortgage lender, commercial banks, or specialized firm will group together many loans and sell grouped loans as securities called collateralized mortgage obligations (CMOs). The risk of the individual loans is reduced by that aggregation process.
Fannie Mae	The Federal National Mortgage Association (FNMA; OTCQB: FNMA), commonly known as Fannie Mae, was founded in 1938 during the Great Depression as part of the New Deal. It is a government-sponsored enterprise (GSE), though it has been a publicly traded company since 1968. The corporation's purpose is to expand the secondary mortgage market by securitizing mortgages in the form of mortgage-backed securities (MBS), allowing lenders to reinvest their assets into more lending and in effect increasing the number of lenders in the mortgage market by reducing the reliance on thrifts. The Federal National Mortgage Association (FNMA), colloquially known as Fannie Mae, was established in 1938 by amendments to the National Housing Act after the Great Depression as part of Franklin Delano Roosevelt's New Deal.
AD-AS model	The AD-AS or Aggregate Demand-Aggregate Supply model is a macroeconomic model that explains price level and output through the relationship of aggregate demand and aggregate supply. It is based on the theory of John Maynard Keynes presented in his work The General Theory of Employment, Interest, and Money. It is one of the primary simplified representations in the modern field of macroeconomics, and is used by a broad array of economists, from libertarian, Monetarist supporters of laissez-faire, such as Milton Friedman to Post-Keynesian supporters of economic interventionism, such as Joan Robinson. The conventional 'aggregate supply and demand' model is, in actuality, a Keynesian visualization that has come to be a widely accepted image of the theory. The Classical supply and demand model, which is largely based on Say's Law, or that supply creates its own demand, depicts the aggregate supply curve as being vertical at all times (not just in the long-run)Modeling The AD/AS model is used to illustrate the Keynesian model of the business cycle.

Chapter 28. Income, Inequaltiy and Poverty

CHAPTER HIGHLIGHTS & NOTES: KEY TERMS, PEOPLE, PLACES, CONCEPTS

	Movements of the two curves can be used to predict the effects that various exogenous events will have on two variables: real GDP and the price level. Furthermore, the model can be incorporated as a component in any of a variety of dynamic models (models of how variables like the price level and others evolve over time). The AD-AS model can be related to the Phillips curve model of wage or price inflation and unemployment.
Structural unemployment	Structural unemployment is a form of unemployment resulting from a mismatch between demand in the labour market and the skills and locations of the workers seeking employment. Even though the number of vacancies may be equal to, or greater than, the number of the unemployed, the unemployed workers may lack the skills needed for the jobs, or they may not live in the part of the country or world where the jobs are available. Structural unemployment is a result of the dynamics of the labor market, such as agricultural workers being displaced by mechanized agriculture, unskilled laborers displaced by both mechanization and automation, or industries with declining employment.
Subprime mortgage	In finance, subprime lending (also referred to as near-prime, non-prime, and second-chance lending) means making loans to people who may have difficulty maintaining the repayment schedule. These loans are characterized by higher interest rates and less favorable terms in order to compensate for higher credit risk. Proponents of subprime lending maintain that the practice extends credit to people who would otherwise not have access to the credit market. Professor Harvey S. Rosen of Princeton University explained, 'The main thing that innovations in the mortgage market have done over the past 30 years is to let in the excluded: the young, the discriminated-against, the people without a lot of money in the bank to use for a down payment.'Defining subprime risk The term subprime refers to the credit quality of particular borrowers, who have weakened credit histories and a greater risk of loan default than prime borrowers. As people become economically active, records are created relating to their borrowing, earning and lending history. This is called a credit rating, and although covered by privacy laws the information is readily available to people with a need to know (in some countries, loan applications specifically allow the lender to access such records). Subprime borrowers have credit ratings that might include:•limited debt experience (so the lender's assessor simply does not know, and assumes the worst), or•no possession of property assets that could be used as security (for the lender to sell in case of default)•excessive debt (the known income of the individual or family is unlikely to be enough to pay living expenses + interest + repayment),•a history of late or sometimes missed payments (morose debt) so that the loan period had to be extended,•failures to pay debts completely (default debt), and•any legal judgments such as 'orders to pay' or bankruptcy (sometimes known in Britain as County Court Judgements or CCJs).

Visit Cram101.com for full Practice Exams

Chapter 28. Income, Inequaltiy and Poverty

CHAPTER HIGHLIGHTS & NOTES: KEY TERMS, PEOPLE, PLACES, CONCEPTS

Lenders' standards for determining risk categories may also consider the size of the proposed loan, and also take into account the way the loan and the repayment plan is structured, if it is a conventional repayment loan, a mortgage loan, an Endowment mortgage interest only loan, Standard repayment loan, amortized loan, credit card limit or some other arrangement. The originator is also taken into consideration. Because of this, it was possible for a loan to a borrower with 'prime' characteristics (e.g. high credit score, low debt) to be classified as subprime. Student loans

In some countries student loans are considered subprime, perhaps because of school drop-outs. In America, the amount of student loan debt recently surpassed credit card debt. In other countries such loans are underwritten by governments or sponsors. Many student loans are structured in special ways because of the difficulty of predicting students' future earnings. These structures may be in the form of Soft loans, Income-Sensitive Repayment loans Income-Contingent Repayment loans and so on. Because student loans provide repayment records for credit rating, and may also indicate their earning potential, Student loan default can cause serious problems later in life as an individual wishes to make a substantial purchase on credit such as purchasing a vehicle or buying a house, since defaulters are likely to be classified as subprime, which means the loan may be refused or more difficult to arrange and certainly more expensive than for someone with a perfect repayment record. United States

Although there is no single, standard definition, in the United States subprime loans are usually classified as those where the borrower has a FICO score below 640. The term was popularized by the media during the Subprime mortgage crisis or 'credit crunch' of 2007. Those loans which do not meet Fannie Mae or Freddie Mac underwriting guidelines for prime mortgages are called 'non-conforming' loans.

Bear Stearns	The Bear Stearns Companies, Inc. (former NYSE ticker symbol BSC) based in New York City, was a global investment bank and securities trading and brokerage, until its sale to JPMorgan Chase in 2008 during the global financial crisis and recession. Its main business areas, based on 2006 net revenue distributions, were capital markets (equities, fixed income, investment banking; just under 80%), wealth management (under 10%), and global clearing services (12%).
Securities and Exchange Commission	The Philippine Securities and Exchange Commission (Filipino: Komisyon sa mga Panagot at Palitan, commonly known as SEC) is a Philippine state commission responsible for securities laws and regulating the securities industry. The SEC is an agency within the Philippine Department of Finance. The SEC is currently headquartered in Mandaluyong City in central Metro Manila.

Visit Cram101.com for full Practice Exams

Chapter 28. Income, Inequaltiy and Poverty

CHAPTER HIGHLIGHTS & NOTES: KEY TERMS, PEOPLE, PLACES, CONCEPTS

Debt-to-capital ratio	A company's debt-to-capital ratio is the ratio of its total debt to its total capital, its debt and equity combined. The ratio measures a company's capital structure, financial solvency, and degree of leverage, at a particular point in time. The data to calculate the ratio are found on the balance sheet.
Tax deduction	Income tax systems generally allow a tax deduction, i.e., a reduction of the income subject to tax, for various items, especially expenses incurred to produce income. Often these deductions are subject to limitations or conditions. Tax deductions generally are allowed only for expenses incurred that produce current benefits, and capitalization of items producing future benefit is required, sometimes with exceptions.
Roaring Twenties	The Roaring Twenties characterizes the distinctive cultural edge of the 1920s in most of the world major cities, for a period of sustained economic prosperity. French speakers called it the 'années folles' ('Crazy Years')., emphasizing the era's social, artistic, and cultural dynamism. 'Normalcy' returned to politics in the wake of hyper-emotional patriotism during World War I, jazz music blossomed, the flapper redefined modern womanhood, Art Deco peaked.
Money supply	In economics, the money supply, is the total amount of money available in an economy at a specific time. There are several ways to define 'money,' but standard measures usually include currency in circulation and demand deposits (depositors' easily accessed assets on the books of financial institutions). Money supply data are recorded and published, usually by the government or the central bank of the country.
Bank reserves	Bank reserves are banks' holdings of deposits in accounts with their central bank (for instance the European Central Bank or the Federal Reserve, in the latter case including federal funds), plus currency that is physically held in the bank's vault (vault cash). The central banks of some nations set minimum reserve requirements. Even when no requirements are set, banks commonly wish to hold some reserves, called desired reserves, against unexpected events such as unusually large net withdrawals by customers or even bank runs.
Trade barrier	Trade barriers are government-induced restrictions on international trade. The barriers can take many forms, including the following:•Tariffs•Non-tariff barriers to trade •Import licenses•Export licenses•Import quotas•Subsidies•Voluntary Export Restraints•Local content requirements•Embargo•Currency devaluation•Trade restriction Most trade barriers work on the same principle: the imposition of some sort of cost on trade that raises the price of the traded products. If two or more nations repeatedly use trade barriers against each other, then a trade war results.

Chapter 28. Income, Inequaltiy and Poverty

CHAPTER HIGHLIGHTS & NOTES: KEY TERMS, PEOPLE, PLACES, CONCEPTS

Kyoto Protocol	The Kyoto Protocol is a protocol to the United Nations Framework Convention on Climate Change (UNFCCC or FCCC), aimed at fighting global warming. The UNFCCC is an international environmental treaty with the goal of achieving the 'stabilisation of greenhouse gas concentrations in the atmosphere at a level that would prevent dangerous anthropogenic interference with the climate system.' The Protocol was initially adopted on 11 December 1997 in Kyoto, Japan, and entered into force on 16 February 2005. As of September 2011, 191 states have signed and ratified the protocol. The only remaining signatory not to have ratified the protocol is the United States.
Labor relations	Labor relations is the study and practice of managing unionized employment situations. In academia, labor relations is frequently a subarea within industrial relations, though scholars from many disciplines--including economics, sociology, history, law, and political science--also study labor unions and labor movements. In practice, labor relations is frequently a subarea within human resource management.
Minimum wage	A minimum wage is the lowest hourly, daily or monthly remuneration that employers may legally pay to workers. Equivalently, it is the lowest wage at which workers may sell their labor. Although minimum wage laws are in effect in many jurisdictions, differences of opinion exist about the benefits and drawbacks of a minimum wage.
Unemployment	Unemployment , as defined by the International Labour Organization, occurs when people are without jobs and they have actively sought work within the past four weeks. The unemployment rate is a measure of the prevalence of unemployment and it is calculated as a percentage by dividing the number of unemployed individuals by all individuals currently in the labor force. In a 2011 news story, BusinessWeek reported, 'More than 200 million people globally are out of work, a record high, as almost two-thirds of advanced economies and half of developing countries are experiencing a slowdown in employment growth'.
Inflation	In economics, inflation is a rise in the general level of prices of goods and services in an economy over a period of time. When the general price level rises, each unit of currency buys fewer goods and services. Consequently, inflation also reflects an erosion in the purchasing power of money - a loss of real value in the internal medium of exchange and unit of account in the economy.
Budget crisis	A budget crisis is an informal name for a situation in which the legislative and the executive in a presidential system deadlock and are unable to pass a budget. In presidential systems, the legislature has the power to pass a budget, but the executive often has a veto in which there are insufficient votes in the legislature to override.

Visit Cram101.com for full Practice Exams

Chapter 28. Income, Inequaltiy and Poverty

CHAPTER HIGHLIGHTS & NOTES: KEY TERMS, PEOPLE, PLACES, CONCEPTS

Debt-to-GDP ratio	In economics, the debt-to-GDP ratio is one of the indicators of the health of an economy. It is the amount of national debt of a country as a percentage of its Gross Domestic Product (GDP). A low debt-to-GDP ratio indicates an economy that produces a large number of goods and services and probably profits that are high enough to pay back debts.
External debt	External debt is that part of the total debt in a country that is owed to creditors outside the country. The debtors can be the government, corporations or private households. The debt includes money owed to private commercial banks, other governments, or international financial institutions such as the International Monetary Fund (IMF) and World Bank.
Government debt	Government debt is the debt owed by a central government. (In the U.S. and other federal states, 'government debt' may also refer to the debt of a state or provincial government, municipal or local government). By contrast, the annual 'government deficit' refers to the difference between government receipts and spending in a single year, that is, the increase of debt over a particular year.
Capital formation	Capital formation is a concept used in macroeconomics, national accounts and financial economics. Occasionally it is also used in corporate accounts. It can be defined in three ways:•It is a specific statistical concept used in national accounts statistics, econometrics and macroeconomics.
Balanced budget	A balanced budget is when there is neither a budget deficit or a budget surplus - when revenues equal expenditure ('the accounts balance') - particularly by a government. More generally, it refers to when there is no deficit, but possibly a surplus. A cyclically balanced budget is a budget that is not necessarily balanced year-to-year, but is balanced over the economic cycle, running a surplus in boom years and running a deficit in lean years, with these offsetting over time.
Political economy	Political economy, buying, and selling, and their relations with law, custom, and government, as well as with the distribution of national income and wealth, including through the budget process. Political economy originated in moral philosophy. It developed in the 18th century as the study of the economies of states, polities, hence political economy.
Health insurance	Health insurance is insurance against the risk of incurring medical expenses among individuals. By estimating the overall risk of health care expenses among a targeted group, an insurer can develop a routine finance structure, such as a monthly premium or payroll tax, to ensure that money is available to pay for the health care benefits specified in the insurance agreement. The benefit is administered by a central organization such as a government agency, private business, or not-for-profit entity.
Competitiveness	Competitiveness is a comparative concept of the ability and performance of a firm, sub-sector or country to sell and supply goods and services in a given market.

Chapter 28. Income, Inequaltiy and Poverty

CHAPTER HIGHLIGHTS & NOTES: KEY TERMS, PEOPLE, PLACES, CONCEPTS

	The term may also be applied to markets, where it is used to refer to the extent to which the market structure may be regarded as perfectly competitive. This usage has nothing to do with the extent to which individual firms are 'competitive'.
Consumer Price Index	The Consumer Price Index (CPI) is the official measure of inflation of consumer prices of the United Kingdom. It is also called the Harmonised Index of Consumer Prices (HICP).
	The traditional measure of inflation in the UK for many years was the Retail Prices Index (RPI), which was first calculated in the early 20th century to evaluate the extent to which workers were affected by price changes during the First World War.
Price index	A price index is a normalized average (typically a weighted average) of prices for a given class of goods or services in a given region, during a given interval of time. It is a statistic designed to help to compare how these prices, taken as a whole, differ between time periods or geographical locations.
	Price indices have several potential uses.
Regulation	Regulation is administrative legislation that constitutes or constrains rights and allocates responsibilities. It can be distinguished from primary legislation (by Parliament or elected legislative body) on the one hand and judge-made law on the other. Regulation can take many forms: legal restrictions promulgated by a government authority, self-regulation by an industry such as through a trade association, social regulation co-regulation, or market regulation.
Health savings account	A health savings account is a tax-advantaged medical savings account available to taxpayers in the United States who are enrolled in a high-deductible health plan (HDHP). The funds contributed to an account are not subject to federal income tax at the time of deposit. Unlike a flexible spending account (FSA), funds roll over and accumulate year to year if not spent.
Savings account	Savings accounts are accounts maintained by retail financial institutions that pay interest but cannot be used directly as money in the narrow sense of a medium of exchange (for example, by writing a check). These accounts let customers set aside a portion of their liquid assets while earning a monetary return. For the bank, money in a savings account may not be callable immediately and therefore often does not incur a reserve requirement freeing up cash from the bank's vault to be lent out with interest.
Property tax	A property tax is a levy on property that the owner is required to pay. The tax is levied by the governing authority of the jurisdiction in which the property is located; it may be paid to a national government, a federated state, a countyregion, or a municipality.

Chapter 28. Income, Inequaltiy and Poverty

CHAPTER HIGHLIGHTS & NOTES: KEY TERMS, PEOPLE, PLACES, CONCEPTS

School choice	School choice is a term used to describe a wide array of programs aimed at giving families the opportunity to choose the school their children will attend. As a matter of form, school choice does not give preference to one form of schooling or another, rather manifests itself whenever a student attends school outside of the one they would have been assigned to by geographic default. The most common options offered by school choice programs are open enrollment laws that allow students to attend other public schools, private schools, charter schools, tax credit and deductions for expenses related to schooling, vouchers, and homeschooling.
Employment discrimination	Employment discrimination is discrimination in hiring, promotion, job assignment, termination, and compensation. It includes various types of harassment. Many jurisdictions prohibit some types of employment discrimination, often by forbidding discrimination based on certain traits ('protected categories').
Labor force	Normally, the labor force of a country consists of everyone of working age (typically above a certain age (around 14 to 16) and below retirement (around 65) who are participating workers, that is people actively employed or seeking employment. People not counted include students, retired people, stay-at-home parents, people in prisons or similar institutions, people employed in jobs or professions with unreported income, as well as discouraged workers who cannot find work. In the United States, the unemployment rate is estimated by a household survey called the Current Population Survey, conducted monthly by the Federal Bureau of Labor Statistics.
Bargaining power	Bargaining power is a concept related to the relative abilities of parties in a situation to exert influence over each other. If both parties are on an equal footing in a debate, then they will have equal bargaining power, such as in a perfectly competitive market, or between an evenly matched monopoly and monopsony. There are a number of fields where the concept of bargaining power has proven crucial to coherent analysis: game theory, labour economics, collective bargaining arrangements, diplomatic negotiations, settlement of litigation, the price of insurance, and any negotiation in general.
Right-to-work law	A 'right-to-work' law is a statute that prohibits union security agreements, or agreements between labor unions and employers that govern the extent to which an established union can require employees' membership, payment of union dues, or fees as a condition of employment, either before or after hiring. Right-to-work laws exist in twenty-three U.S. states, mostly in the southern and western United States. Such laws are allowed under the 1947 federal Taft-Hartley Act.

Chapter 28. Income, Inequaltiy and Poverty

CHAPTER HIGHLIGHTS & NOTES: KEY TERMS, PEOPLE, PLACES, CONCEPTS

Wage	A wage is a compensation, usually financial, received by workers in exchange for their labor.
	Compensation in terms of wages is given to workers and compensation in terms of salary is given to employees. Compensation is a monetary benefit given to employees in return for the services provided by them.
Union	In set theory, the union (denoted as ∪) of a collection of sets is the set of all distinct elements in the collection. The union of a collection of sets $S_1, S_2, S_3, \ldots, S_n$ gives a set $S_1 \cup S_2 \cup S_3 \cup \ldots \cup S_n$.
	The union of two sets A and B is the collection of points which are in A or in B : $A \cup B = \{x : x \in A \text{ or } x \in B\}$
	A simple example: $A = \{1, 2, 3, 4\}$ $B = \{5, 6, 7, 8\}$ $A \cup B = \{1, 2, 3, 4, 5, 6, 7, 8\}$
	Another typical example: $A = \{1, 2, 3, 4, 5, 6\}$ $B = \{5, 6, 7, 8\}$ $A \cup B = \{1, 2, 3, 4, 5, 6, 7, 8\}$
	Other more complex operations can be done including the union, if the set is for example defined by a property rather than a finite or assumed infinite enumeration of elements.
Roger A. Sedjo	Roger A. Sedjo is an economist and senior fellow and director of Resources for the Future. Forestry and land use have been major focuses of his career.
	He has been a consultant for the World Bank, the Asian Development Bank, the U.S. Agency for Internal Development, the Food and Agricultural Organization of the United Nations, and the Organisation for Economic Cooperation and Development.
Land management	Land management is the process of managing the use and development (in both urban and rural settings) of land resources. Land resources are used for a variety of purposes which may include organic agriculture, reforestation, water resource management and eco-tourism projects.
Land use	'Land use' is also often used to refer to the distinct land use types in zoning.
	Land use is the human use of land. Land use involves the management and modification of natural environment or wilderness into built environment such as fields, pastures, and settlements.

Visit Cram101.com for full Practice Exams

Chapter 28. Income, Inequaltiy and Poverty

CHAPTER HIGHLIGHTS & NOTES: KEY TERMS, PEOPLE, PLACES, CONCEPTS

Environmental protection	Environmental protection is a practice of protecting the environment, on individual, organizational or governmental levels, for the benefit of the natural environment and (or) humans. Due to the pressures of population and technology, the biophysical environment is being degraded, sometimes permanently. This has been recognized, and governments have begun placing restraints on activities that cause environmental degradation.
Global warming	Global warming is the rising average temperature of Earth's atmosphere and oceans since the late 19th century and its projected continuation. Since the early 20th century, Earth's average surface temperature has increased by about 0.8 °C (1.4 °F), with about two thirds of the increase occurring since 1980. Warming of the climate system is unequivocal, and scientists are more than 90% certain that most of it is caused by increasing concentrations of greenhouse gases produced by human activities such as deforestation and the burning of fossil fuels. These findings are recognized by the national science academies of all major industrialized nations.[A] Climate model projections are summarized in the 2007 Fourth Assessment Report (AR4) by the Intergovernmental Panel on Climate Change (IPCC).
Open market	The term open market is used generally to refer to a situation close to free trade and in a more specific technical sense to interbank trade in securities. In a general sense used in economics and political economy, an open market refers to a market which is accessible to all economic actors. In an open market so defined, all economic actors have an equal opportunity of entry in that market.
Total cost	In economics, and cost accounting, total cost describes the total economic cost of production and is made up of variable costs, which vary according to the quantity of a good produced and include inputs such as labor and raw materials, plus fixed costs, which are independent of the quantity of a good produced and include inputs (capital) that cannot be varied in the short term, such as buildings and machinery. Total cost in economics includes the total opportunity cost of each factor of production as part of its fixed or variable costs. The rate at which total cost changes as the amount produced changes is called marginal cost.
The commons	Commons are resources that are owned in common or shared among communities. These resources are said to be 'held in common' and can include everything from natural resources and common land to software. The commons contains public property and private property, over which people have certain traditional rights.

Visit Cram101.com for full Practice Exams

Chapter 28. Income, Inequaltiy and Poverty

CHAPTER HIGHLIGHTS & NOTES: KEY TERMS, PEOPLE, PLACES, CONCEPTS

Tragedy of the commons	The tragedy of the commons is a dilemma arising from the situation in which multiple individuals, acting independently and rationally consulting their own self-interest, will ultimately deplete a shared limited resource, even when it is clear that it is not in anyone's long-term interest for this to happen Central to Hardin's article is an example (first sketched in an 1833 pamphlet by William Forster Lloyd) involving medieval land tenure in Europe, of herders sharing a common parcel of land, on which they are each entitled to let their cows graze.
Stock market crash	A stock market crash is a sudden dramatic decline of stock prices across a significant cross-section of a stock market, resulting in a significant loss of paper wealth. Crashes are driven by panic as much as by underlying economic factors. They often follow speculative stock market bubbles.
Free trade	Free trade is a policy by which a government does not discriminate against imports or interfere with exports by applying tariffs (to imports) or subsidies (to exports) or quotas. According to the law of comparative advantage the policy permits trading partners mutual gains from trade of goods and services. Under a free trade policy, prices emerge from supply and demand, and are the sole determinant of resource allocation.

CHAPTER QUIZ: KEY TERMS, PEOPLE, PLACES, CONCEPTS

1. _____ is the stock of competencies, knowledge, social and personality attributes, including creativity, embodied in the ability to perform labor so as to produce economic value. It is an aggregate economic view of the human being acting within economies, which is an attempt to capture the social, biological, cultural and psychological complexity as they interact in explicit and/or economic transactions.

   It was assumed in early economic theories, reflecting the context in which the secondary sector of the economy was producing much more than the tertiary sector was able to produce at the time in most countries - to be a fungible resource, homogeneous, and easily interchangeable, and it was referred to simply as workforce or labor, one of three factors of production (the others being land, and assumed-interchangeable assets of money and physical equipment).

   a. Knowledge capital
   b. Human capital
   c. Means of production
   d. Natural capital

2. . A _____ is a loan secured by real property through the use of a mortgage note which evidences the existence of the loan and the encumbrance of that realty through the granting of a mortgage which secures the loan. However, the word mortgage alone, in everyday usage, is most often used to mean _____.

Chapter 28. Income, Inequaltiy and Poverty

Visit Cram101.com for full Practice Exams

CHAPTER QUIZ: KEY TERMS, PEOPLE, PLACES, CONCEPTS

The word mortgage is a Law French term meaning 'death contract,' meaning that the pledge ends (dies) when either the obligation is fulfilled or the property is taken through foreclosure.

a. Balloon payment mortgage
b. Mortgage loan
c. Bank walkaway
d. Mortgage belt

3. _____ Holdings Inc. (former NYSE ticker symbol LEH) ( ) was a global financial services firm. Before declaring bankruptcy in 2008, Lehman was the fourth largest investment bank in the USA (behind Goldman Sachs, Morgan Stanley, and Merrill Lynch), doing business in investment banking, equity and fixed-income sales and trading (especially U.S. Treasury securities), research, investment management, private equity, and private banking.

a. 15th century
b. Generalized entropy index
c. Genuine progress indicator
d. Lehman Brothers

4. In economics, a _____ is a good that is both non-excludable and non-rivalrous in that individuals can not be effectively excluded from use and where use by one individual does not reduce availability to others. Examples of _____s include fresh air, clean water, knowledge, lighthouses, open source software, radio and television broadcasts, roads, street lighting. _____s that are available everywhere are sometimes referred to as global _____s.

a. Public sector
b. Quasi-market
c. Public good
d. Reprivatization

5. In the United States, the _____ is a fund operated by the Social Security Administration into which are paid payroll tax contributions from workers and employers under the Social Security system and out of which benefit payments are made to retirees, survivors, and the disabled, and for general administrative expenses. The fund also earns interest. There technically are two component funds, the Old-Age and Survivors Insurance (OASI) and Disability Insurance (DI) Trust Funds, referred to collectively as the OASDI funds.

a. Vaccines for Children Program
b. Windfall Elimination Provision
c. Years of coverage
d. Social Security Trust Fund

ANSWER KEY
Chapter 28. Income, Inequaltiy and Poverty

1. b
2. b
3. d
4. c
5. d

You can take the complete Chapter Practice Test

for Chapter 28. Income, Inequaltiy and Poverty
on all key terms, persons, places, and concepts.

Online 99 Cents

http://www.epub40.13.20514.28.cram101.com/

Use www.Cram101.com for all your study needs

including Cram101's online interactive problem solving labs in

chemistry, statistics, mathematics, and more.

Visit Cram101.com for full Practice Exams

Other Cram101 e-Books and Tests

Want More?
Cram101.com...

Cram101.com provides the outlines and highlights of your textbooks, just like this e-StudyGuide, but also gives you the **PRACTICE TESTS**, and other exclusive study tools for all of your textbooks.

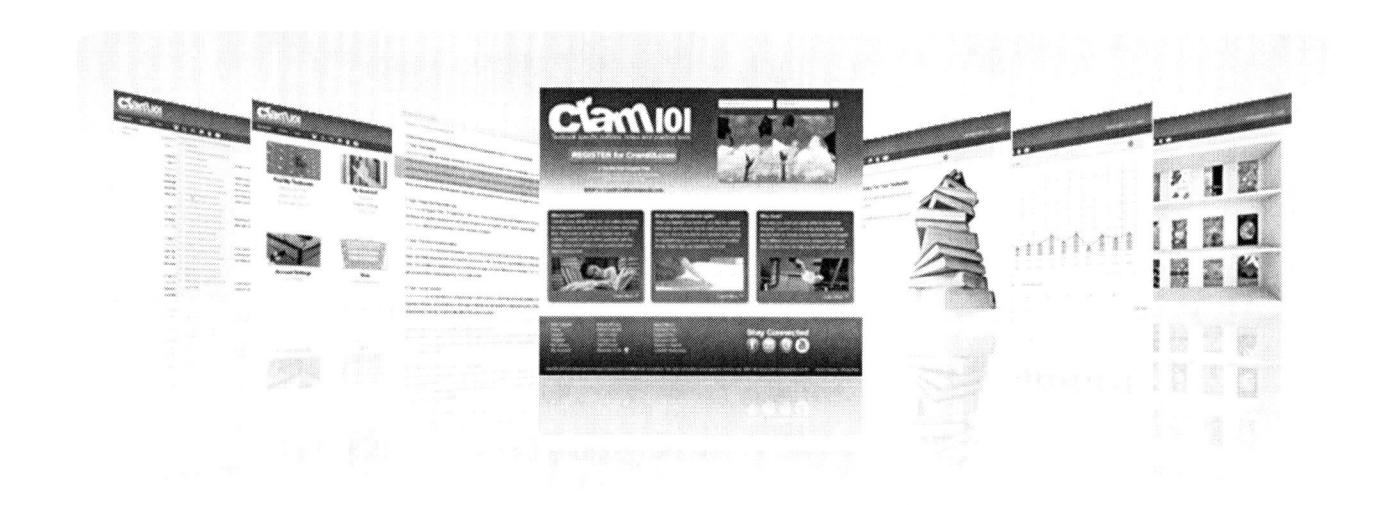

Learn More. *Just click*
http://www.cram101.com/

Other Cram101 e-Books and Tests

Visit *Cram101.com* for full Practice Exams

CPSIA information can be obtained at www.ICGtesting.com
Printed in the USA
BVOW050532160113

310752BV00001B/257/P

9 781478 416333